KiNGofBANDiTJiNG

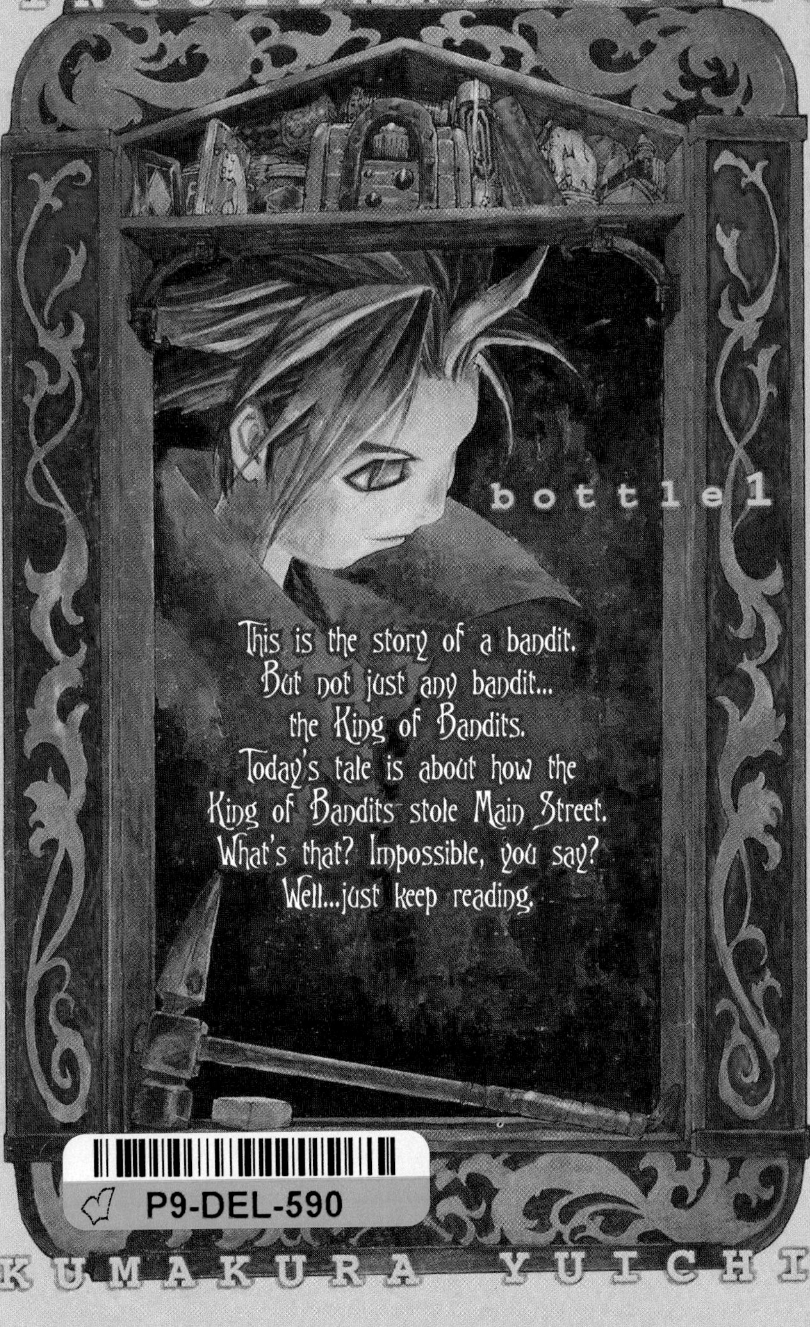
bottle 1
This is the story of a bandit.
But not just any bandit...
the King of Bandits.
Today's tale is about how the
King of Bandits stole Main Street.
What's that? Impossible, you say?
Well...just keep reading.

KUMAKURA YUICHI

N D i T j i N G

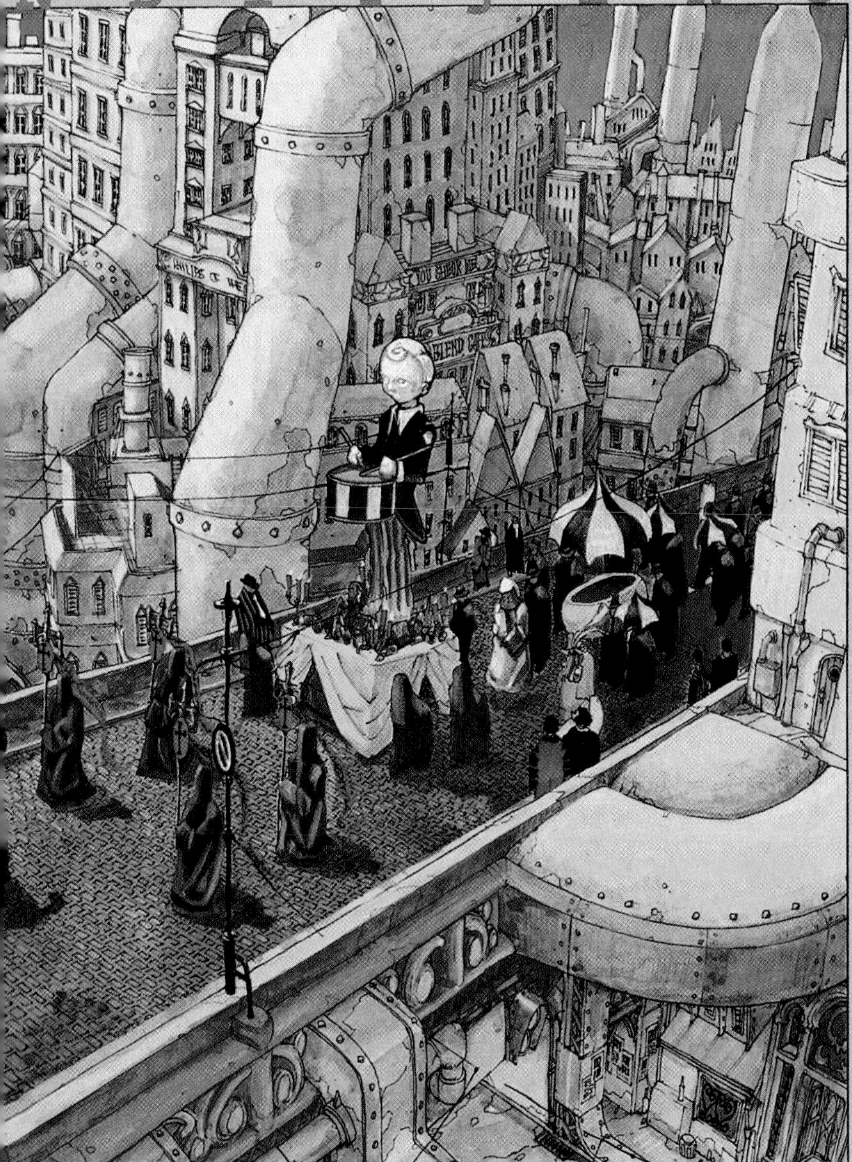

fants du paradis #1

of Paradise - Part 1)

KiNG of BA

楽園のこどもたち前編

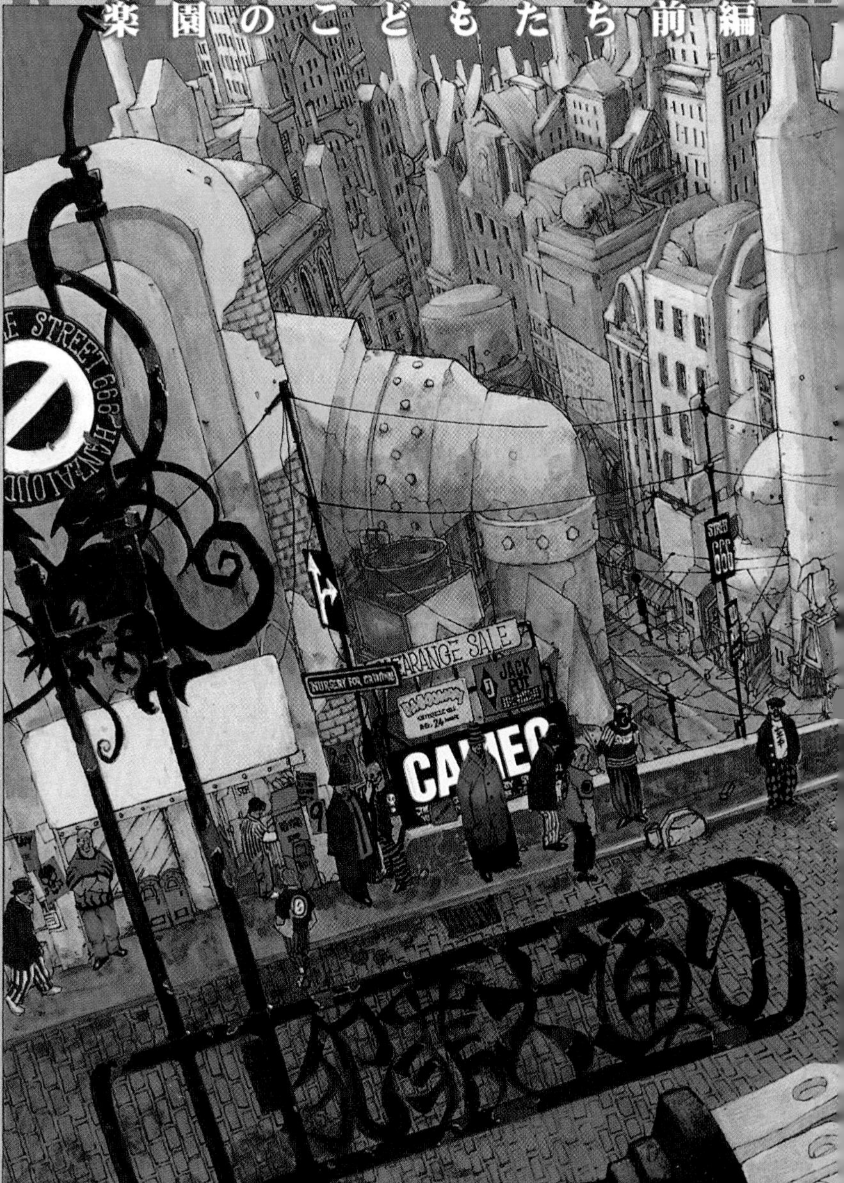

JACK POT

1st shot

Les en

(The Children

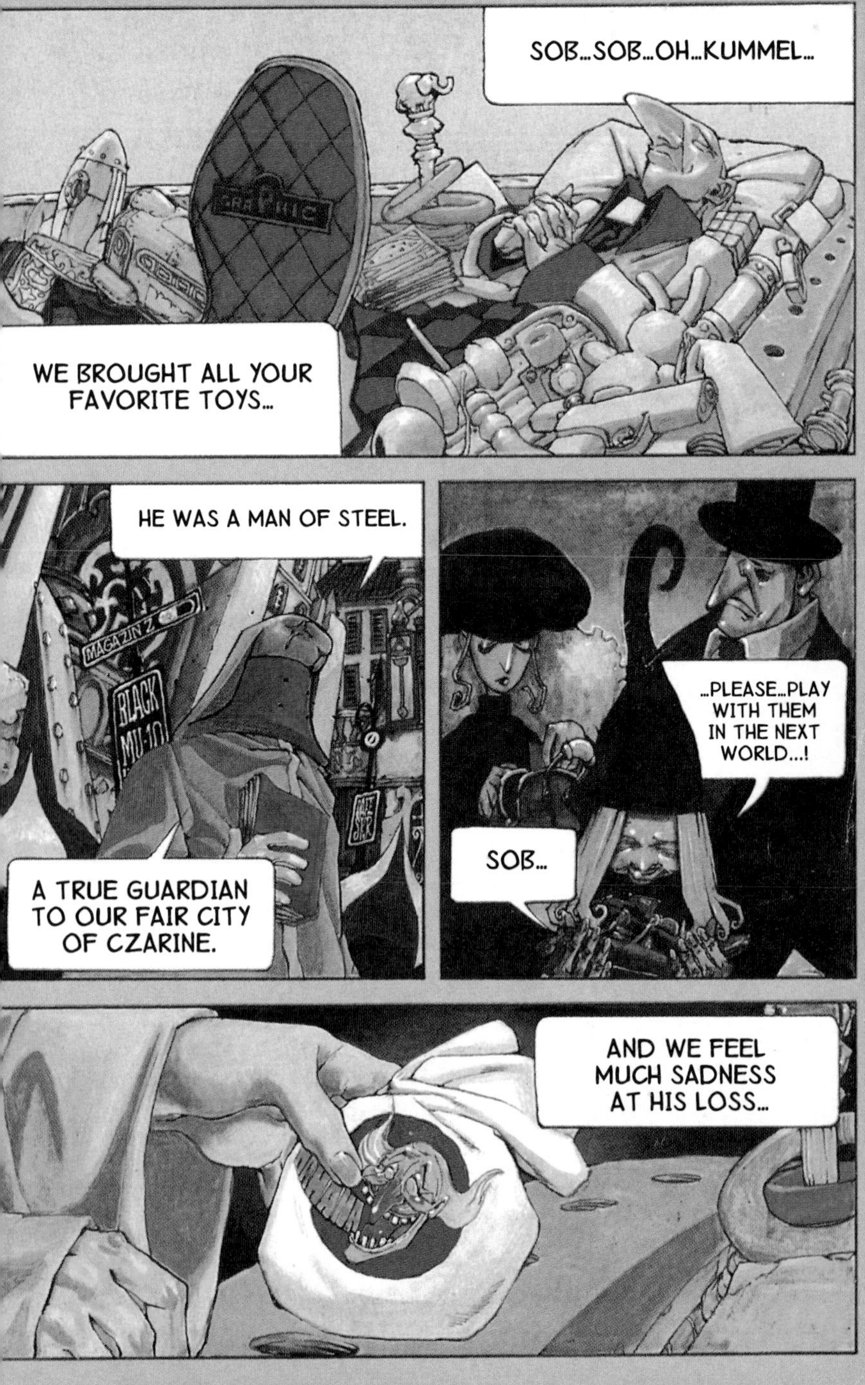
SOB...SOB...OH...KUMMEL...
WE BROUGHT ALL YOUR FAVORITE TOYS...
HE WAS A MAN OF STEEL.
MAGAZIN Z
A TRUE GUARDIAN TO OUR FAIR CITY OF CZARINE.
...PLEASE...PLAY WITH THEM IN THE NEXT WORLD...!
SOB...
AND WE FEEL MUCH SADNESS AT HIS LOSS...

All that glitters...

Even the stars

All things precious...

Even your life

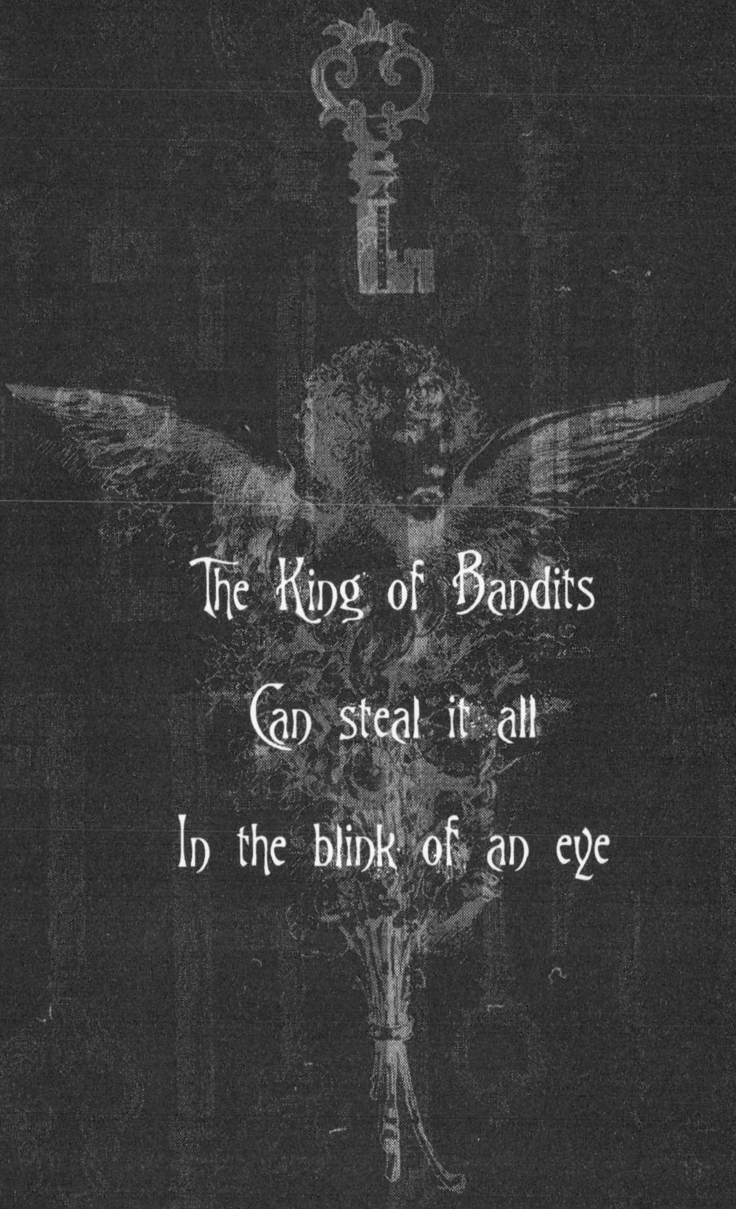
The King of Bandits
Can steal it all
In the blink of an eye

KING OF BANDITS JING
TWILIGHT TALES

VOLUME 1 OF 6

STORY AND ART BY
YUICHI KUMAKURA

HAMBURG // LONDON // LOS ANGELES // TOKYO

Jing: King of Bandits - Twilight Tales Vol. 1

Created by Yuichi Kumakura

Translation - Alexis Kirsch
English Adaptation - Carol Fox
Copy Editor - Hope Donovan
Retouch and Lettering - Vicente Rivera, Jr.
Cover Design - Gary Shum

Editor - Paul Morrissey
Digital Imaging Manager - Chris Buford
Pre-Press Manager - Antonio DePietro
Production Managers - Jennifer Miller and Mutsumi Miyazaki
Art Director - Matt Alford
Managing Editor - Jill Freshney
VP of Production - Ron Klamert
President and C.O.O. - John Parker
Publisher and C.E.O. - Stuart Levy

A  **TOKYOPOP**® Manga

TOKYOPOP Inc.
5900 Wilshire Blvd. Suite 2000
Los Angeles, CA 90036

E-mail: info@TOKYOPOP.com
Come visit us online at www.TOKYOPOP.com

ISBN: 1-59182-469-9

First TOKYOPOP printing: September 2004
10 9 8 7 6 5 4 3 2 1
Printed in the USA

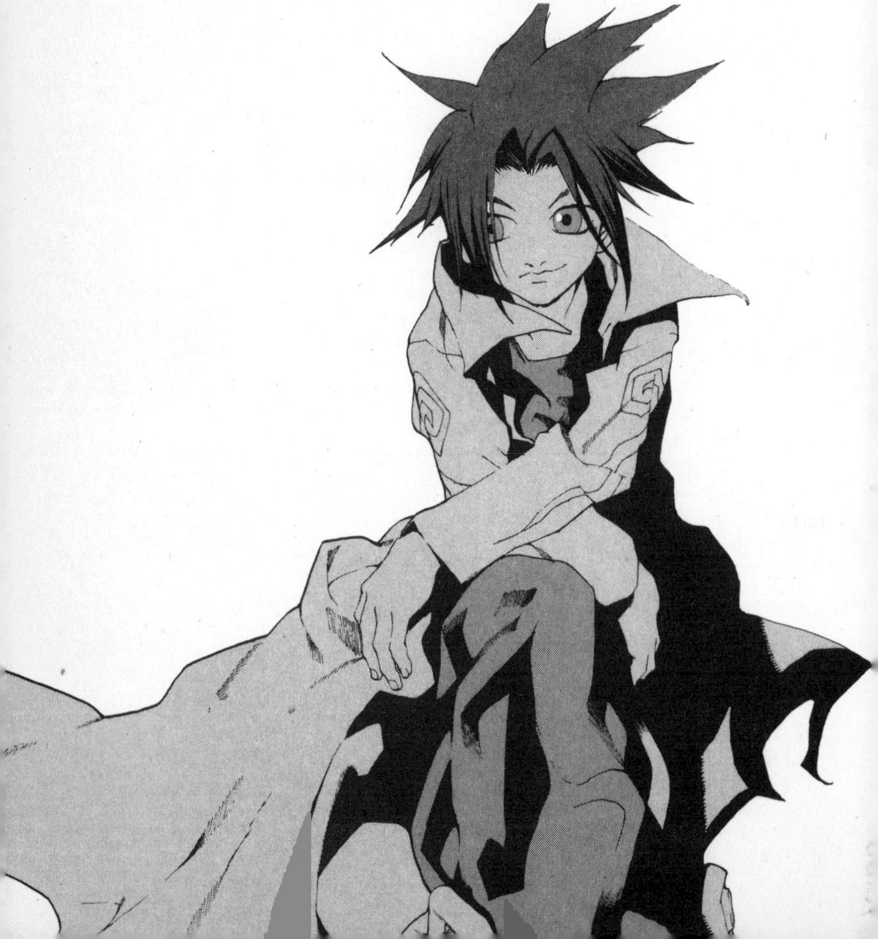

JING: KING OF BANDITS
TWILIGHT TALES
VOL. ONE CONTENTS

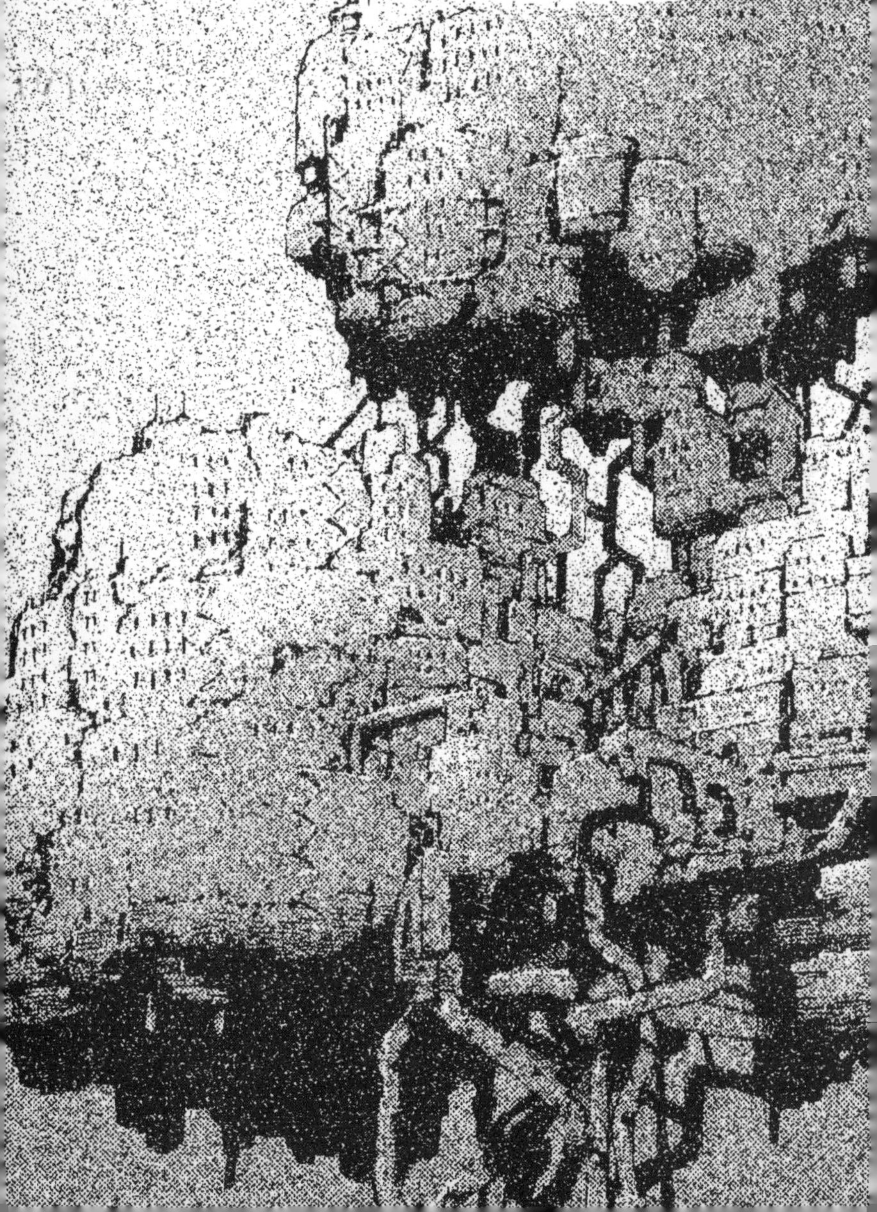

Once upon a midnight dreary, a thief named Jing was weak and weary,
Many strange and forgotten lands he did traverse and explore.
His companion was a bird named Kir, his black wings a-flapping,
While Jing nodded, nearly napping, Kir saw booty galore.
"Wake up, Jing," Kir muttered, "all around us is loot galore."
Treasure from ceiling to floor!

Thus, this ebony bird's wiling, sent Jing's sad face into smiling,
For Jing could steal the stars from the sky, thievery he truly did adore.
The albatross sat proudly on Jing's placid bust, his beady eyes did implore,
One more thing Kir did utter, his feathers all a greedy flutter, his voice a roar,
Quoth the albatross, "Let's steal some more!"

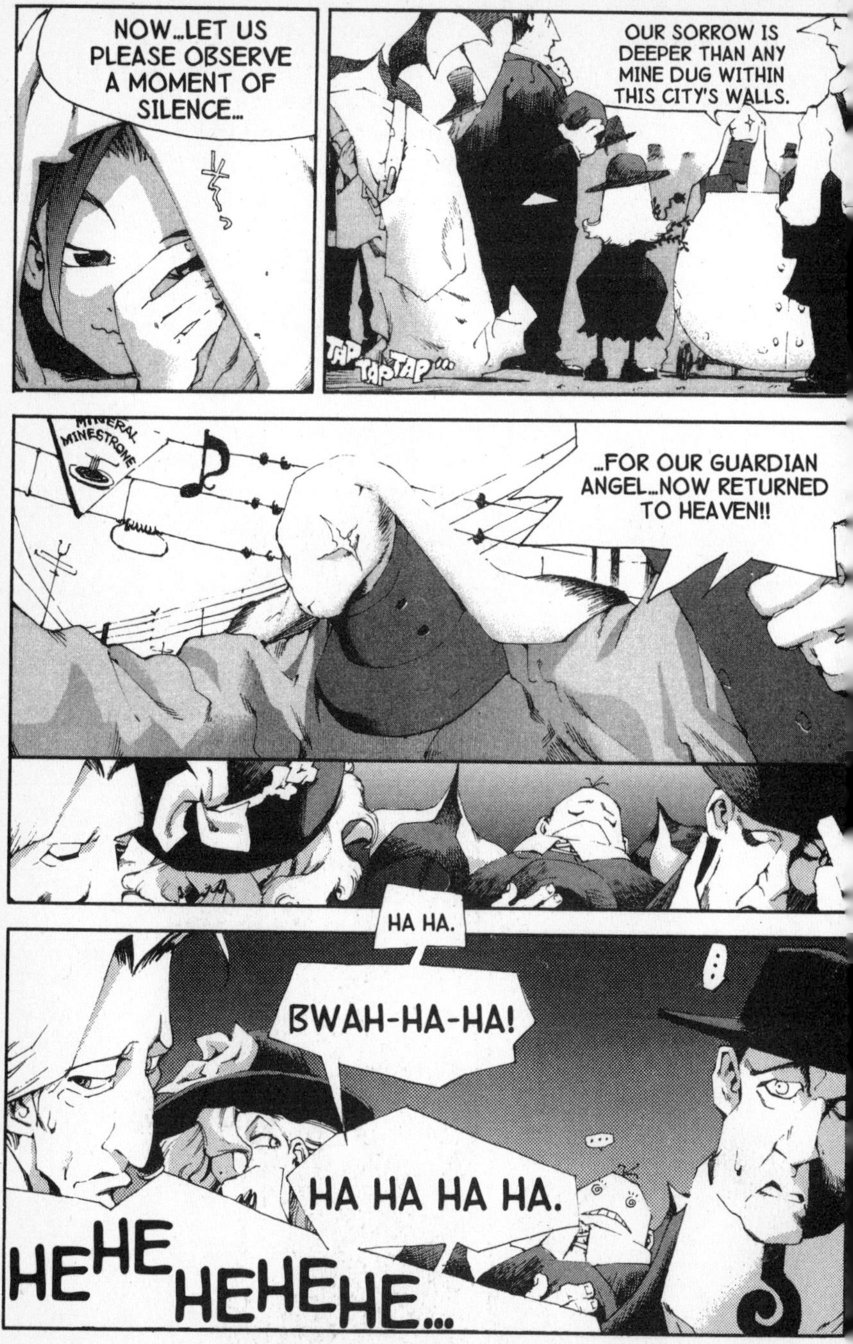
NOW...LET US PLEASE OBSERVE A MOMENT OF SILENCE...
OUR SORROW IS DEEPER THAN ANY MINE DUG WITHIN THIS CITY'S WALLS.
TAP TAP TAP...
MINERAL MINESTRONE
...FOR OUR GUARDIAN ANGEL...NOW RETURNED TO HEAVEN!!
HA HA.
BWAH-HA-HA!
HA HA HA HA.
...
HEHE HEHEHEHE...

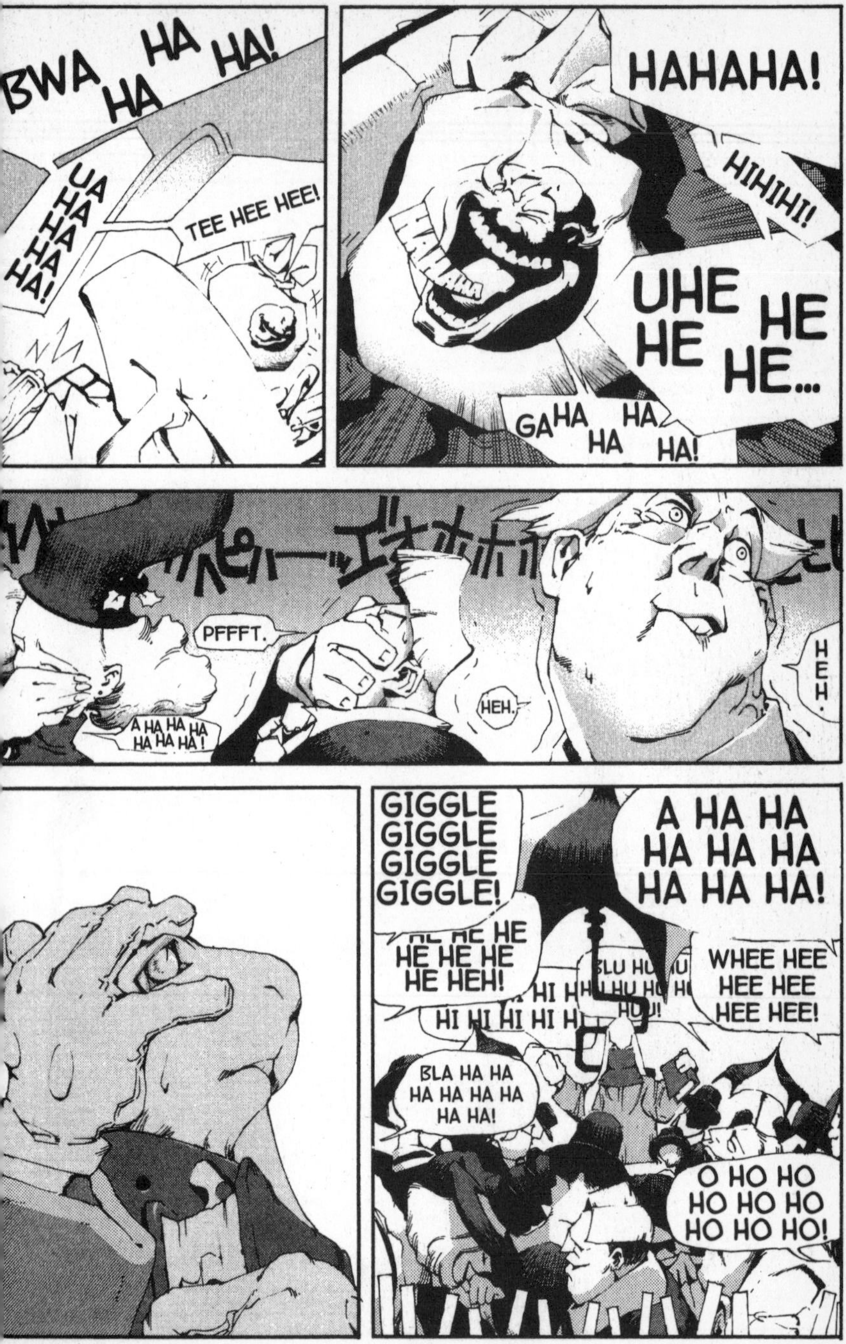
HAHAHA!
HIHIHI!
UHE HE HE HE...
GA HA HA HA HA!
BWA HA HA HA!
UA HA HA HA HA HA!
TEE HEE HEE!
HEH.
HEH.
PFFFT.
A HA HA HA HA HA HA!
A HA HA HA HA HA HA HA HA!
GIGGLE GIGGLE GIGGLE GIGGLE!
WHEE HEE HEE HEE HEE HEE!
HE HE HE HE HEH!
BLA HA HA HA HA HA HA HA HA!
O HO HO HO HO HO HO HO HO!

SHUT UP!!
STOP
LAUGHING!!!!
THE SURVIVOR

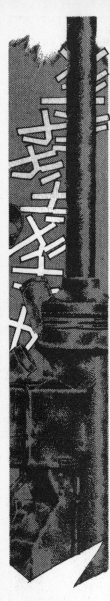

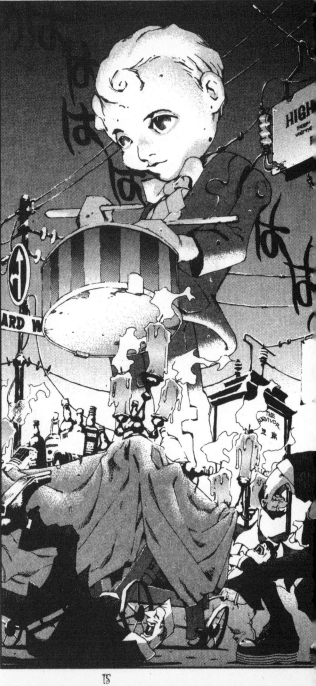

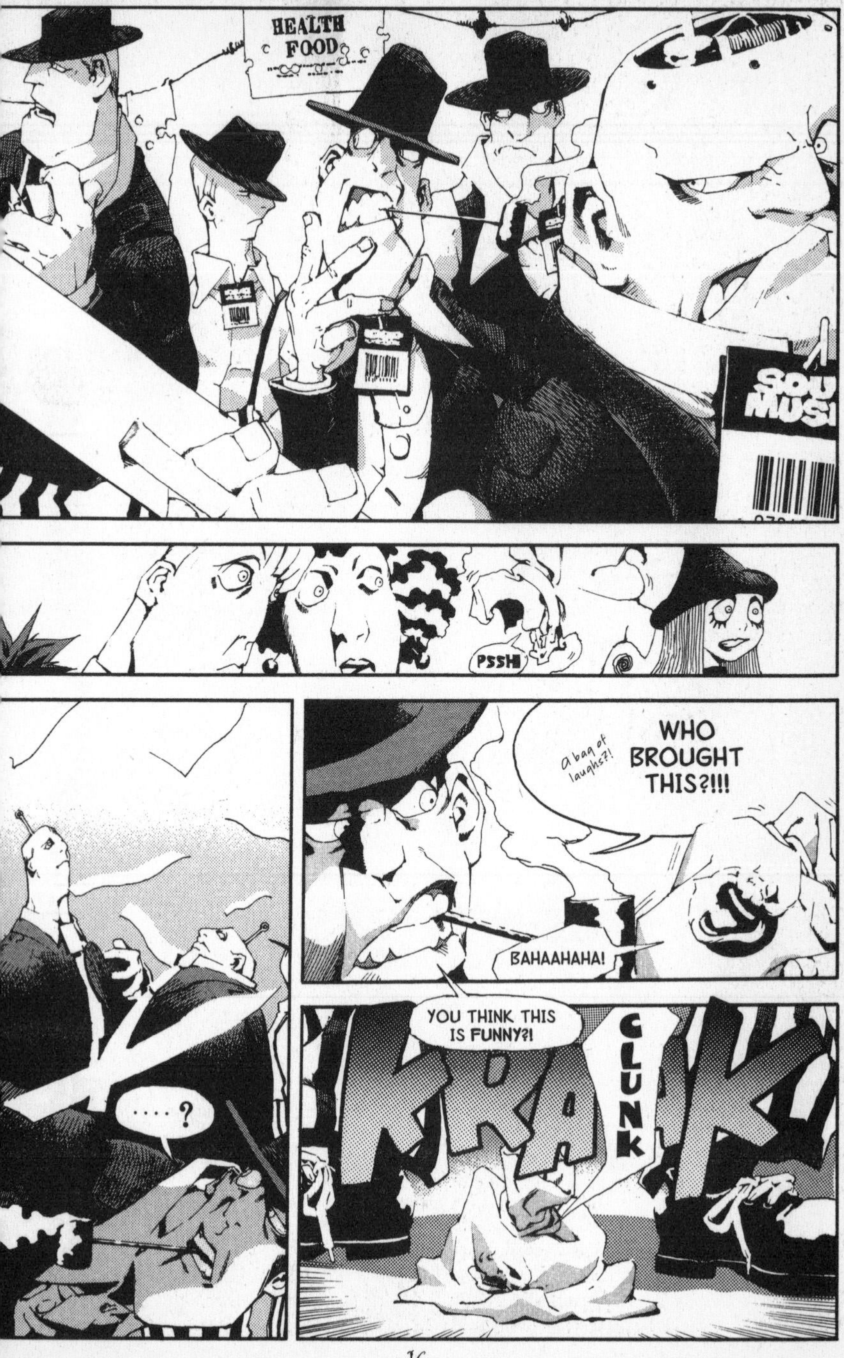
HEALTH FOOD
PSSH
....?
WHO BROUGHT THIS?!!!
A bag of laughs?!
BAHAAHAHA!
YOU THINK THIS IS FUNNY?!
KRAK
CLUNK

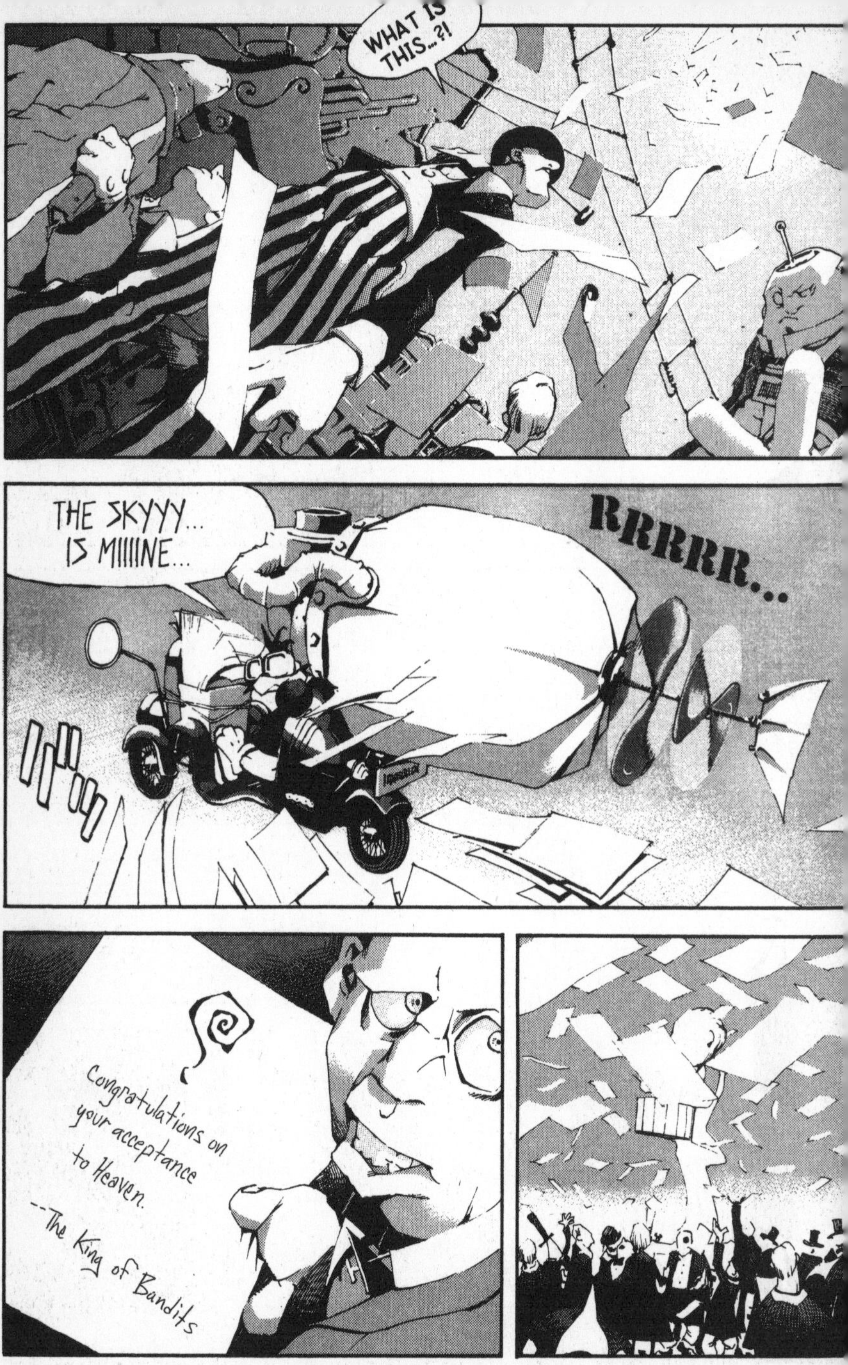
WHAT IS THIS...?!
THE SKYYY... IS MIIIINE...
RRRRRR...
Congratulations on your acceptance to Heaven.
--The King of Bandits

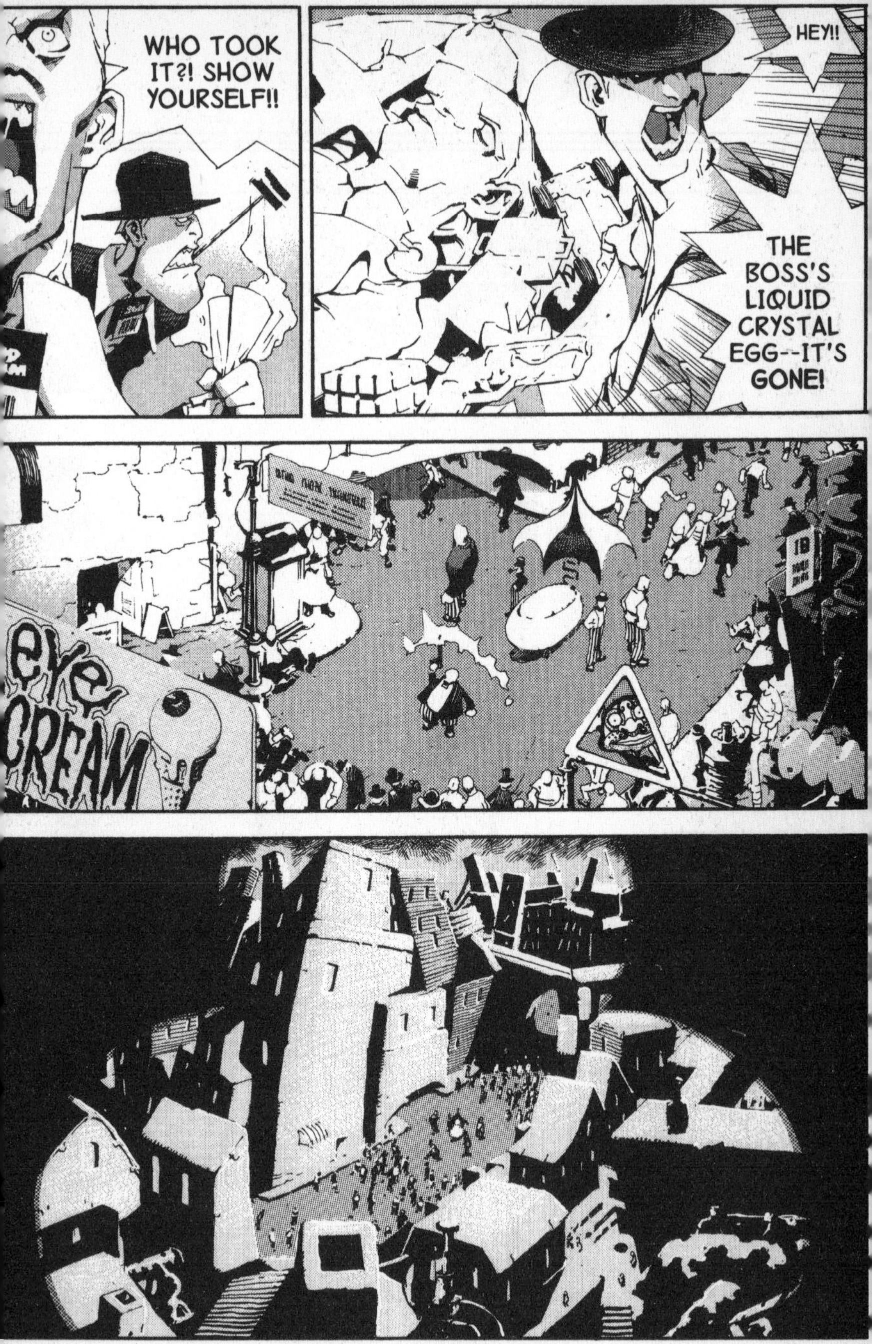
WHO TOOK IT?! SHOW YOURSELF!!
HEY!!
THE BOSS'S LIQUID CRYSTAL EGG--IT'S GONE!
eye CREAM

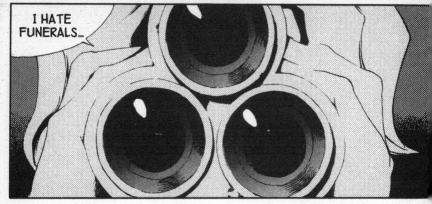

I HATE FUNERALS...

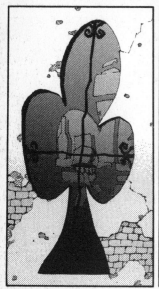

...AND NOISY FUNERALS ARE THE WORST.

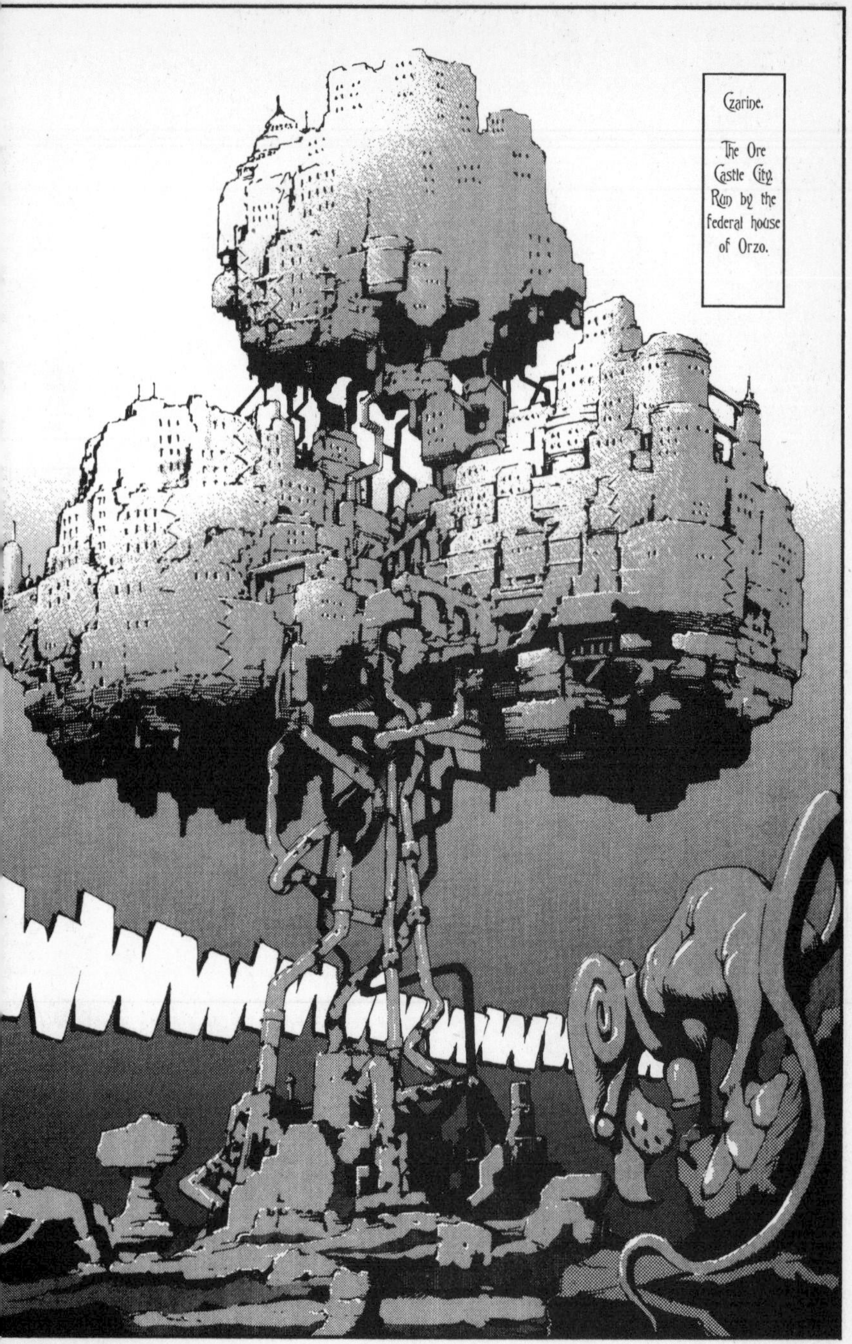
Czarine.
The Ore Castle City. Run by the federal house of Orzo.

A CITY WITH ORE AND A CASTLE, I'D THINK.
ORE CASTLE CITY? WHAT'S THAT S'POSED TO MEAN?
...AND THAT PHONE? THIS CITY WAS BUILT ON THE STUFF THAT MADE BOTH OF 'EM.
YOU'RE SO CRUEL...
SEE THIS EGG...
REMEMBER WHEN YOU ONLY HAD EYES FOR ME?!
SYCAMORE

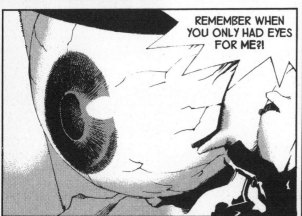

I AIN'T INTO COLLECTIN' CORPSES OF MY OWN KIND!

BUT---JING---DID WE REALLY COME ALL THIS WAY TO STEAL A FOSSILIZED EGG?!

OF COURSE NOT, KIR... SOMETHING MUCH GREATER IS IN STORE.

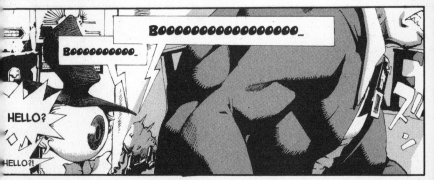

Booooooooooooooooooooo_

Booooooooooo_

HELLO?

HELLO?!

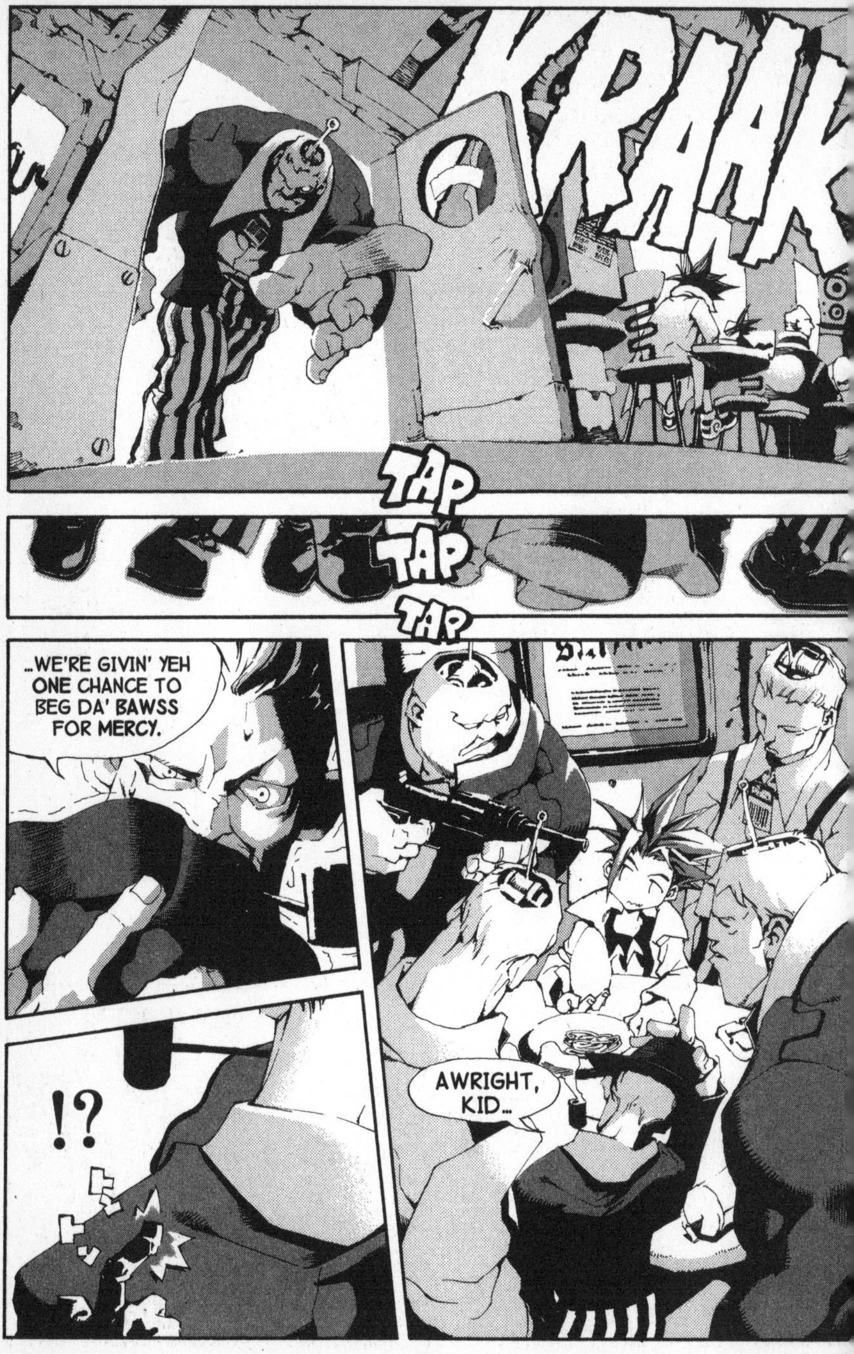
KRAAK
TAP
TAP
TAP
...WE'RE GIVIN' YEH ONE CHANCE TO BEG DA' BAWSS FOR MERCY.
!?
AWRIGHT, KID...

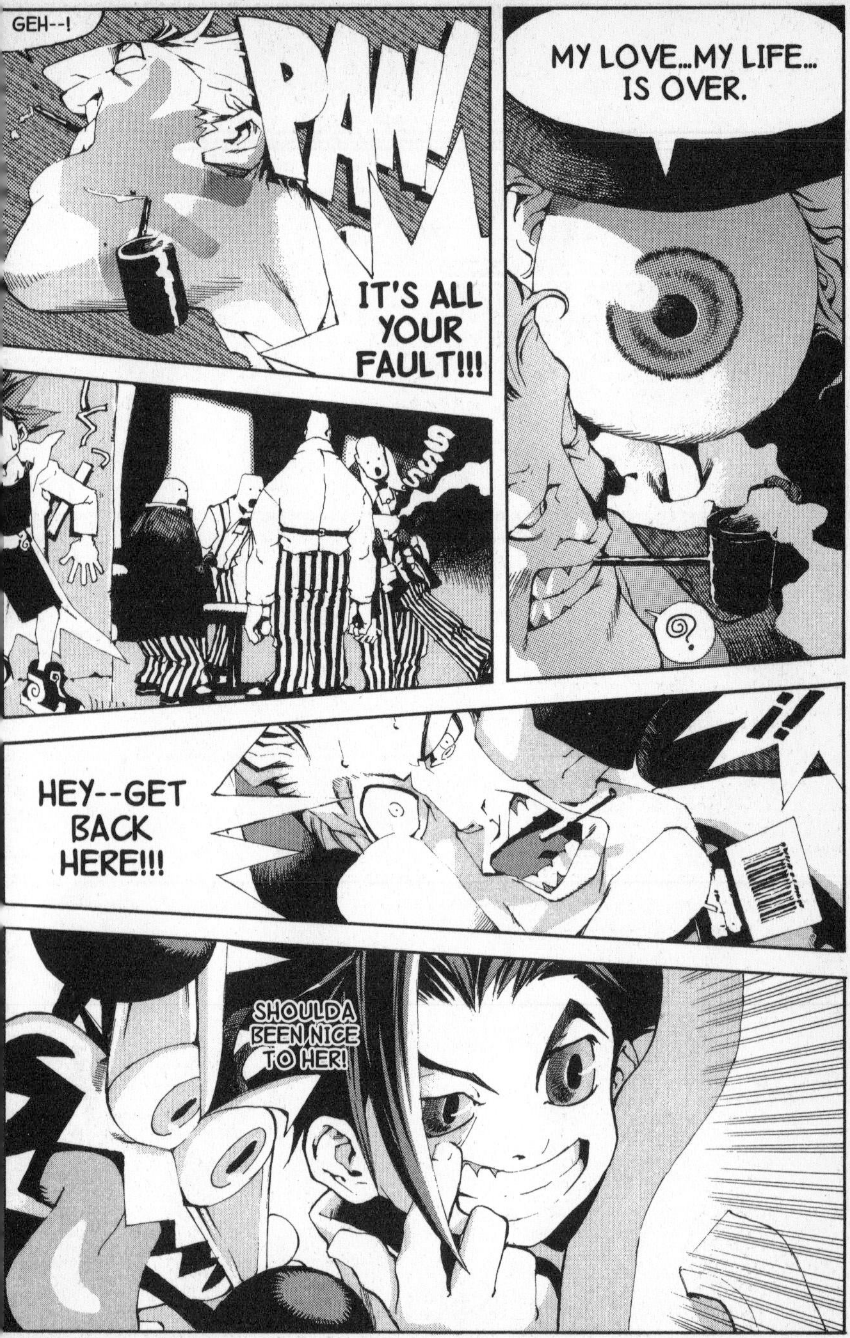
GEH--!
PAN!
IT'S ALL YOUR FAULT!!!
MY LOVE...MY LIFE... IS OVER.
!!
HEY--GET BACK HERE!!!
SHOULDA BEEN NICE TO HER!

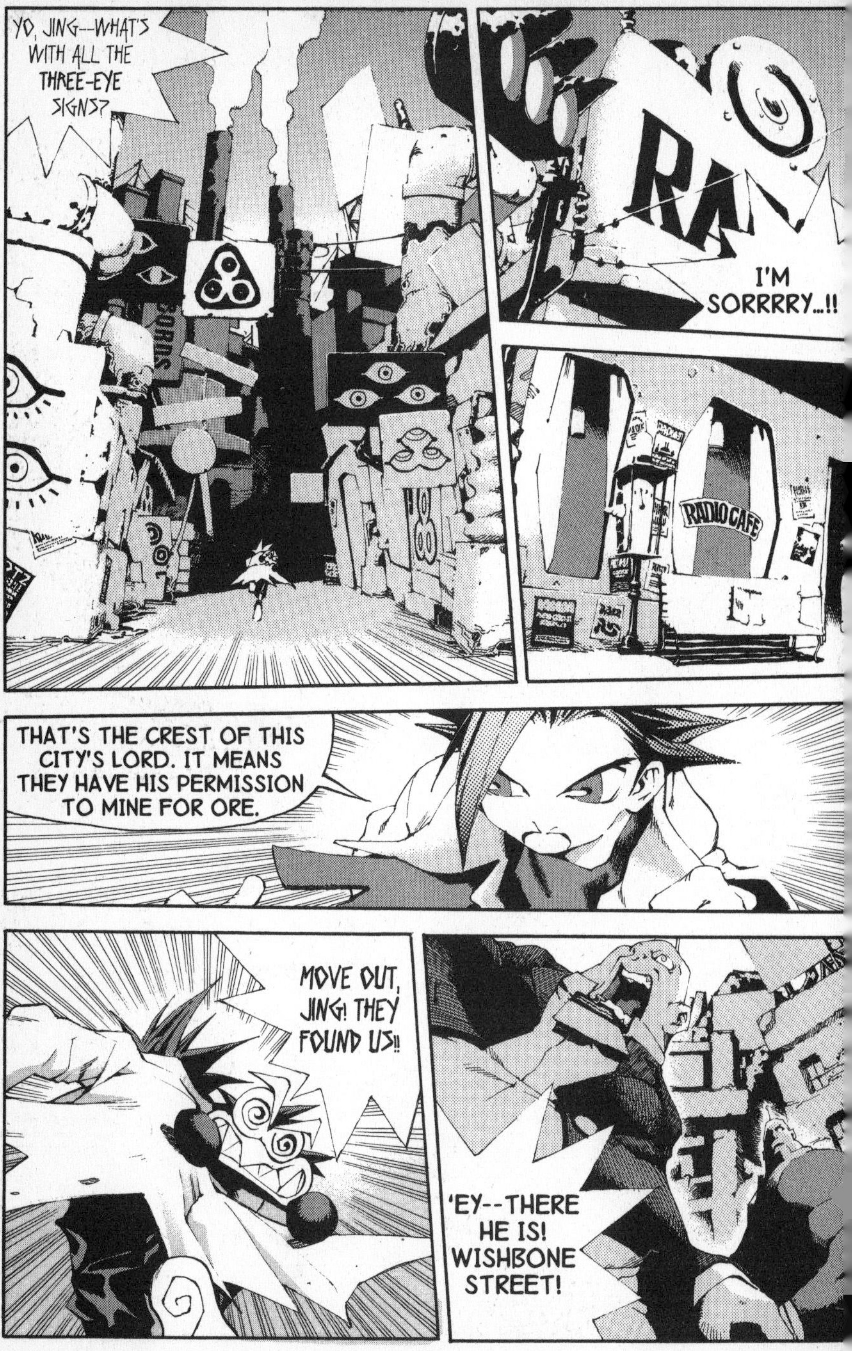
I'M SORRRRY...!!
YO, JING--WHAT'S WITH ALL THE THREE-EYE SIGNS?
RADIO CAFE
THAT'S THE CREST OF THIS CITY'S LORD. IT MEANS THEY HAVE HIS PERMISSION TO MINE FOR ORE.
'EY--THERE HE IS! WISHBONE STREET!
MOVE OUT, JING! THEY FOUND US!!

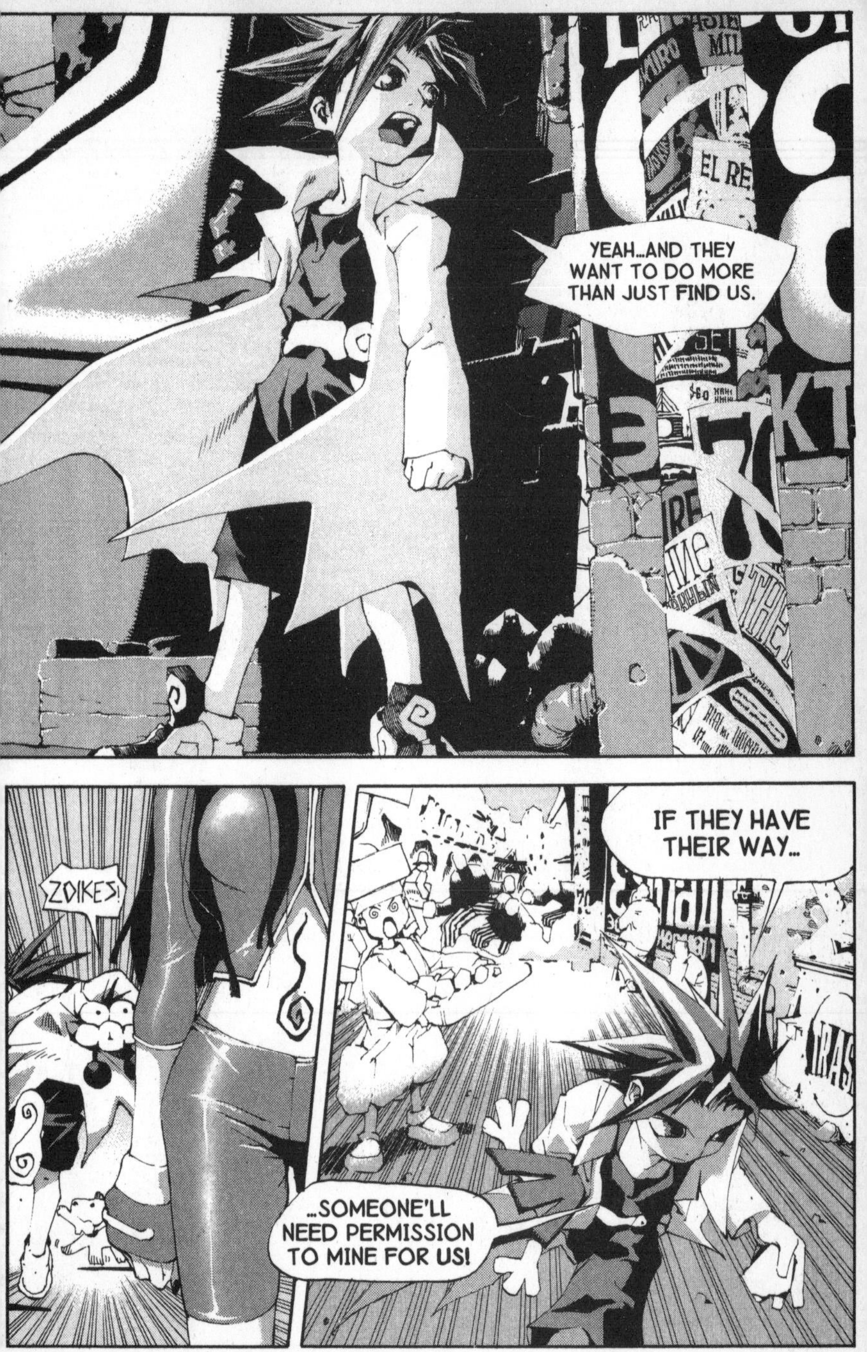
YEAH...AND THEY WANT TO DO MORE THAN JUST FIND US.
ZOIKES!
IF THEY HAVE THEIR WAY...
...SOMEONE'LL NEED PERMISSION TO MINE FOR US!

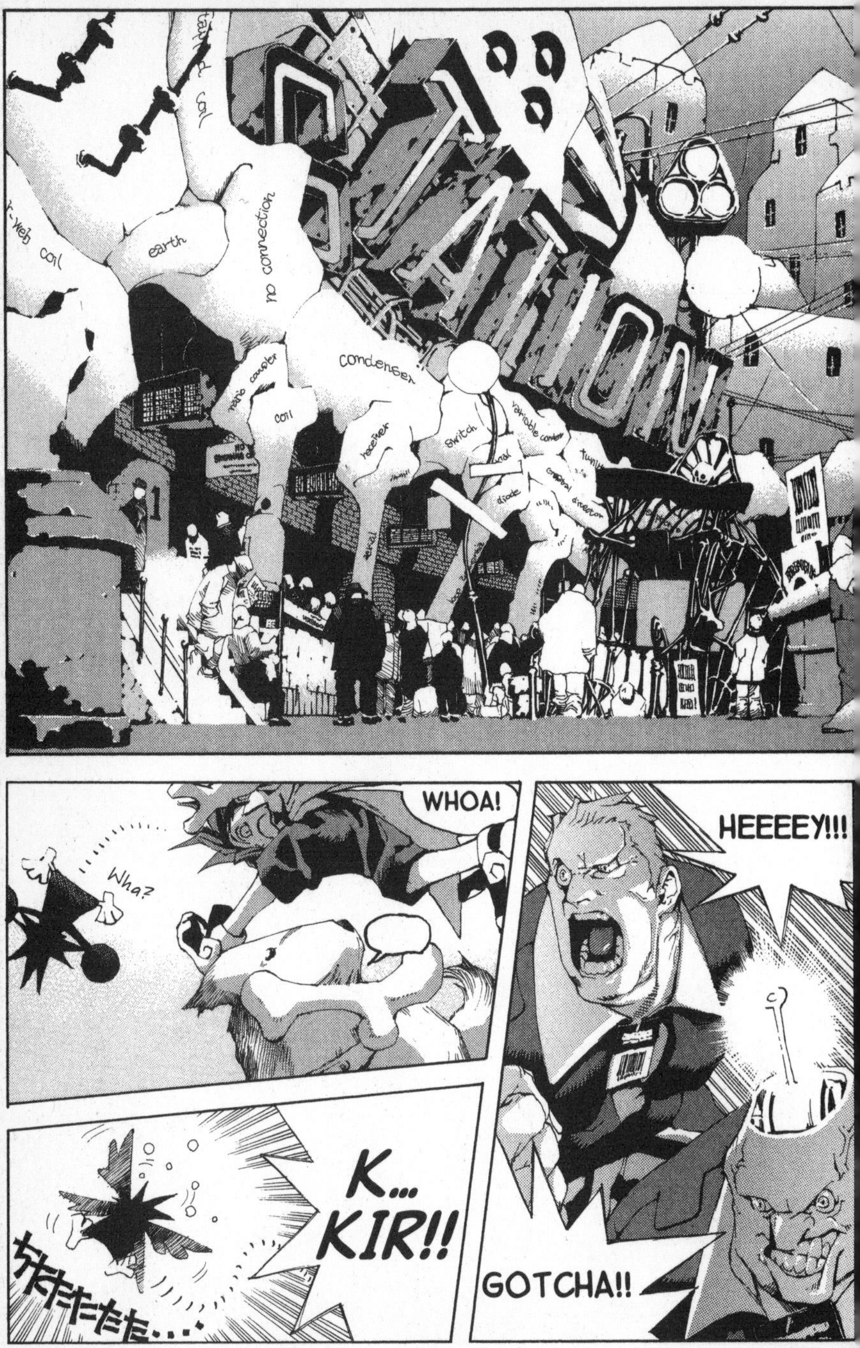
tapped coil
earth
no connection
condenser
coil
receiver
switch
diode
director
HEEEEY!!!
WHOA!
Wha?
GOTCHA!!
K... KIR!!

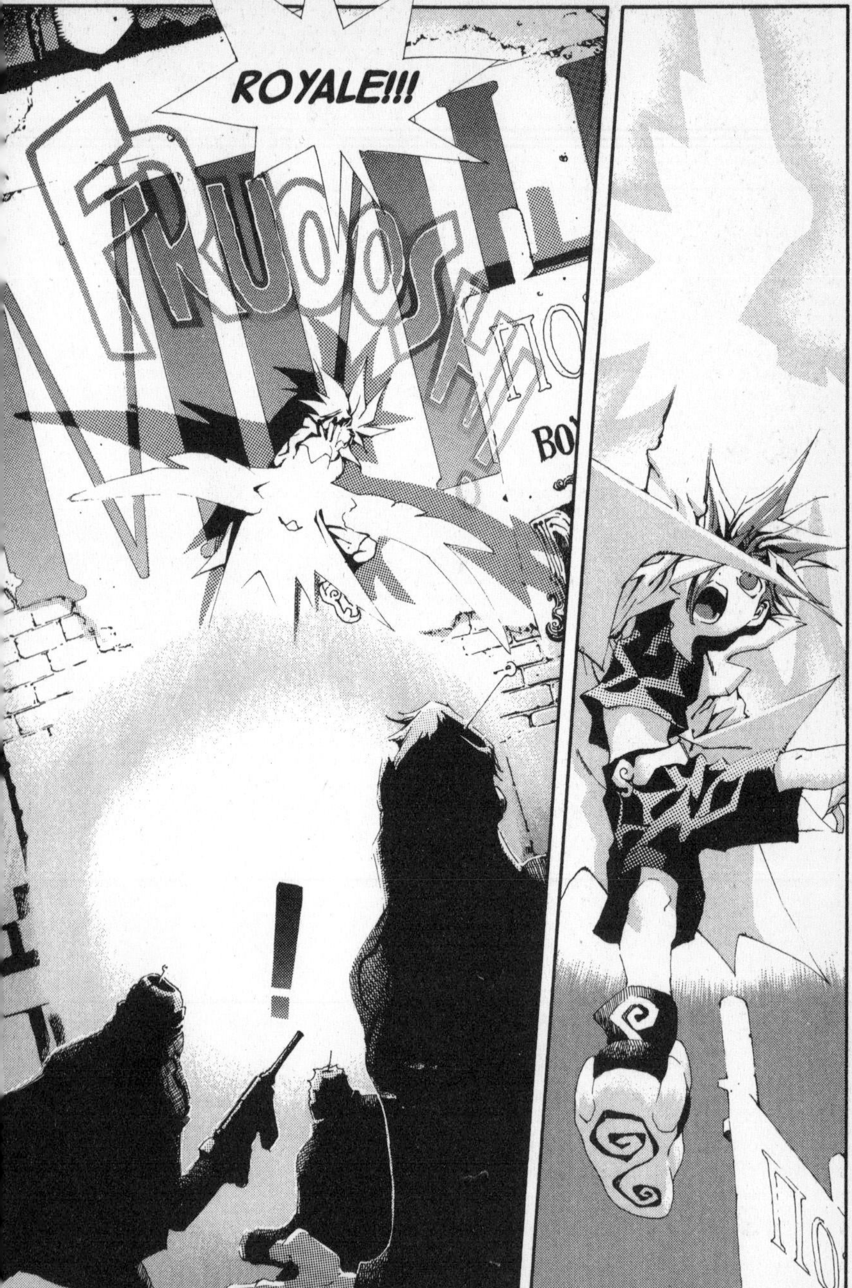
ROYALE!!!
!

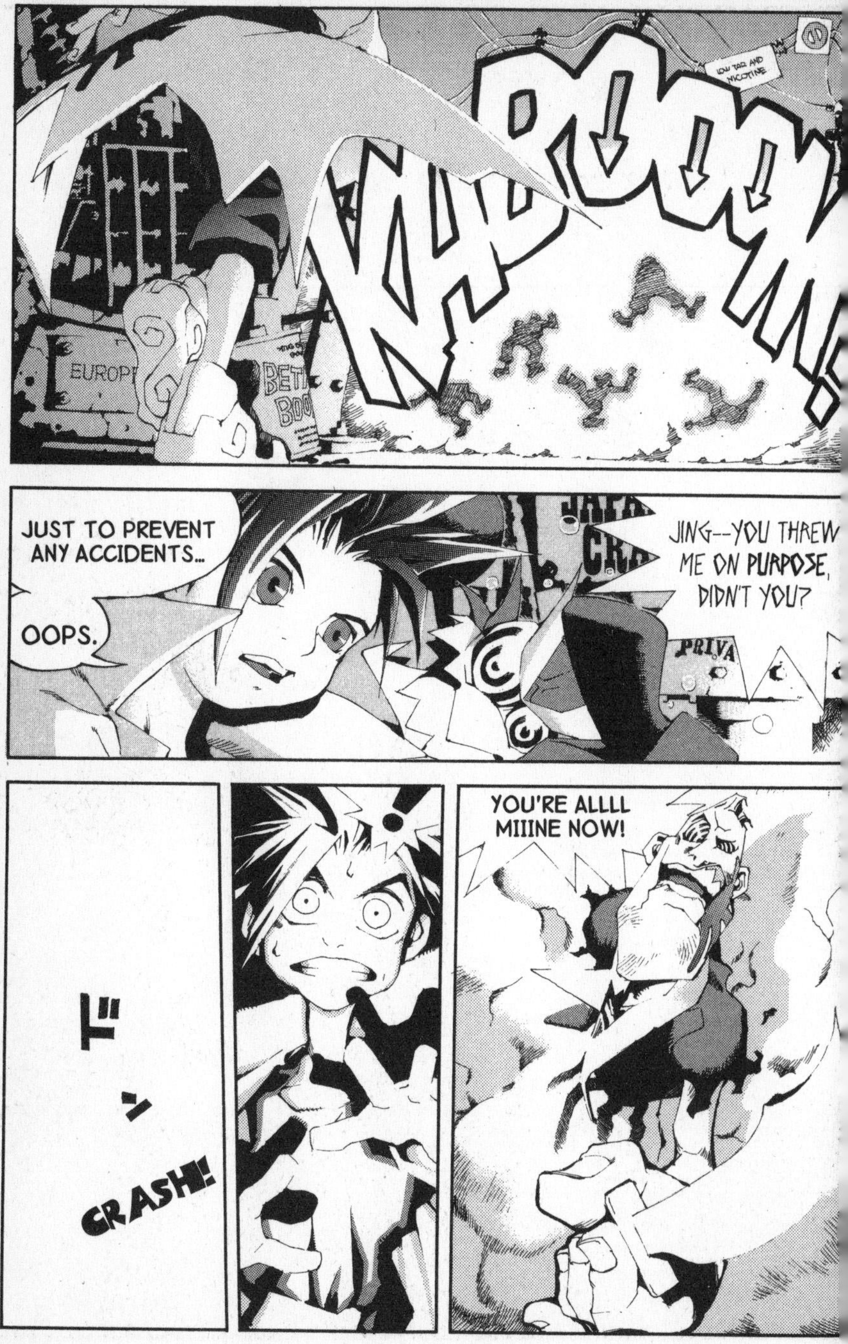
LOW TAR AND NICOTINE
KABOOM
EUROP
JING--YOU THREW ME ON PURPOSE, DIDN'T YOU?
JUST TO PREVENT ANY ACCIDENTS...
OOPS.
PRIVA
YOU'RE ALLLL MIIINE NOW!
ドン
CRASH!

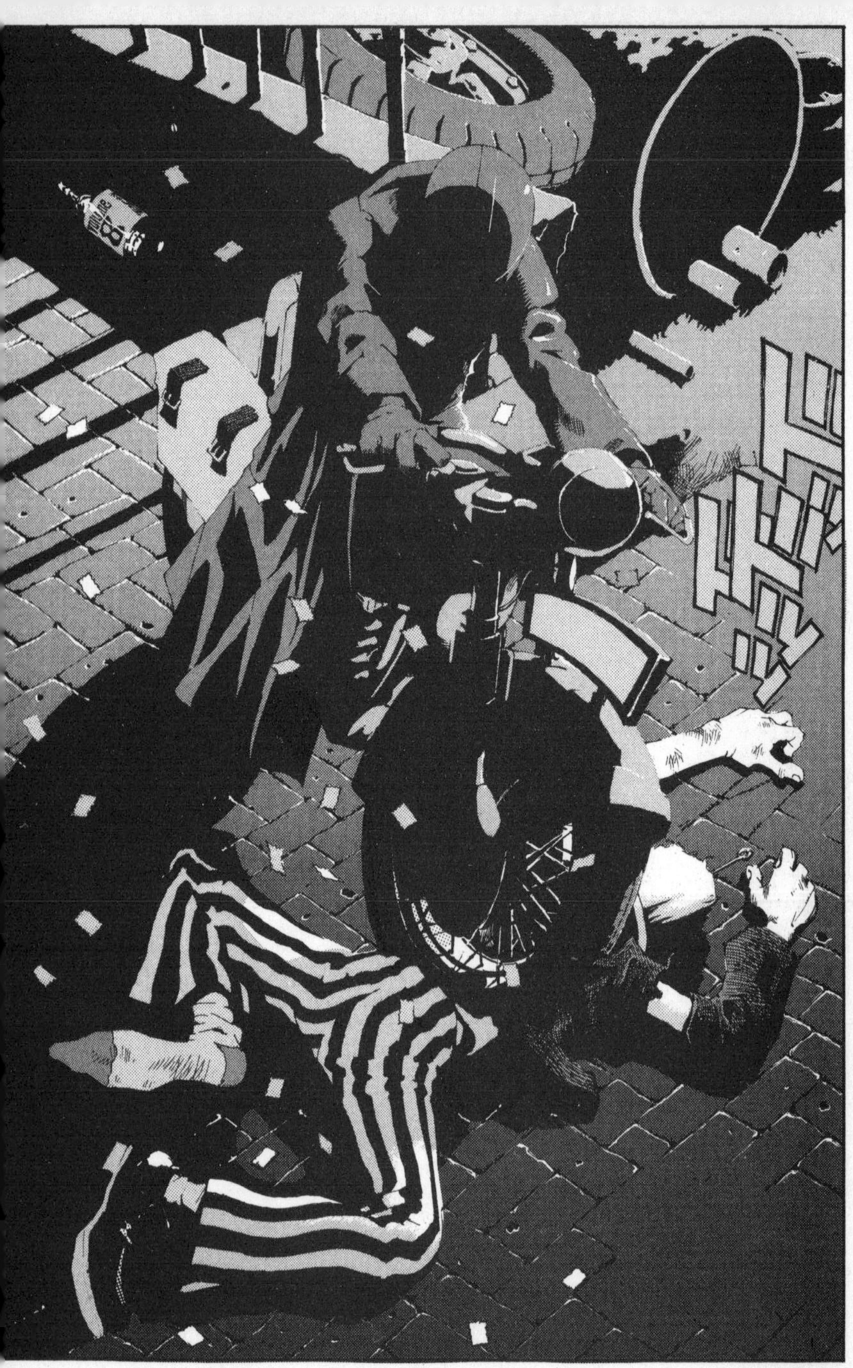

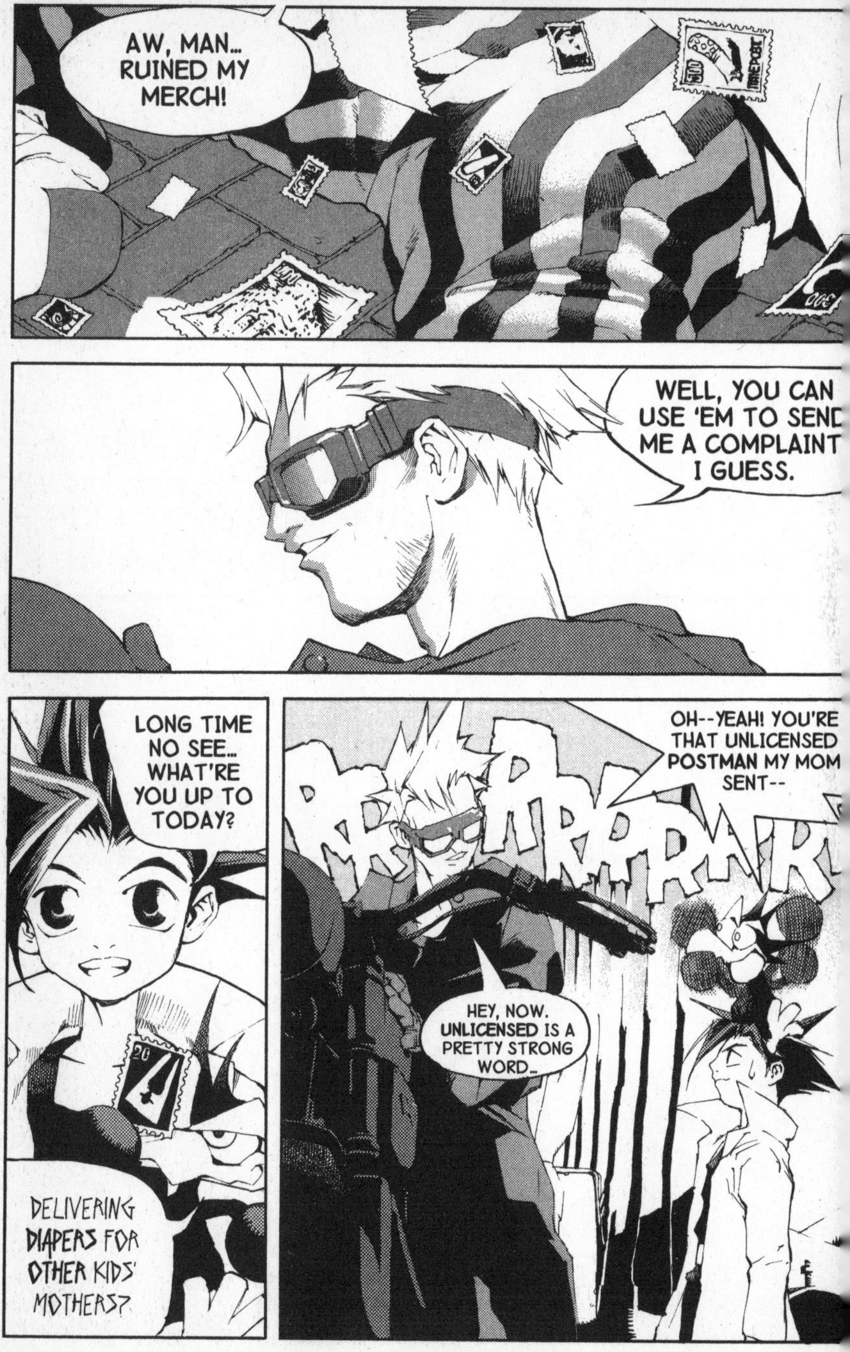
AW, MAN... RUINED MY MERCH!
WELL, YOU CAN USE 'EM TO SEND ME A COMPLAINT I GUESS.
OH--YEAH! YOU'RE THAT UNLICENSED POSTMAN MY MOM SENT--
HEY, NOW. UNLICENSED IS A PRETTY STRONG WORD...
LONG TIME NO SEE... WHAT'RE YOU UP TO TODAY?
DELIVERING DIAPERS FOR OTHER KIDS' MOTHERS?

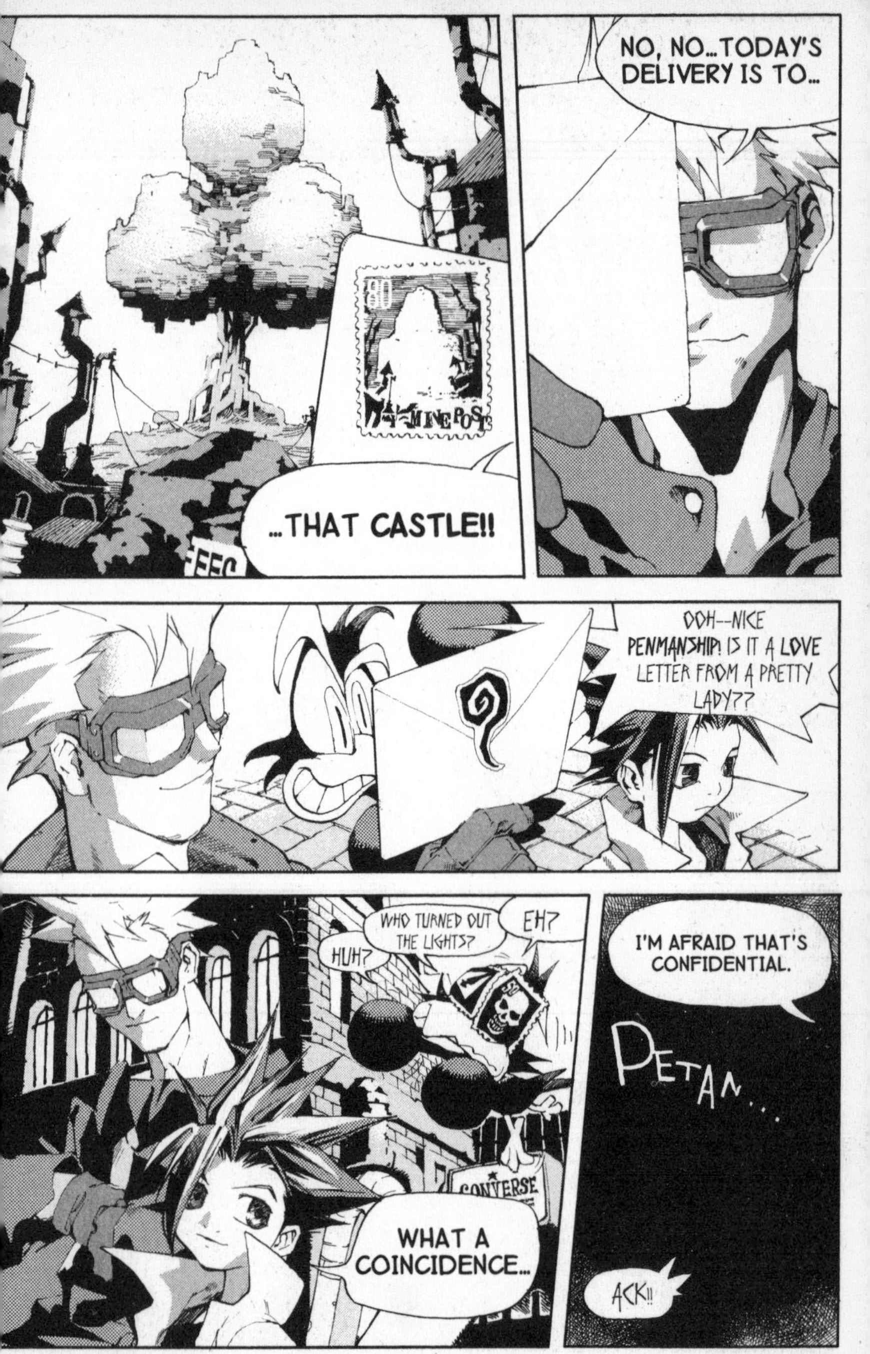
NO, NO...TODAY'S DELIVERY IS TO...
80
MINE POST
...THAT CASTLE!!
OOH--NICE PENMANSHIP! IS IT A LOVE LETTER FROM A PRETTY LADY??
I'M AFRAID THAT'S CONFIDENTIAL.
PETAN...
ACK!!
EH?
WHO TURNED OUT THE LIGHTS?
HUH?
CONVERSE
WHAT A COINCIDENCE...

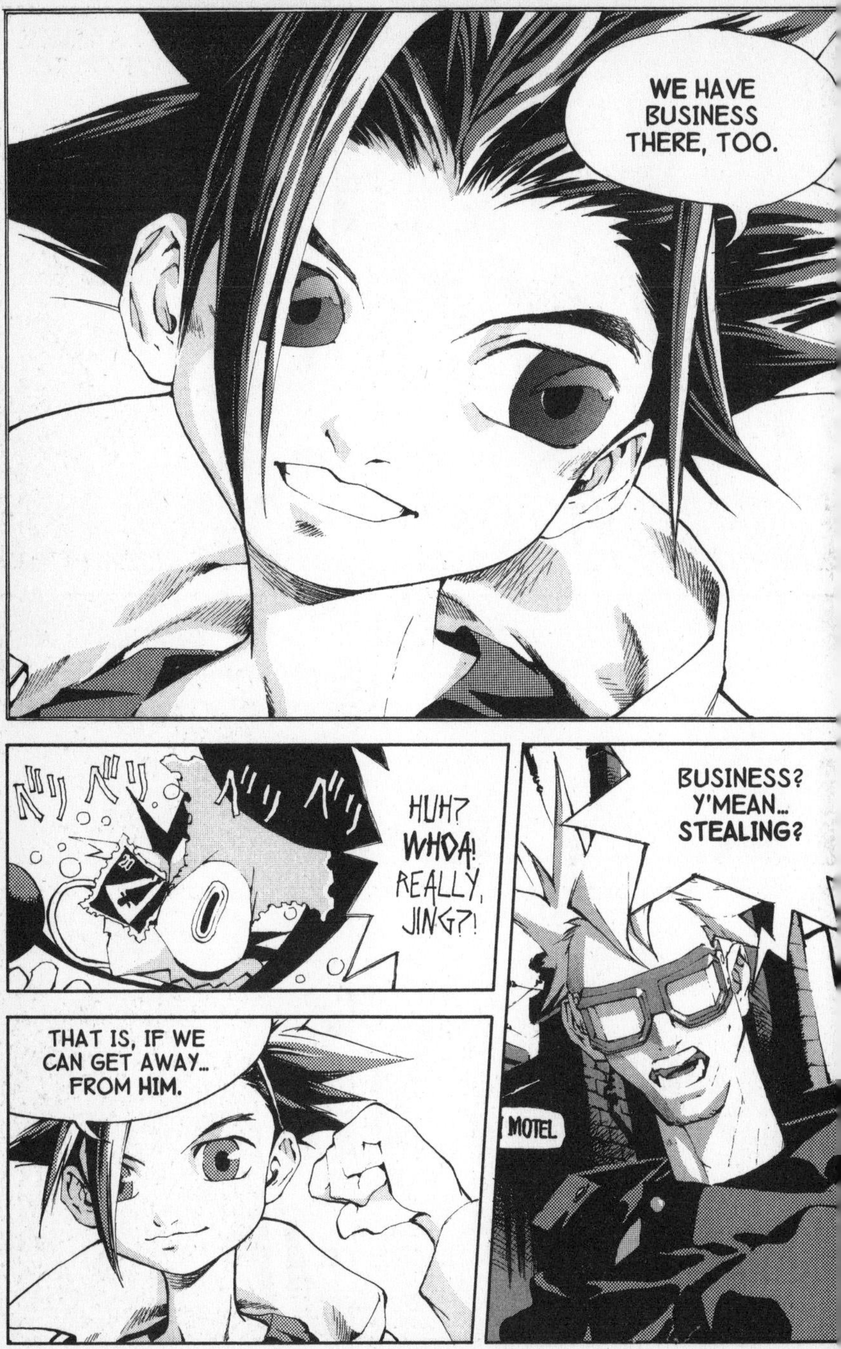

WE HAVE BUSINESS THERE, TOO.
BUSINESS? Y'MEAN... STEALING?
MOTEL
HUH? WHOA! REALLY, JING?!
THAT IS, IF WE CAN GET AWAY... FROM HIM.

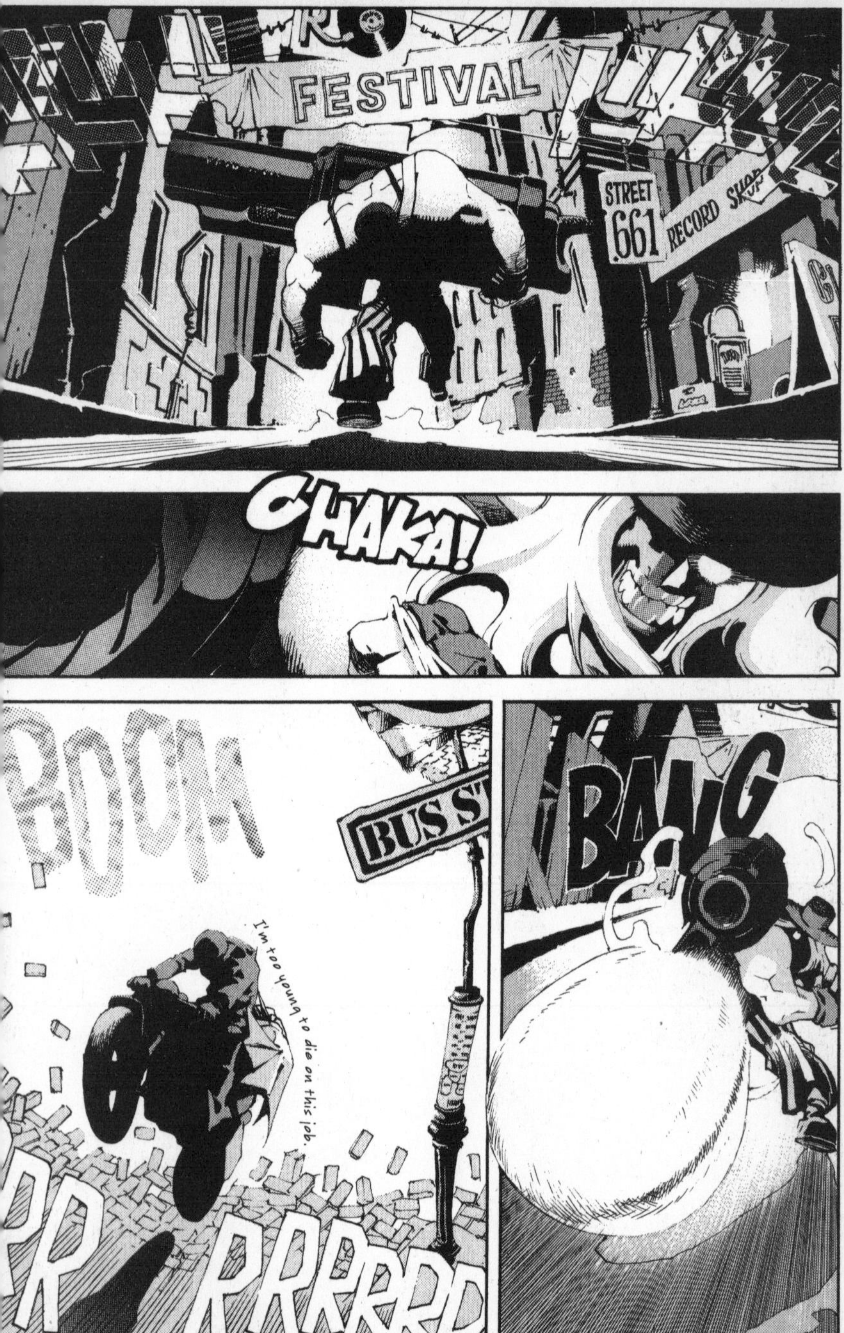
FESTIVAL
STREET 661
RECORD
CHAKA!
BOOM
BUS S
I'm too young to die on this job.
RRRRRD
BANG

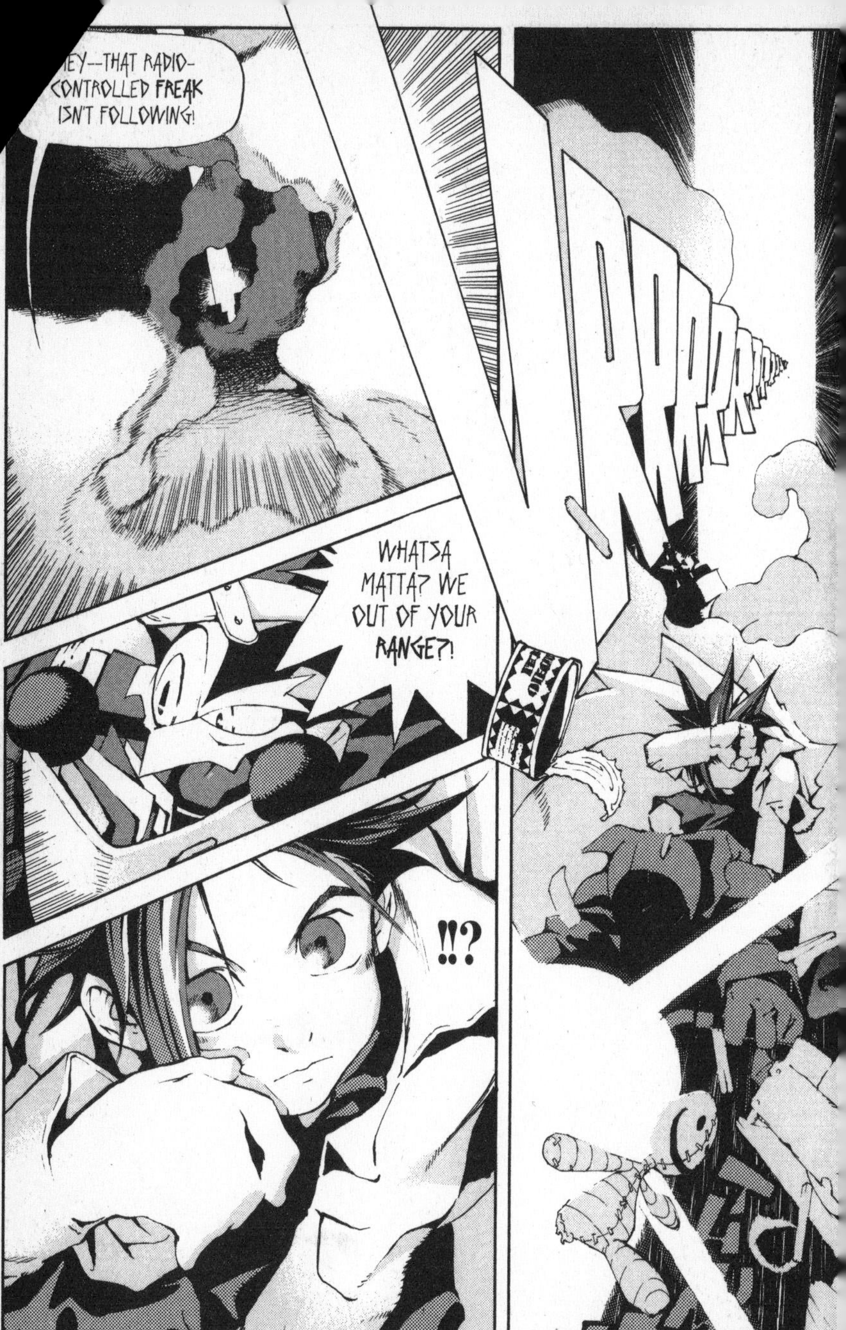
EY--THAT RADIO-CONTROLLED FREAK ISN'T FOLLOWING!
WHATSA MATTA? WE OUT OF YOUR RANGE?!
!!?

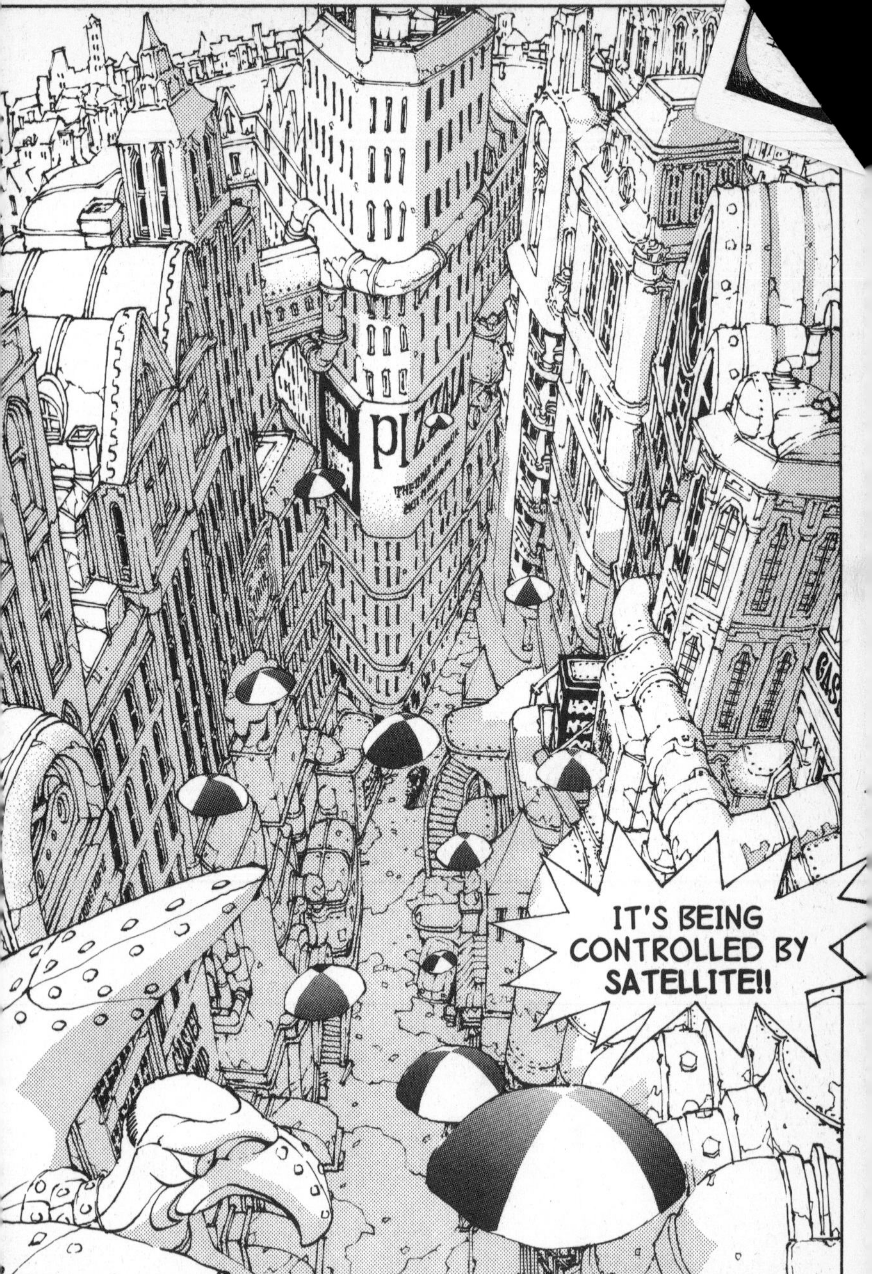

PIZ
IT'S BEING CONTROLLED BY SATELLITE!!

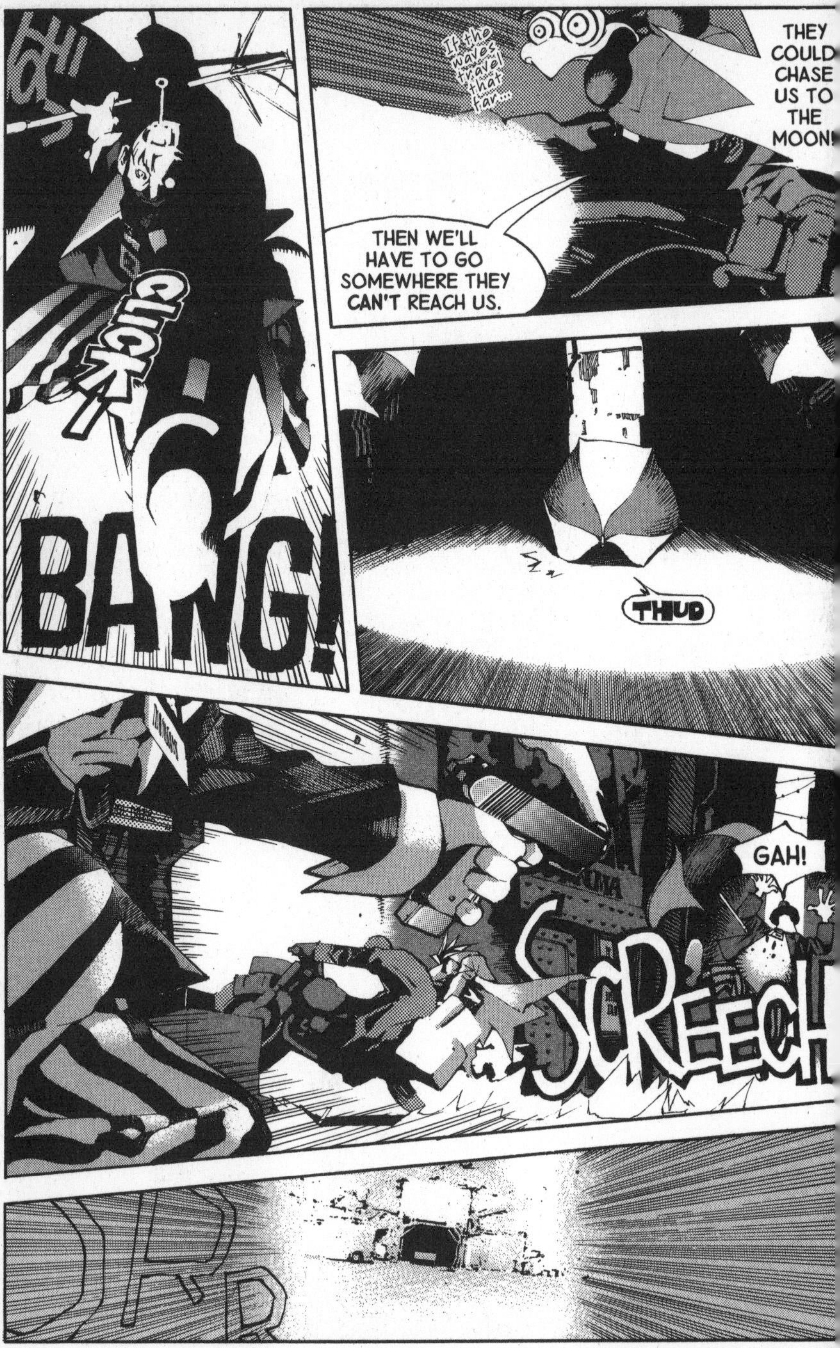
THEY COULD CHASE US TO THE MOON!
If the waves travel that far...
THEN WE'LL HAVE TO GO SOMEWHERE THEY CAN'T REACH US.
CLICK
BANG!
THUD
GAH!
SCREECH

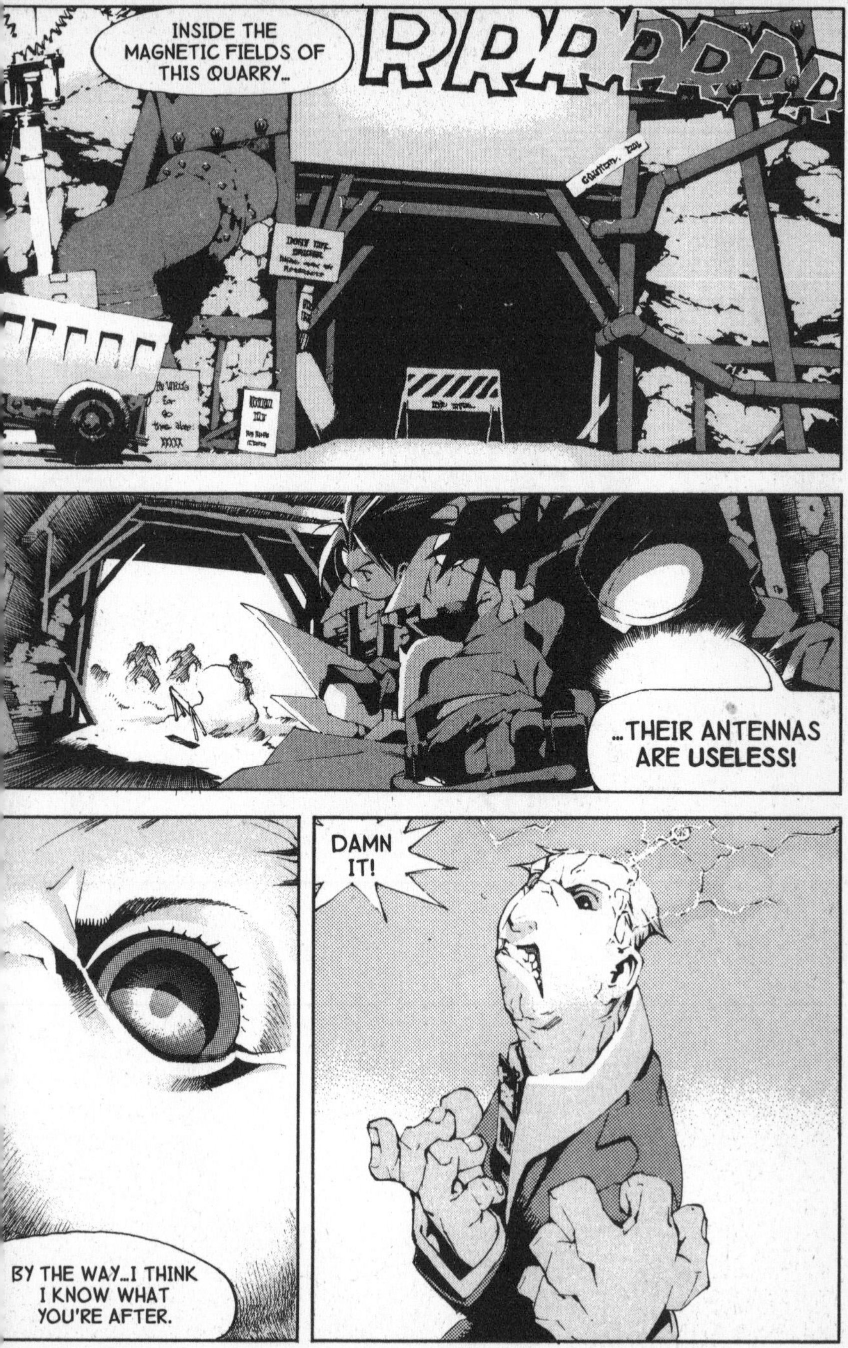

INSIDE THE MAGNETIC FIELDS OF THIS QUARRY...
RRRRRRR
...THEIR ANTENNAS ARE USELESS!
BY THE WAY...I THINK I KNOW WHAT YOU'RE AFTER.
DAMN IT!

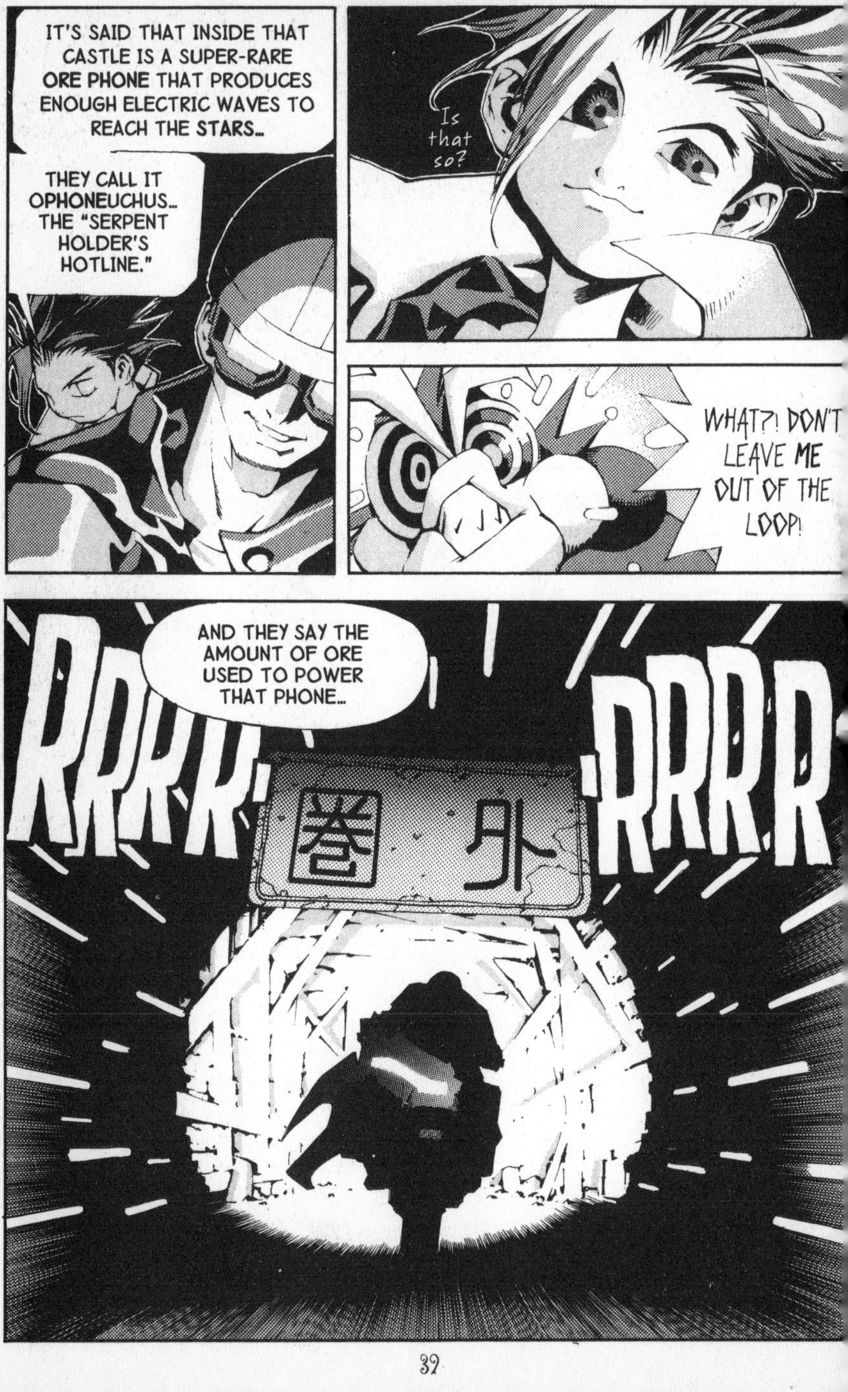
IT'S SAID THAT INSIDE THAT CASTLE IS A SUPER-RARE ORE PHONE THAT PRODUCES ENOUGH ELECTRIC WAVES TO REACH THE STARS...
THEY CALL IT OPHONEUCHUS... THE "SERPENT HOLDER'S HOTLINE."
Is that so?
WHAT?! DON'T LEAVE ME OUT OF THE LOOP!
AND THEY SAY THE AMOUNT OF ORE USED TO POWER THAT PHONE...
RRRRR
RRRR
圏外

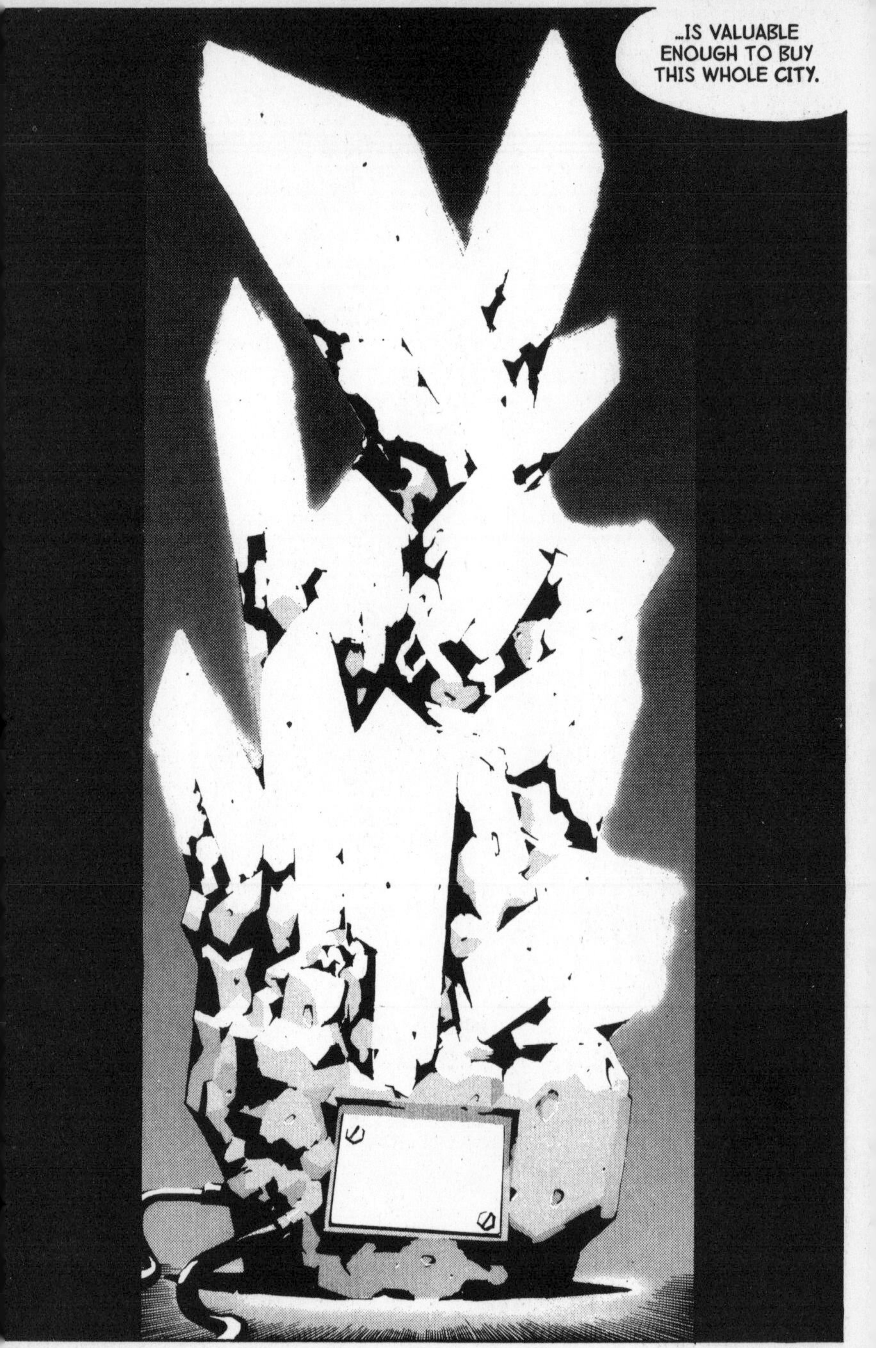
...IS VALUABLE ENOUGH TO BUY THIS WHOLE CITY.

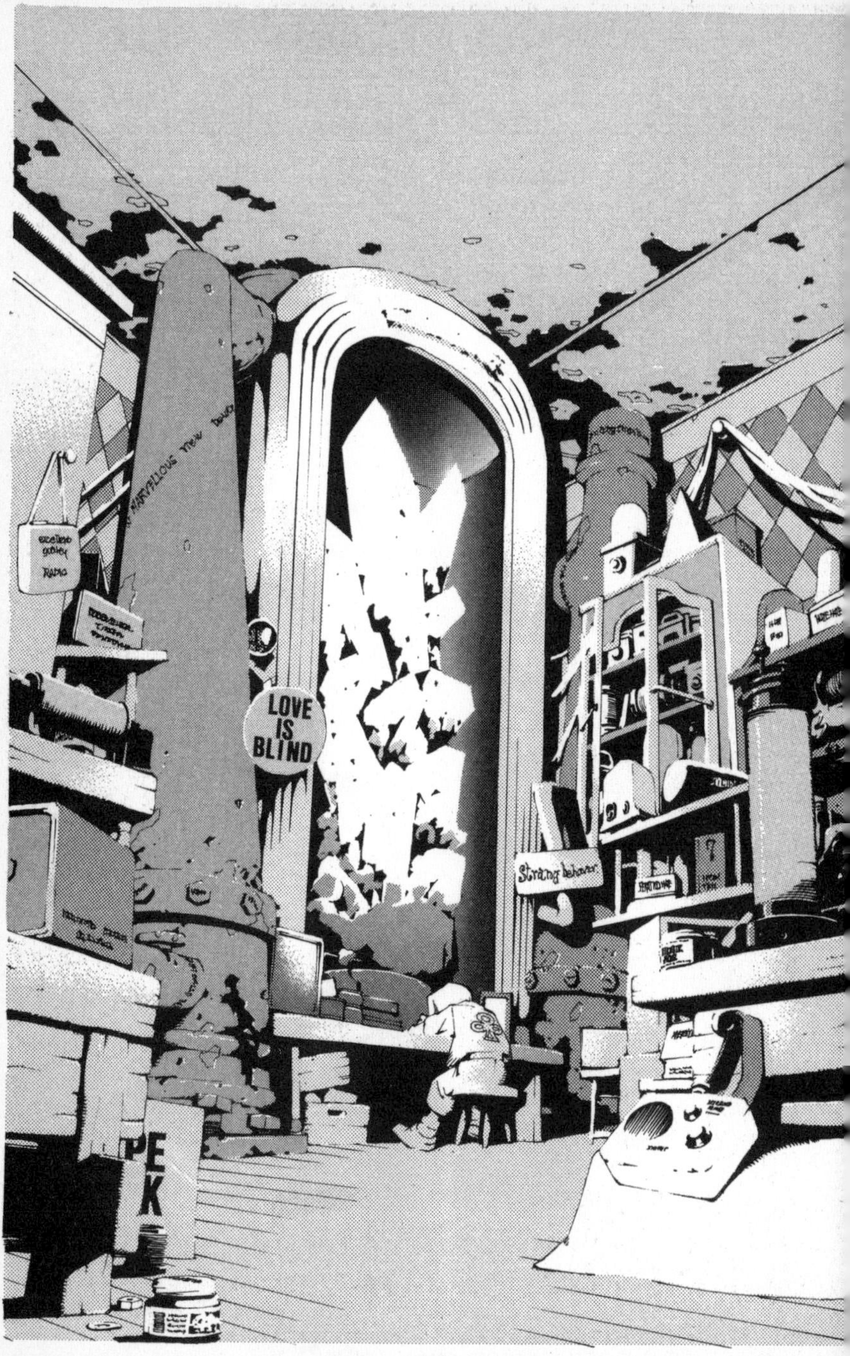
LOVE IS BLIND
Strang behavior
RADIO

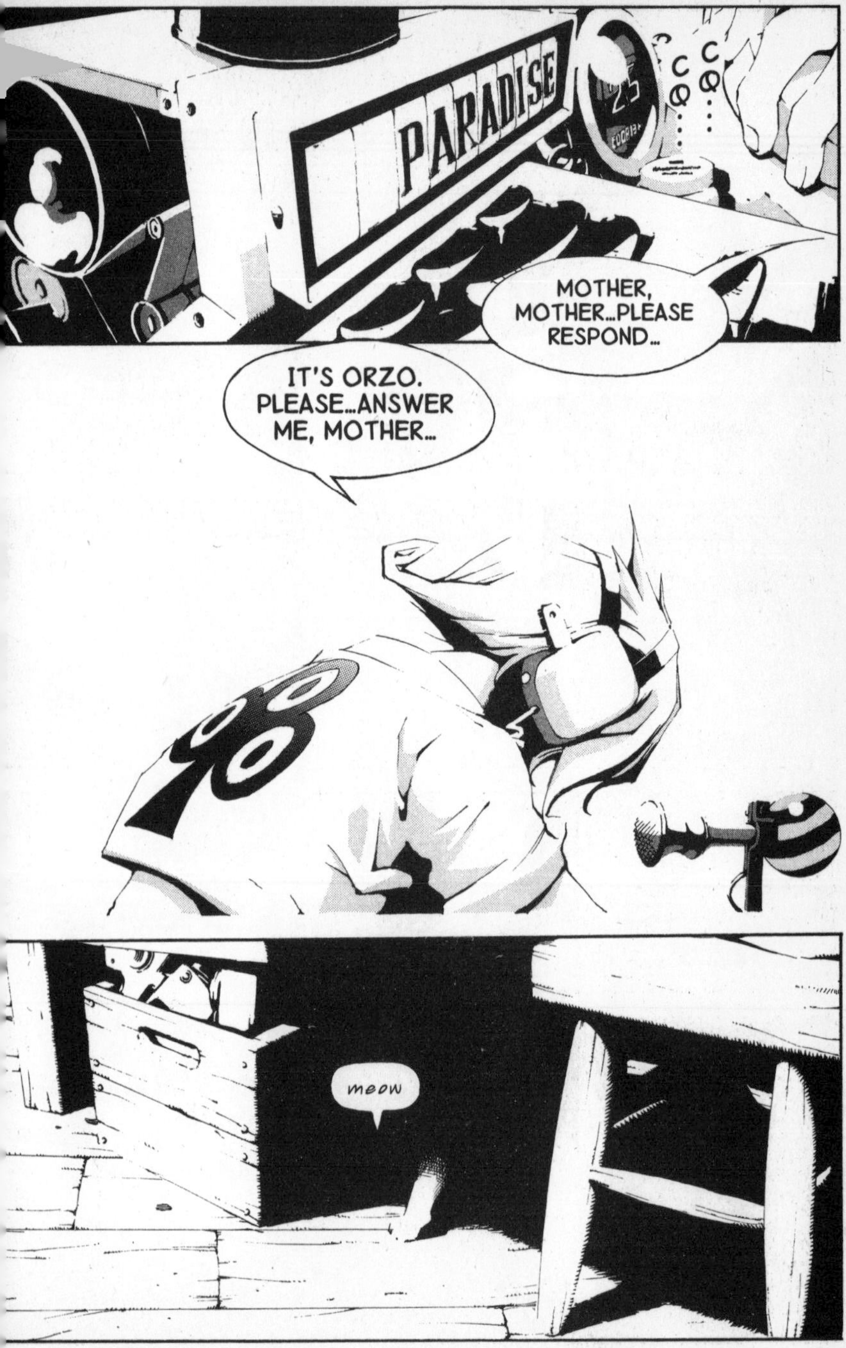
PARADISE
MOTHER, MOTHER...PLEASE RESPOND...
IT'S ORZO. PLEASE...ANSWER ME, MOTHER...
meow

CQ...
CQ...

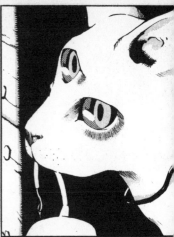

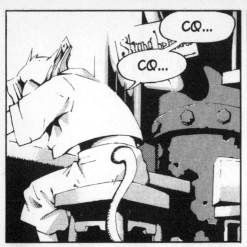

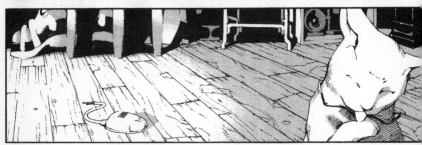

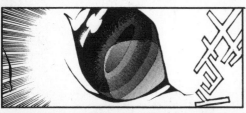

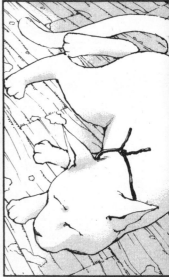

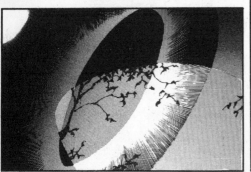

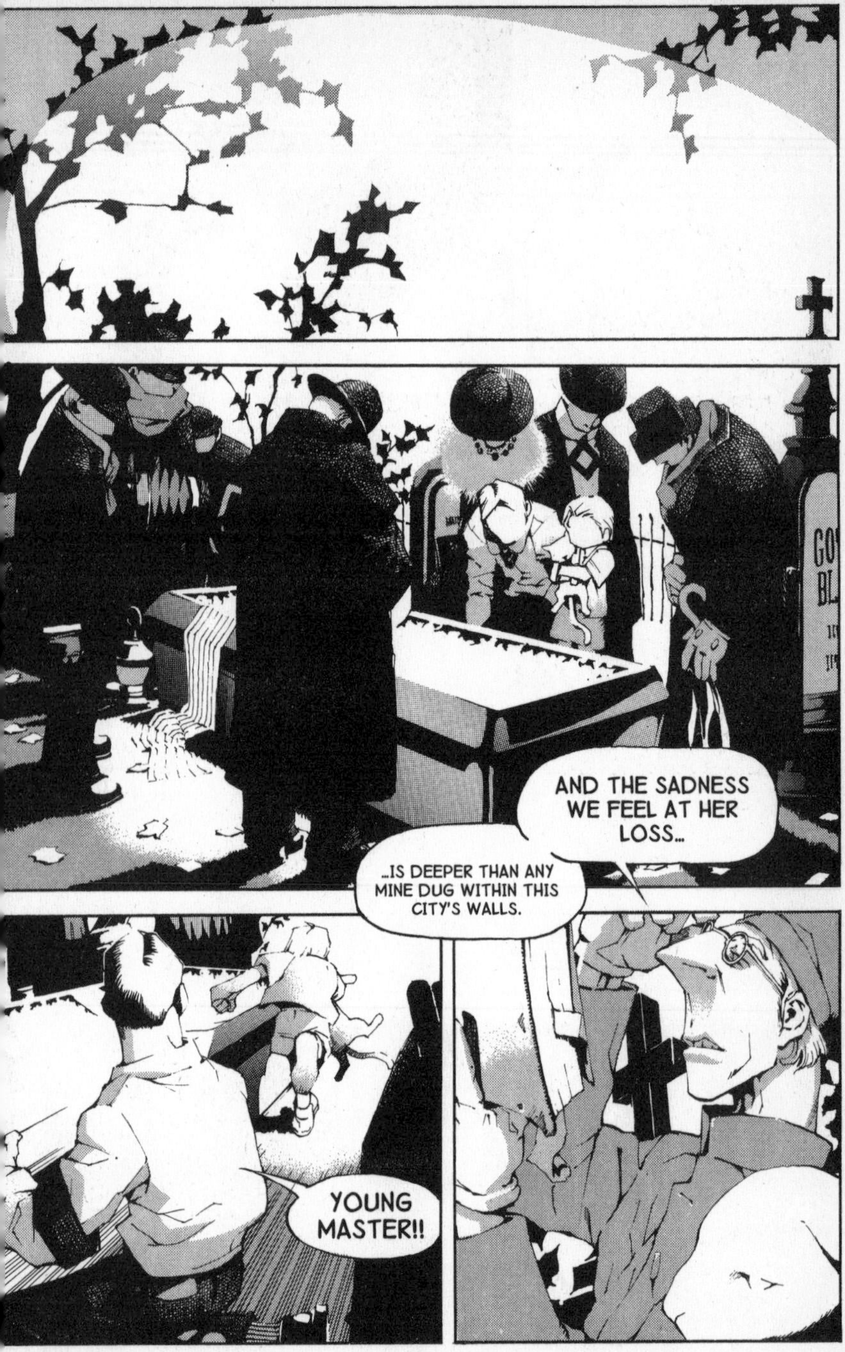
AND THE SADNESS WE FEEL AT HER LOSS...
...IS DEEPER THAN ANY MINE DUG WITHIN THIS CITY'S WALLS.
YOUNG MASTER!!

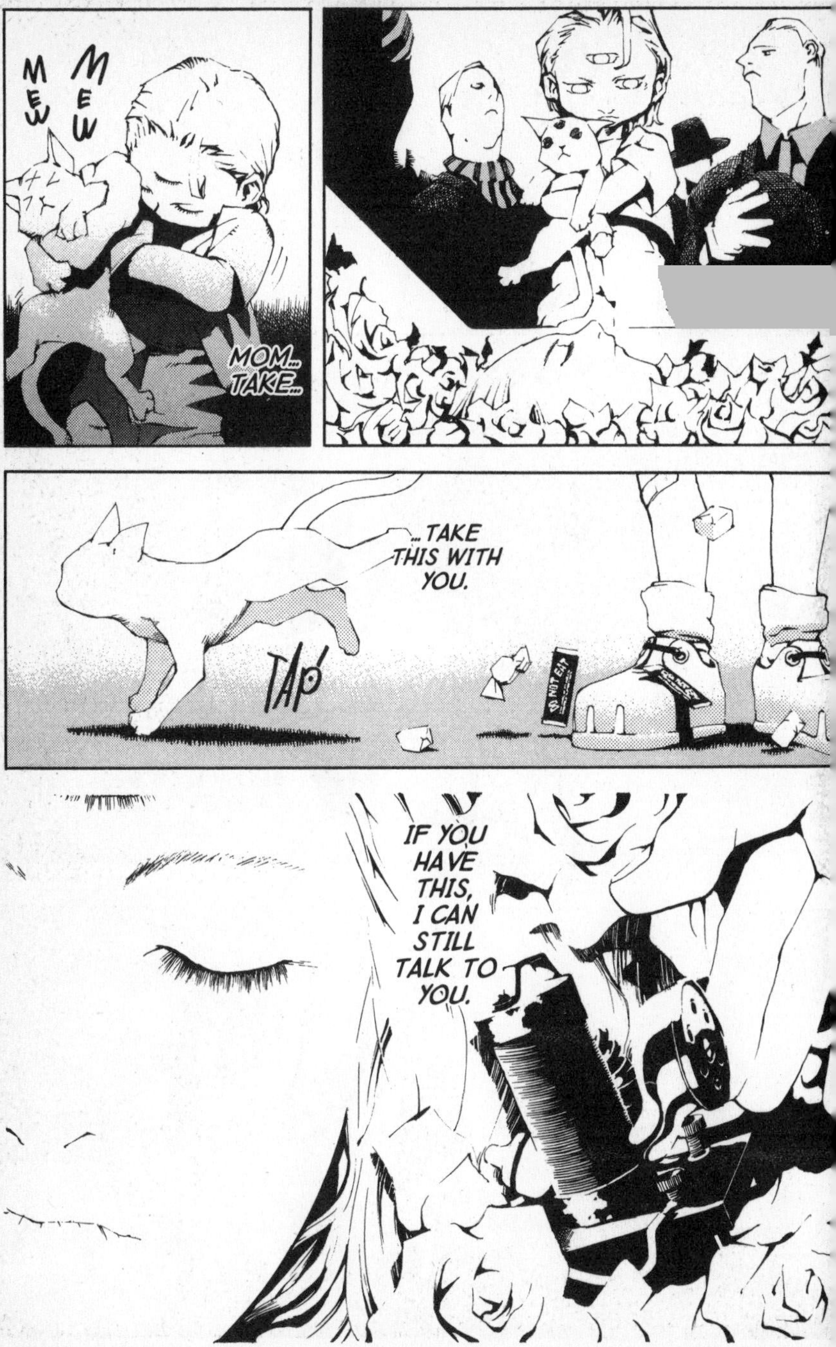
MEW
MEW
MOM... TAKE...
...TAKE THIS WITH YOU.
TAP
DO NOT EAT
IF YOU HAVE THIS, I CAN STILL TALK TO YOU.

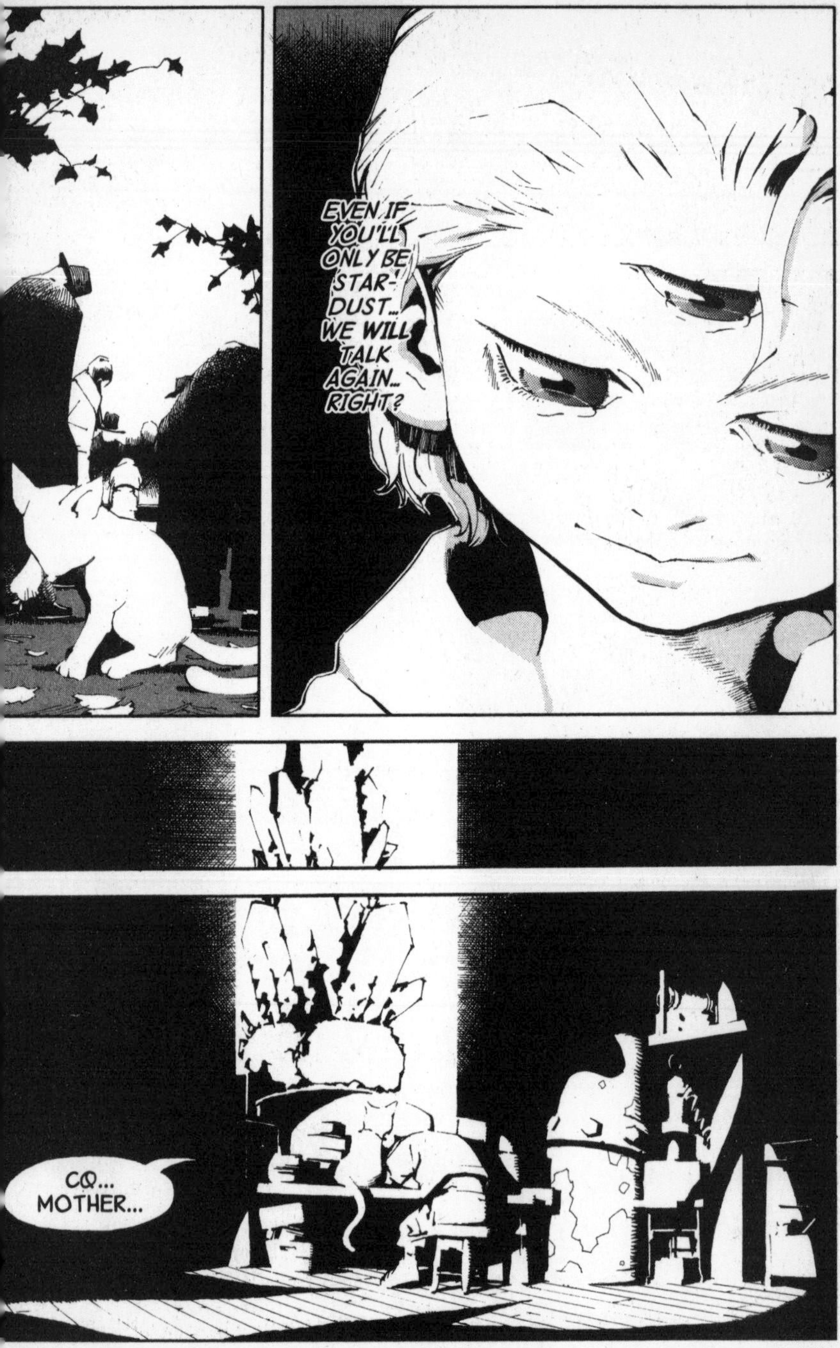
EVEN IF YOU'LL ONLY BE STAR-DUST... WE WILL TALK AGAIN... RIGHT?
CQ... MOTHER...

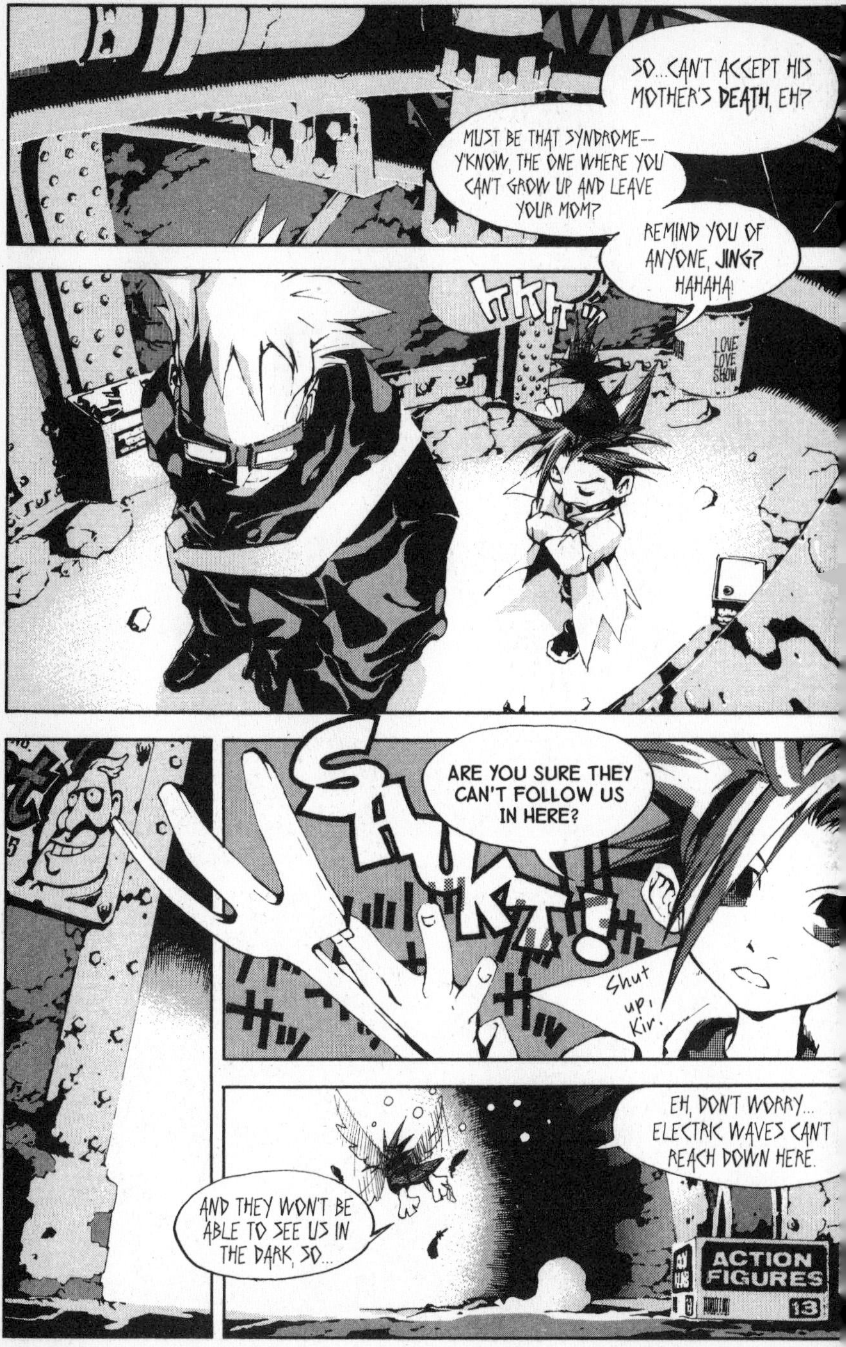

SO...CAN'T ACCEPT HIS MOTHER'S DEATH, EH?
MUST BE THAT SYNDROME-- Y'KNOW, THE ONE WHERE YOU CAN'T GROW UP AND LEAVE YOUR MOM?
REMIND YOU OF ANYONE, JING? HAHAHA!
LOVE LOVE SHOW
ARE YOU SURE THEY CAN'T FOLLOW US IN HERE?
Shut up, Kir.
EH, DON'T WORRY... ELECTRIC WAVES CAN'T REACH DOWN HERE.
AND THEY WON'T BE ABLE TO SEE US IN THE DARK, SO...
ACTION FIGURES
13

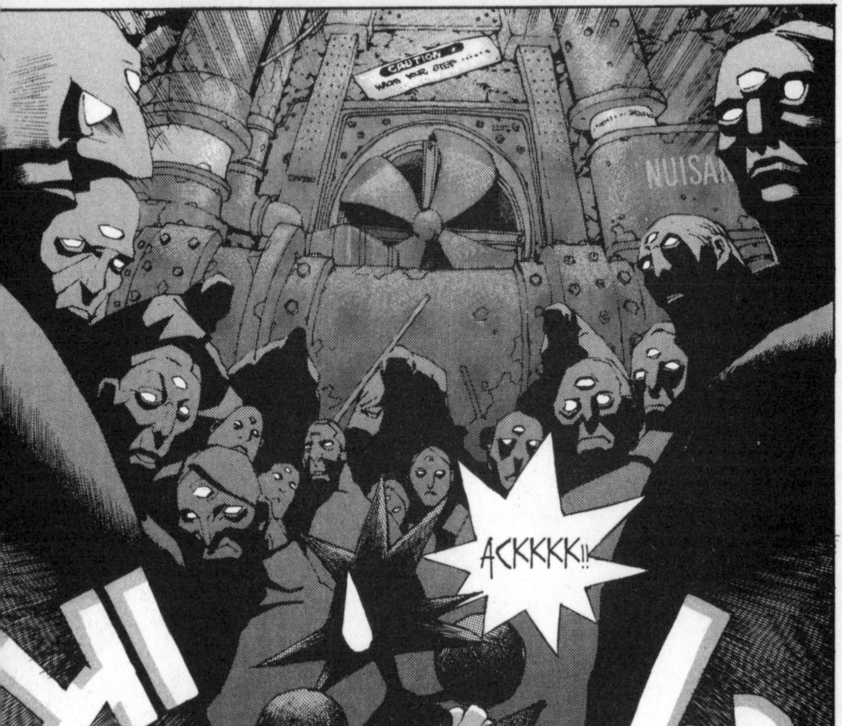
CAUTION
WATCH YOUR STEP
NUISA
ACKKKK!!

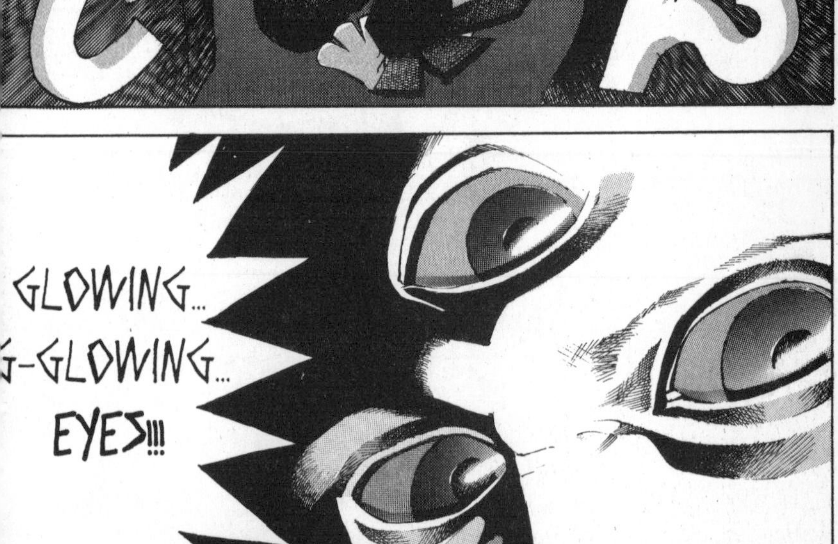
GLOWING...
G-GLOWING...
EYES!!!

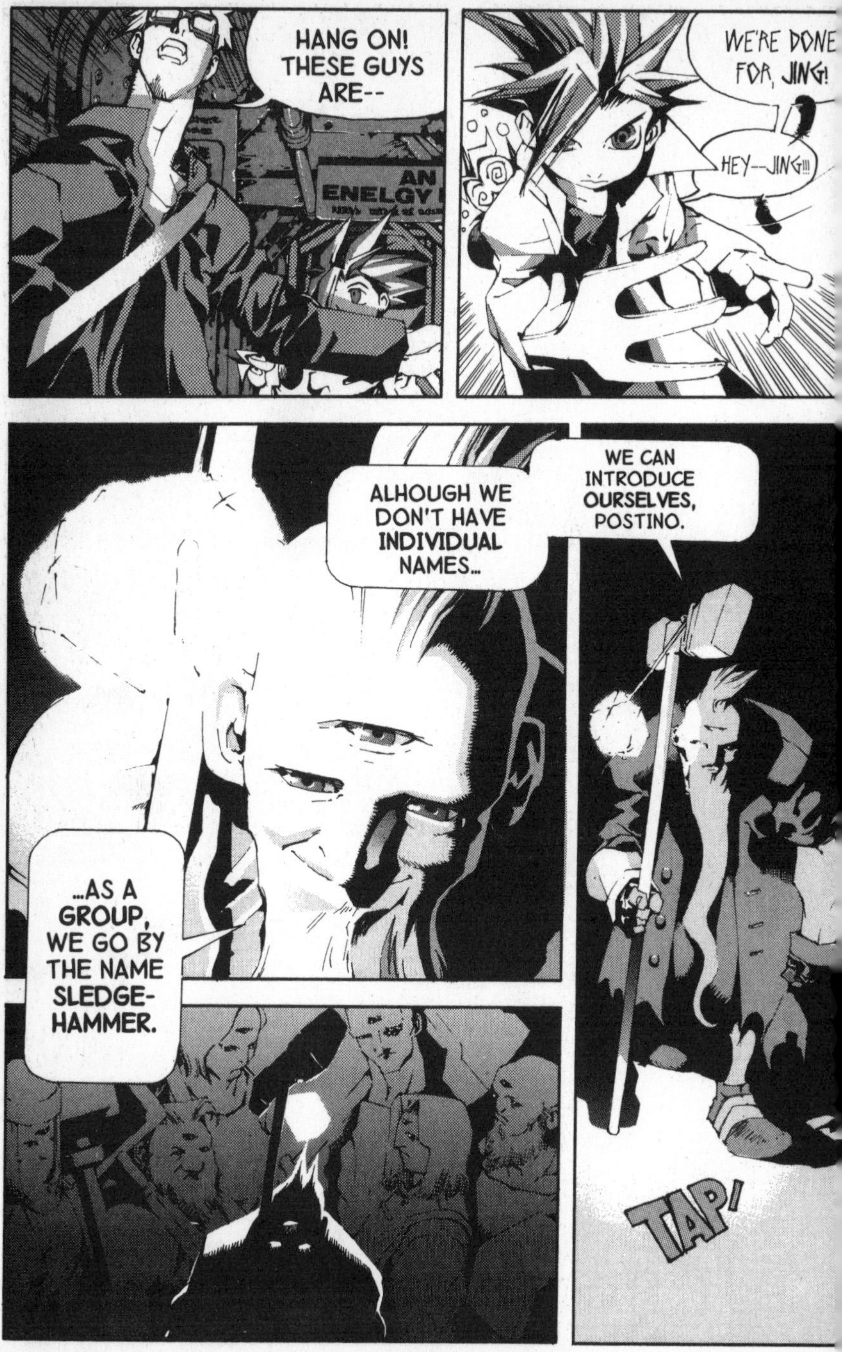
HANG ON! THESE GUYS ARE--
AN
ENELGY
WE'RE DONE FOR, JING!
HEY--JING!!!
WE CAN INTRODUCE OURSELVES, POSTINO.
ALHOUGH WE DON'T HAVE INDIVIDUAL NAMES...
...AS A GROUP, WE GO BY THE NAME SLEDGE-HAMMER.
TAP!

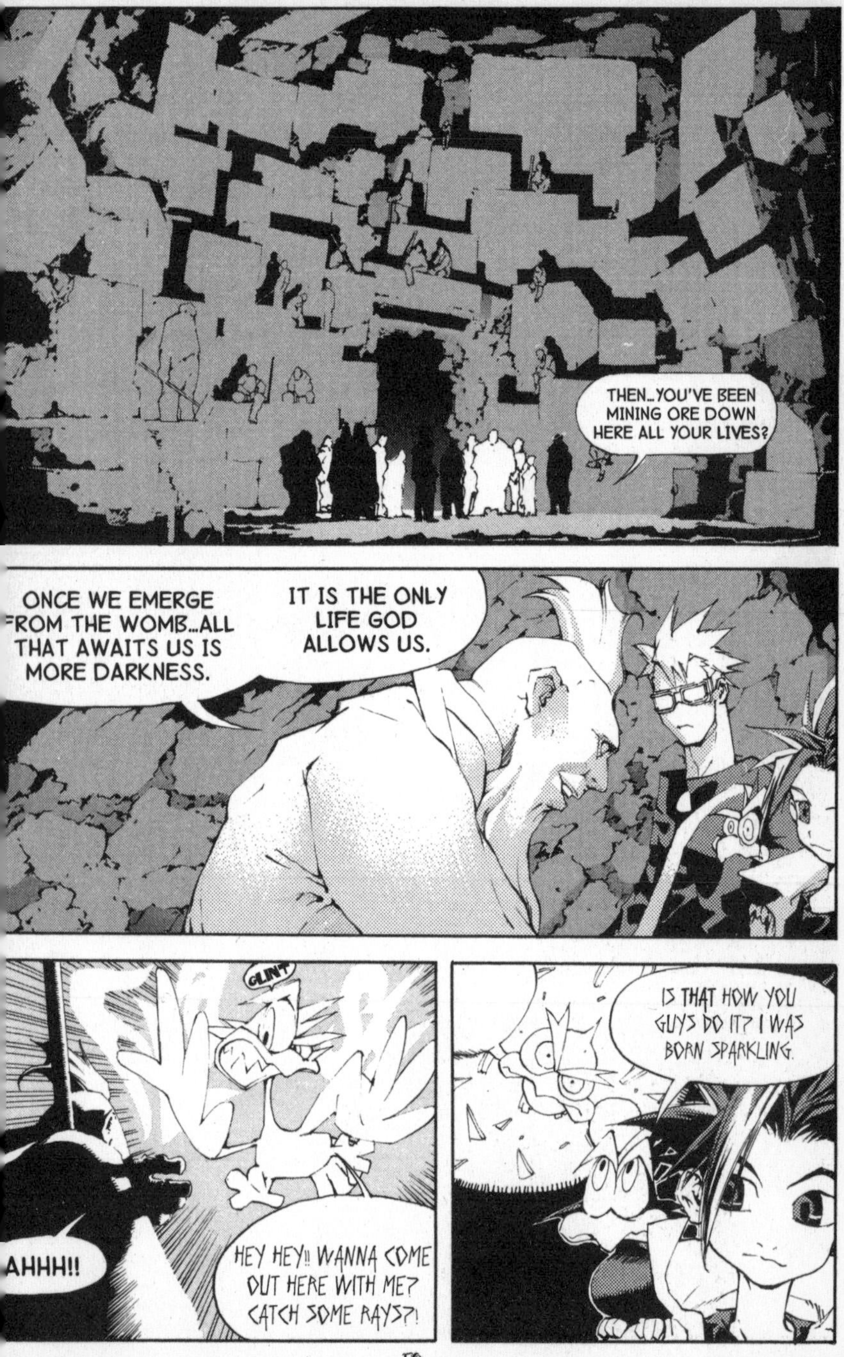
THEN...YOU'VE BEEN MINING ORE DOWN HERE ALL YOUR LIVES?
ONCE WE EMERGE FROM THE WOMB...ALL THAT AWAITS US IS MORE DARKNESS.
IT IS THE ONLY LIFE GOD ALLOWS US.
GLINT
HEY HEY!! WANNA COME OUT HERE WITH ME? CATCH SOME RAYS?!
AHHH!!
IS THAT HOW YOU GUYS DO IT? I WAS BORN SPARKLING.

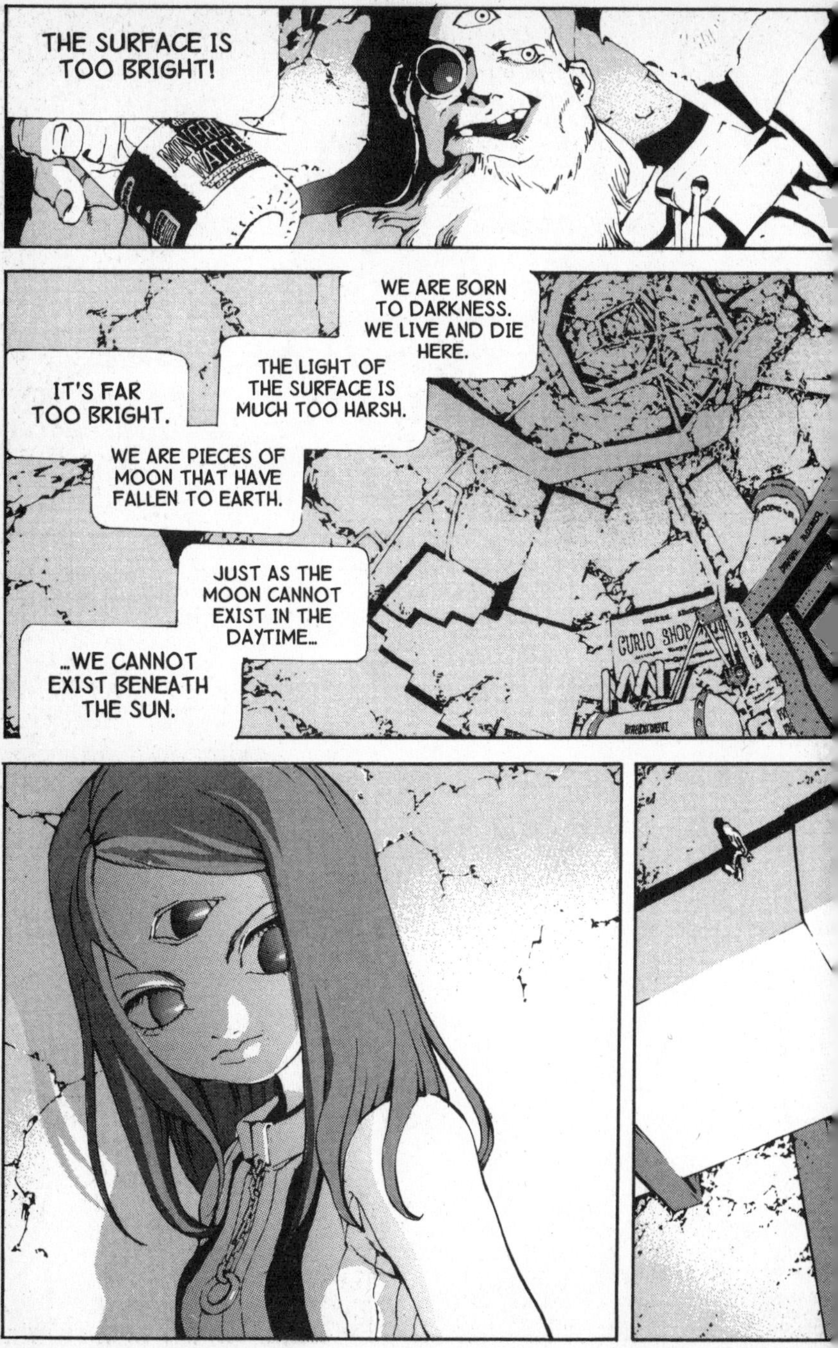
THE SURFACE IS TOO BRIGHT!
WE ARE BORN TO DARKNESS. WE LIVE AND DIE HERE.
THE LIGHT OF THE SURFACE IS MUCH TOO HARSH.
IT'S FAR TOO BRIGHT.
WE ARE PIECES OF MOON THAT HAVE FALLEN TO EARTH.
JUST AS THE MOON CANNOT EXIST IN THE DAYTIME...
...WE CANNOT EXIST BENEATH THE SUN.
CURIO SHOP

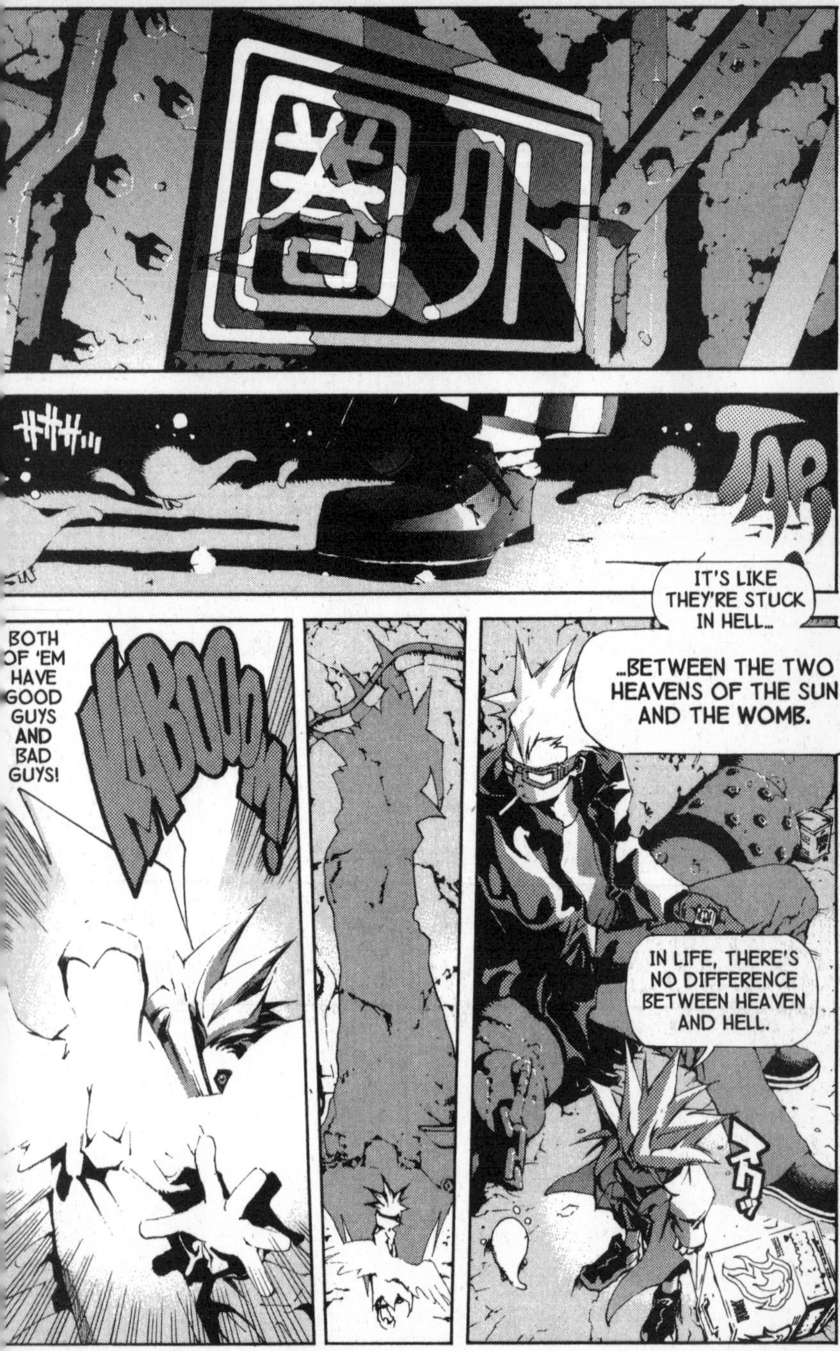
圏外
TAP
IT'S LIKE THEY'RE STUCK IN HELL...
...BETWEEN THE TWO HEAVENS OF THE SUN AND THE WOMB.
IN LIFE, THERE'S NO DIFFERENCE BETWEEN HEAVEN AND HELL.
BOTH OF 'EM HAVE GOOD GUYS AND BAD GUYS!
KABOOOM

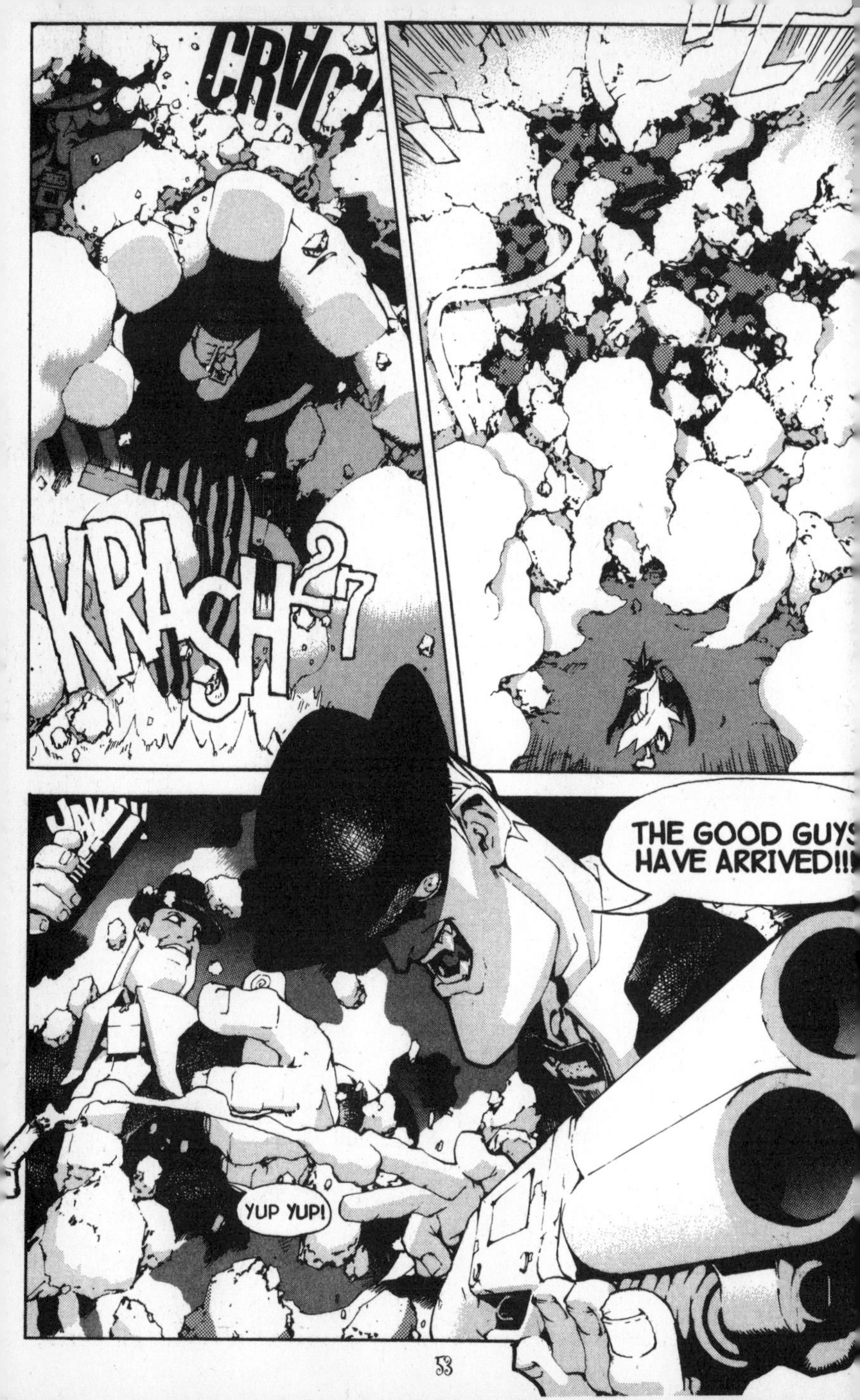
CRACK
KRASH
THE GOOD GUYS HAVE ARRIVED!!!
YUP YUP!

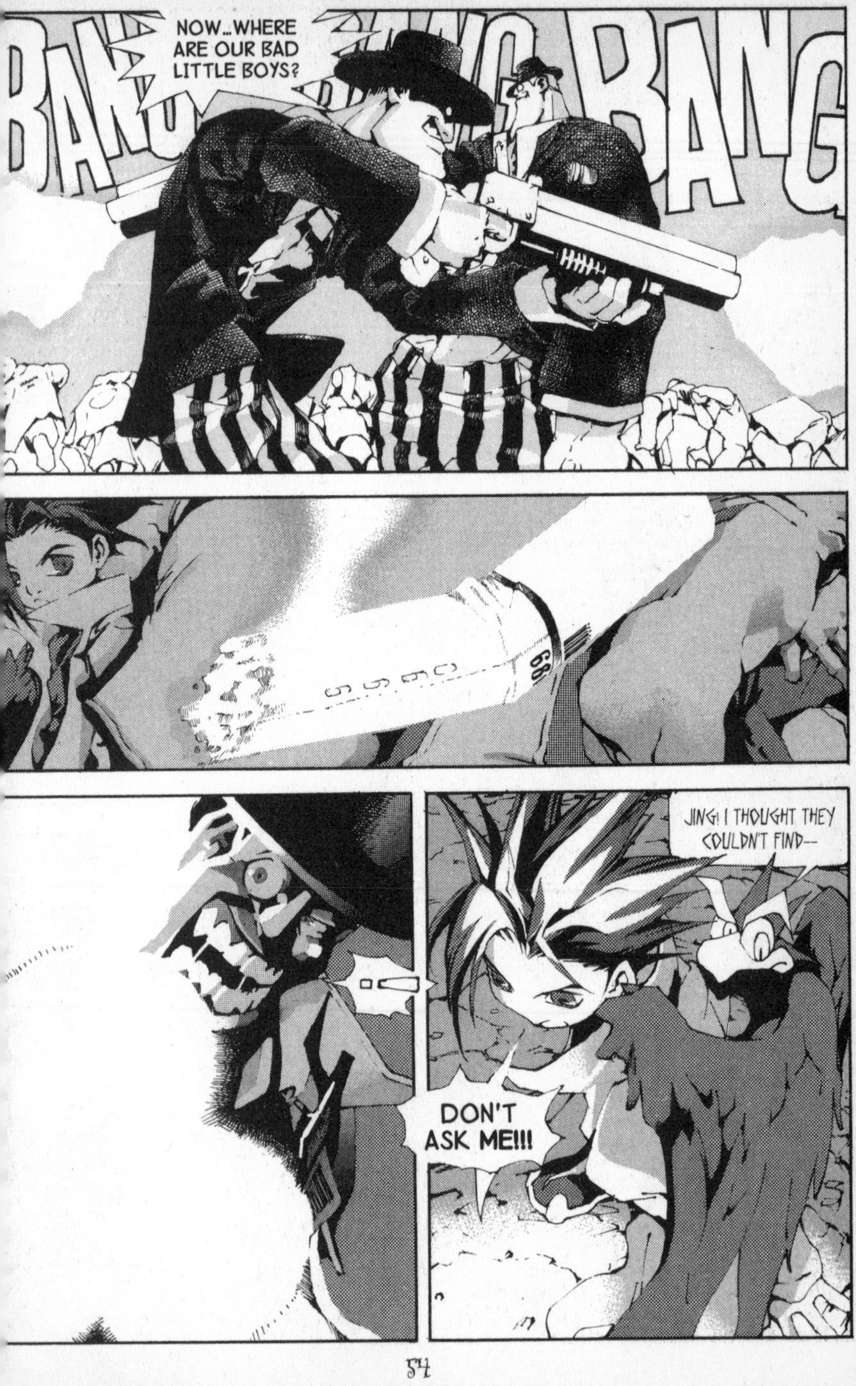

BANG BANG BANG
NOW...WHERE ARE OUR BAD LITTLE BOYS?
JING! I THOUGHT THEY COULDN'T FIND--
DON'T ASK ME!!!
!

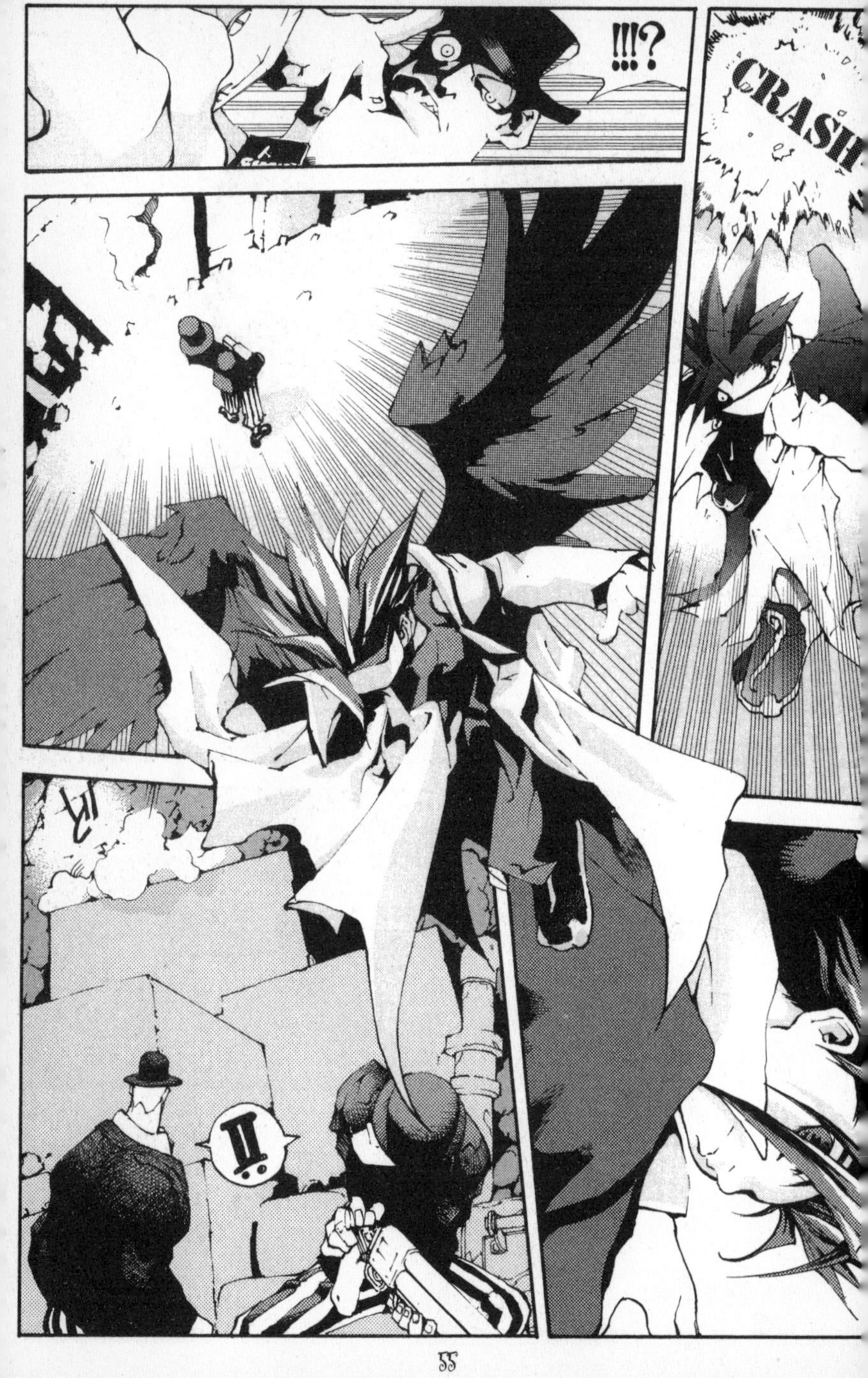
CRASH
!!!?
!!

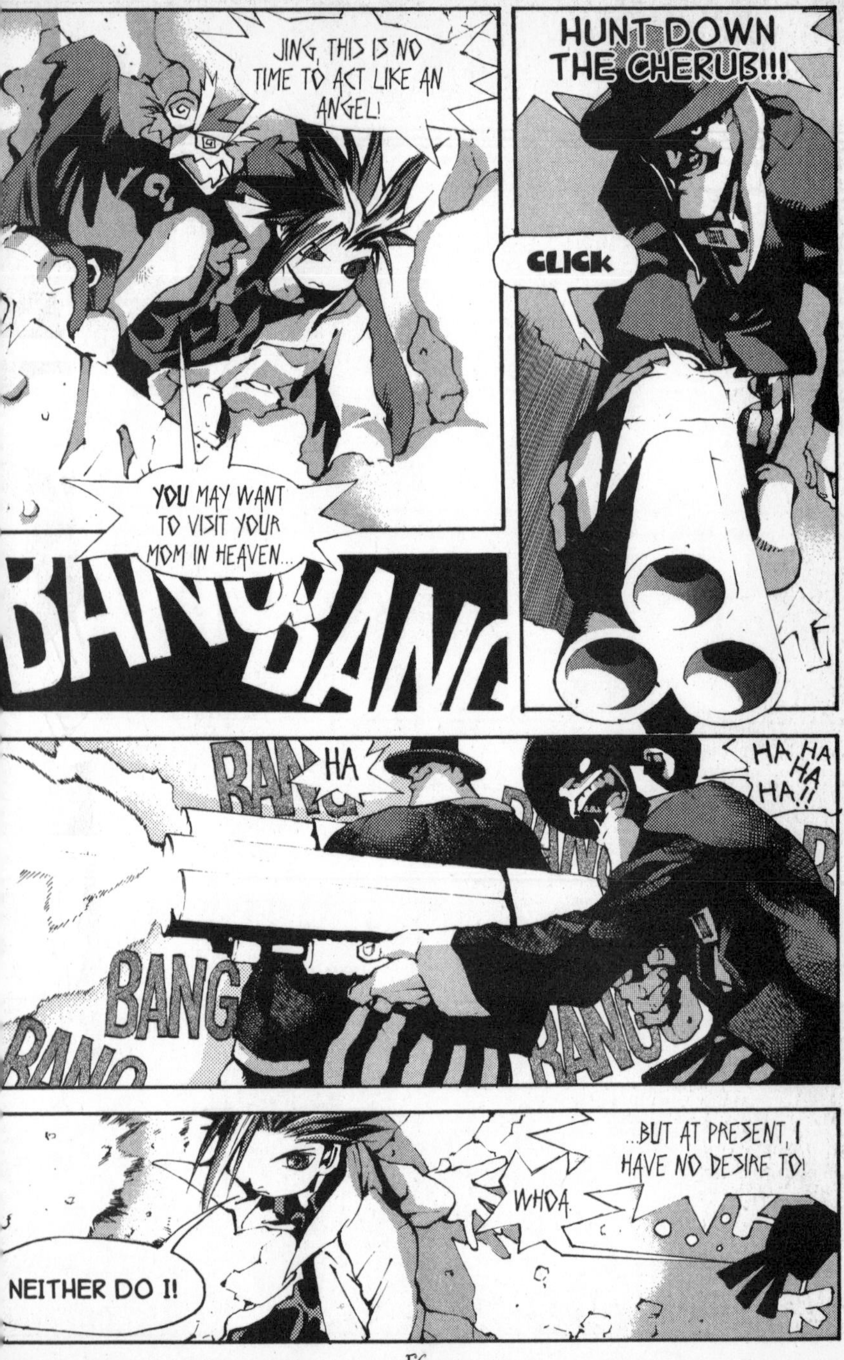
HUNT DOWN THE CHERUB!!!
CLICK
JING, THIS IS NO TIME TO ACT LIKE AN ANGEL!
YOU MAY WANT TO VISIT YOUR MOM IN HEAVEN...
BANG BANG
HA HA HA HA!!
HA
BANG
BANG
...BUT AT PRESENT, I HAVE NO DESIRE TO!
WHOA.
NEITHER DO I!

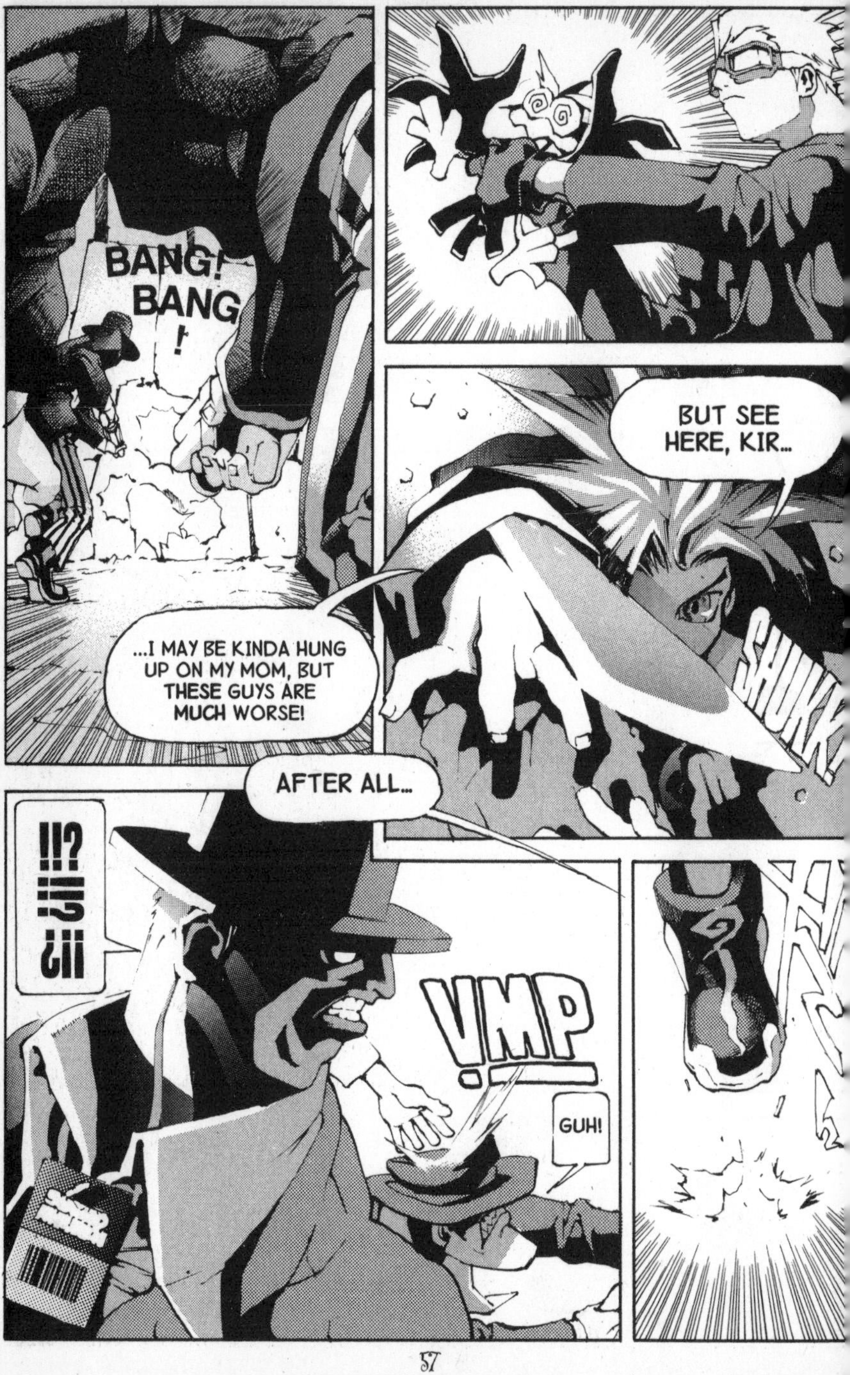
BUT SEE HERE, KIR...
SHUKK!
BANG! BANG!
...I MAY BE KINDA HUNG UP ON MY MOM, BUT THESE GUYS ARE MUCH WORSE!
AFTER ALL...
VMP
GUH!

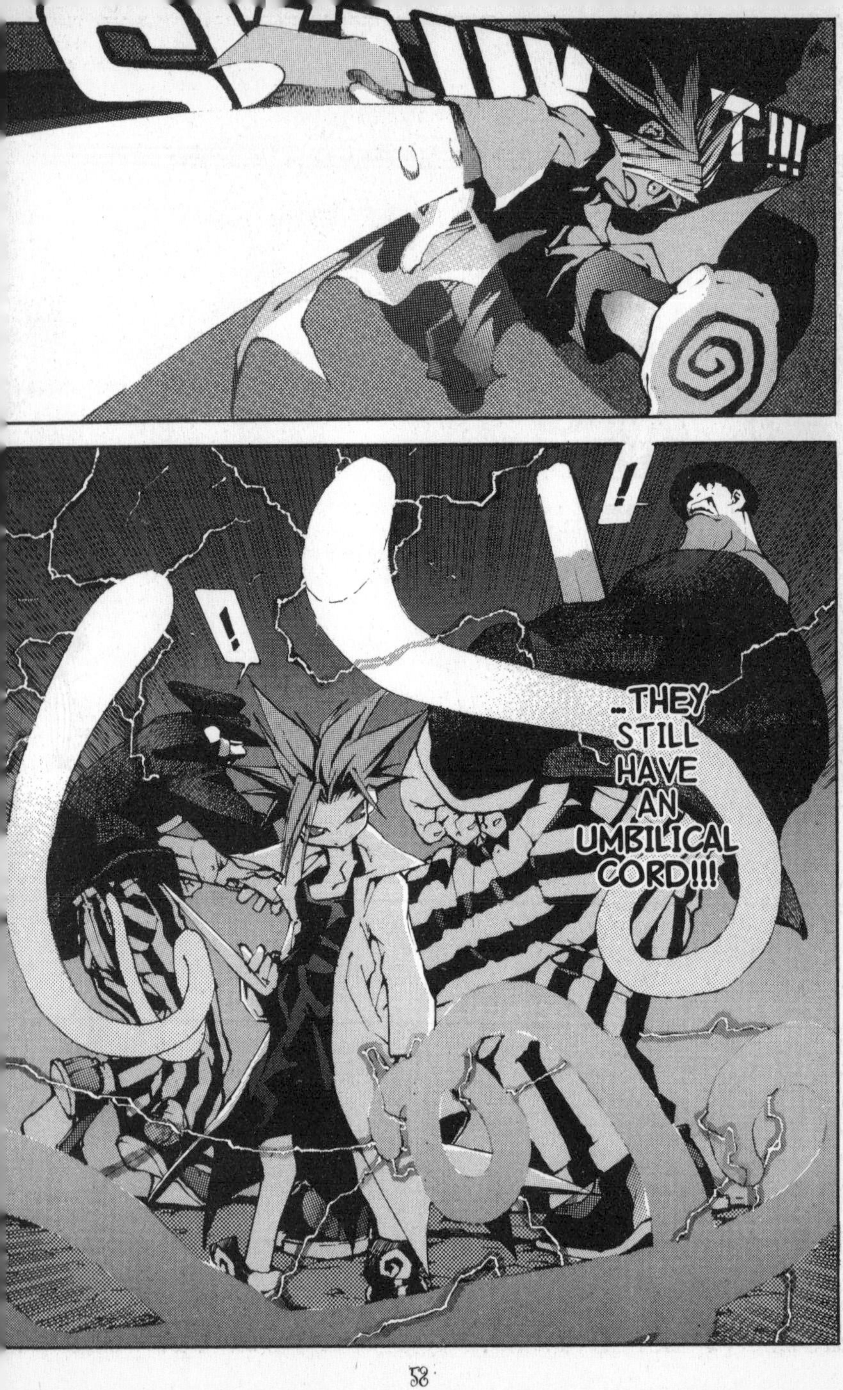
!
!
...THEY STILL HAVE AN UMBILICAL CORD!!!

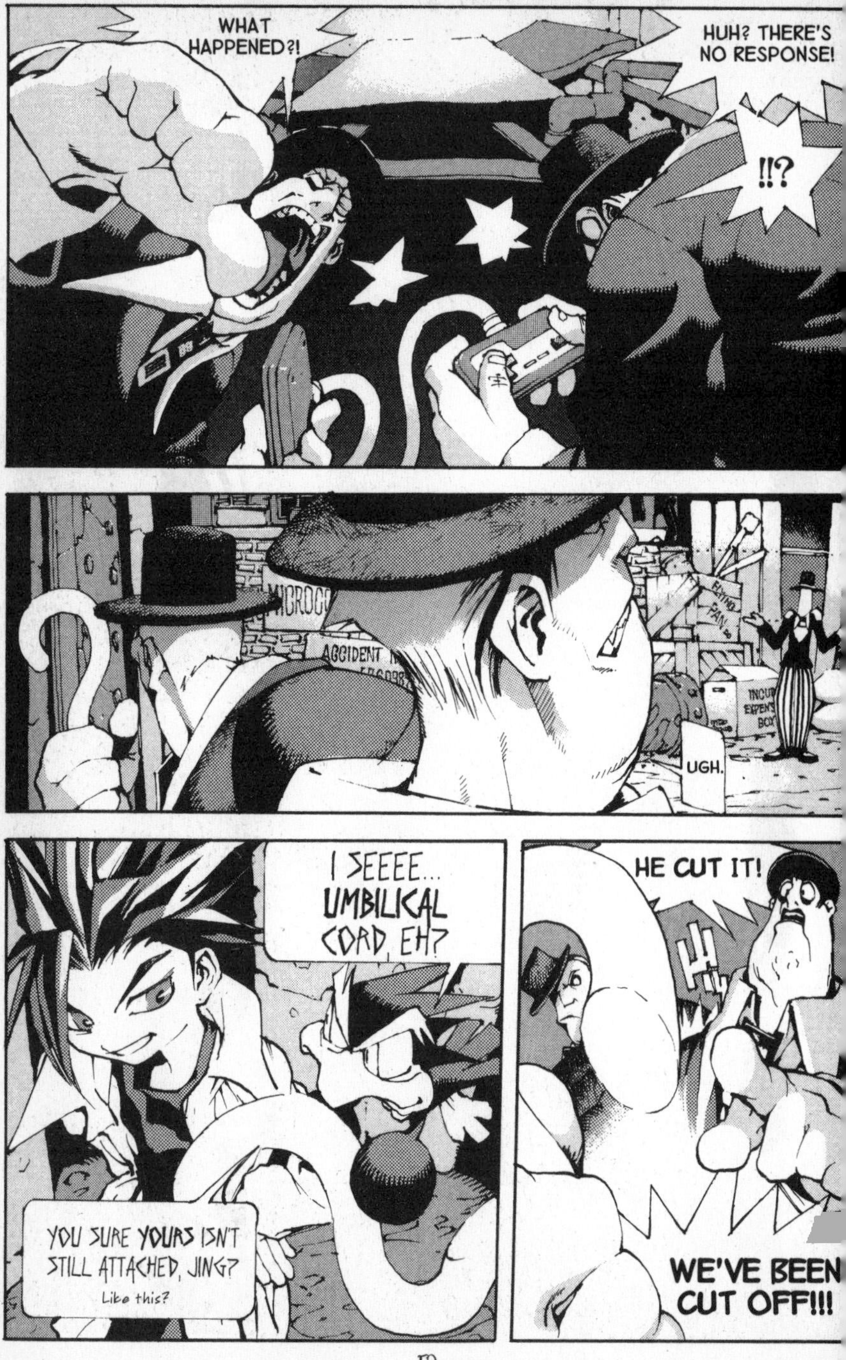

WHAT HAPPENED?!
HUH? THERE'S NO RESPONSE!
!!?
UGH.
I SEEEE... UMBILICAL CORD, EH?
HE CUT IT!
YOU SURE YOURS ISN'T STILL ATTACHED, JING?
Like this?
WE'VE BEEN CUT OFF!!!

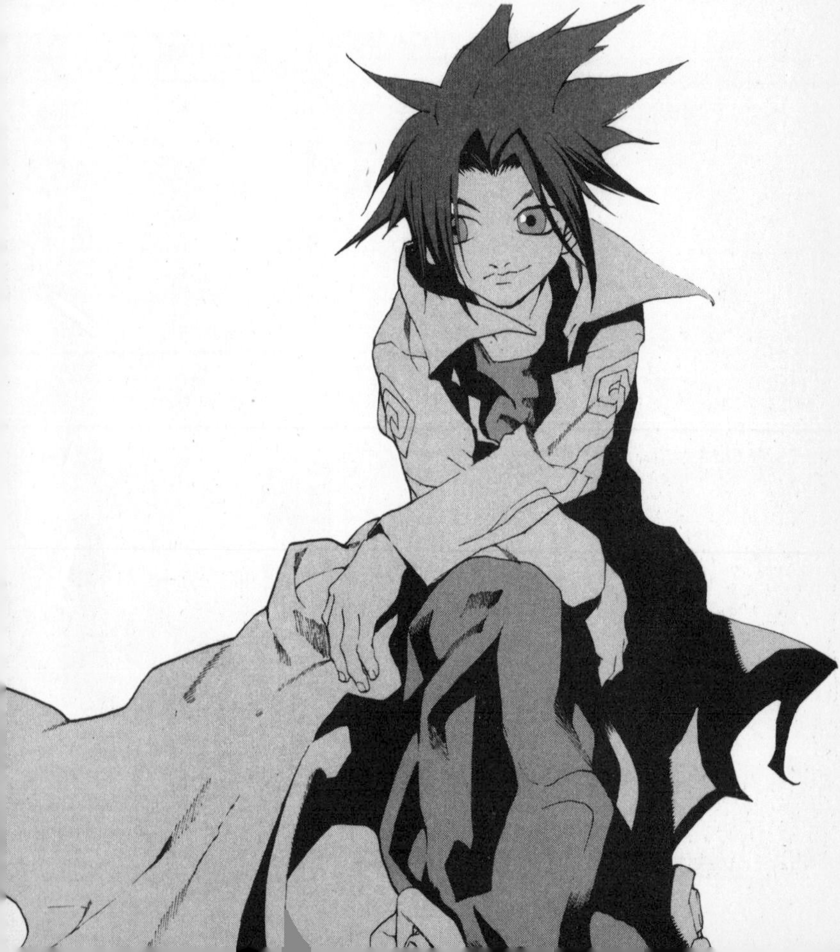

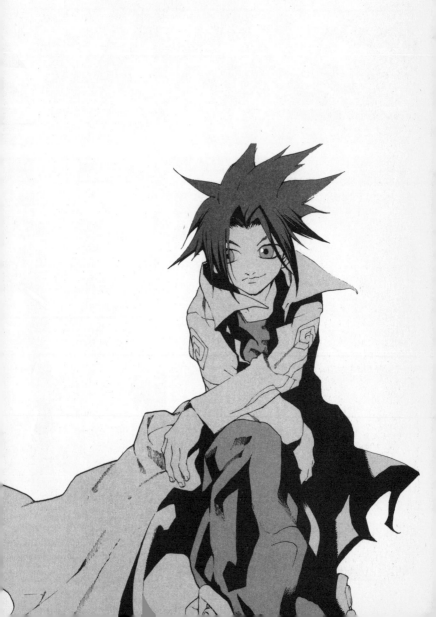

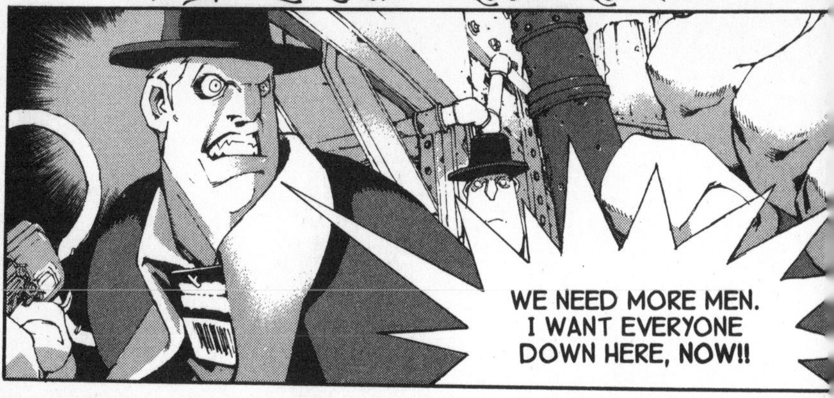
WE NEED MORE MEN.
I WANT EVERYONE
DOWN HERE, NOW!!

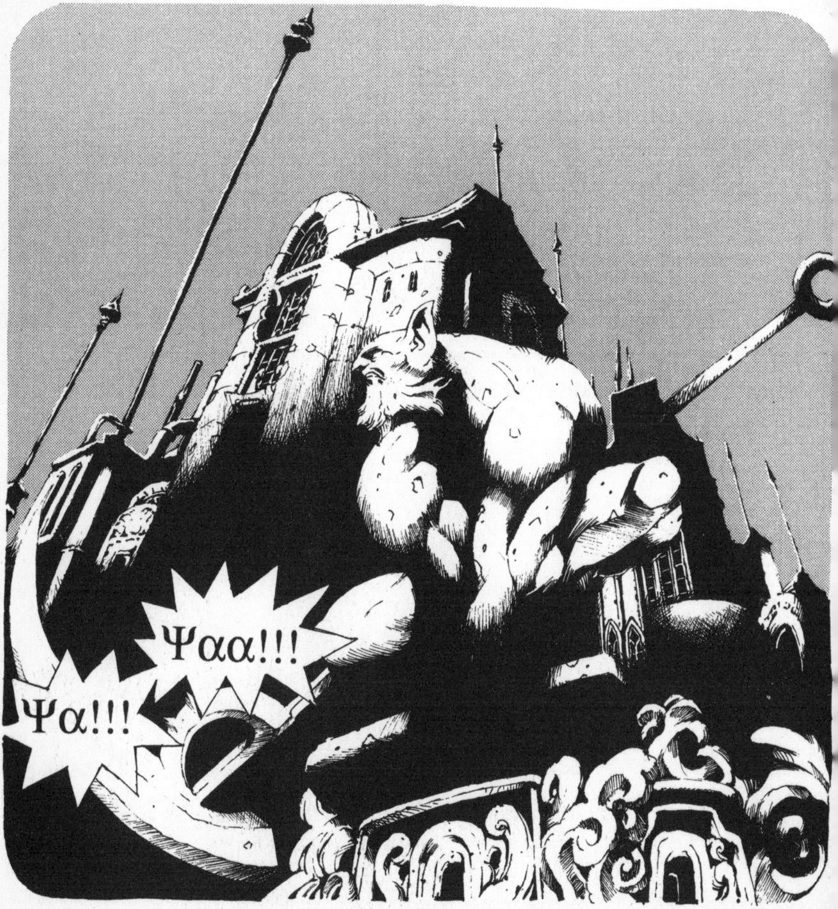
Ψαα!!!
Ψα!!!

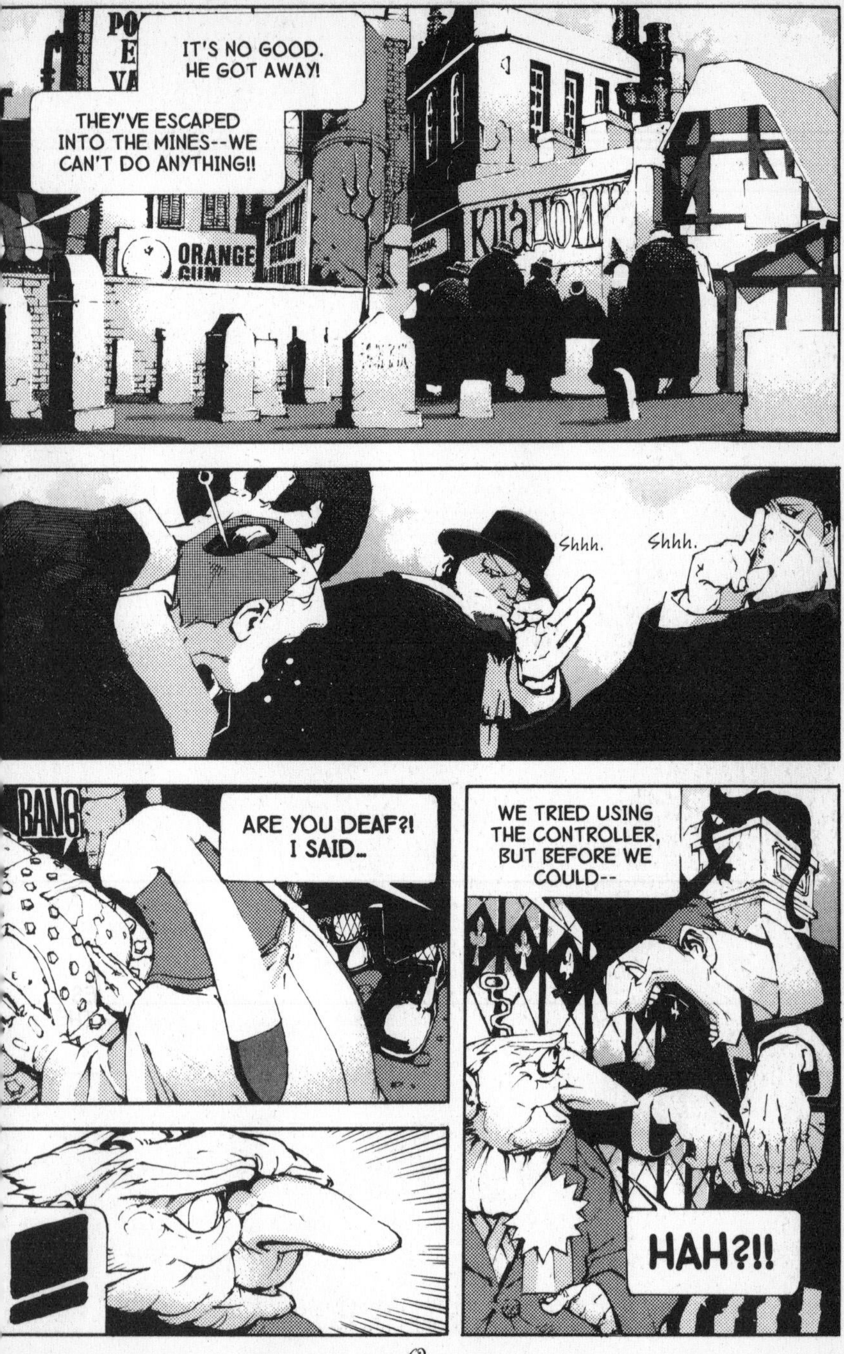
IT'S NO GOOD. HE GOT AWAY!
THEY'VE ESCAPED INTO THE MINES--WE CAN'T DO ANYTHING!!
ORANGE
Shhh.
Shhh.
BANG
ARE YOU DEAF?! I SAID..
WE TRIED USING THE CONTROLLER, BUT BEFORE WE COULD--
HAH?!!

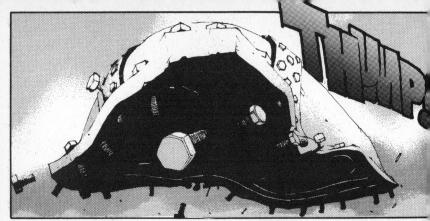

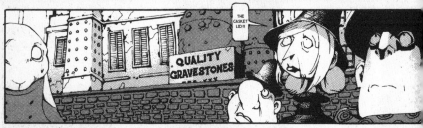

THUMP
THE CASKET LID?!
QUALITY GRAVESTONES
SWING
YOUR FOOLISH WHINING REACHES ALL THE WAY TO THE AFTERLIFE.
EVEN MY DEAD ANTENNA IS REACTING.
IF THIS IS HOW YOU'RE GONNA RUN THINGS WITHOUT ME...
DEVILMAN ALLEY

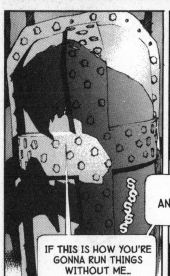

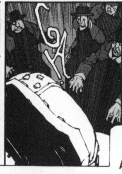

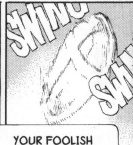

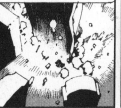

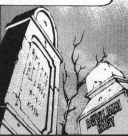

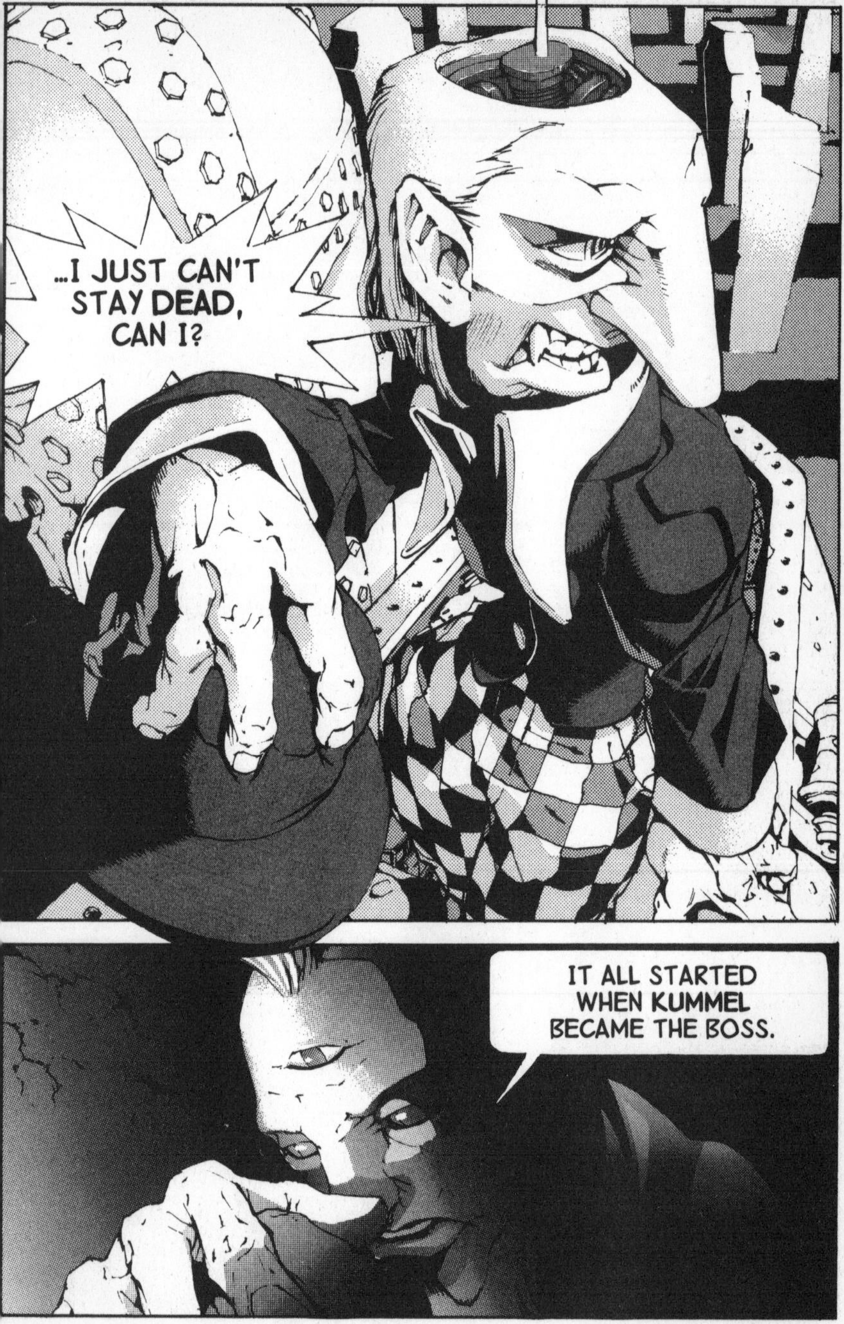
...I JUST CAN'T STAY DEAD, CAN I?
IT ALL STARTED WHEN KUMMEL BECAME THE BOSS.

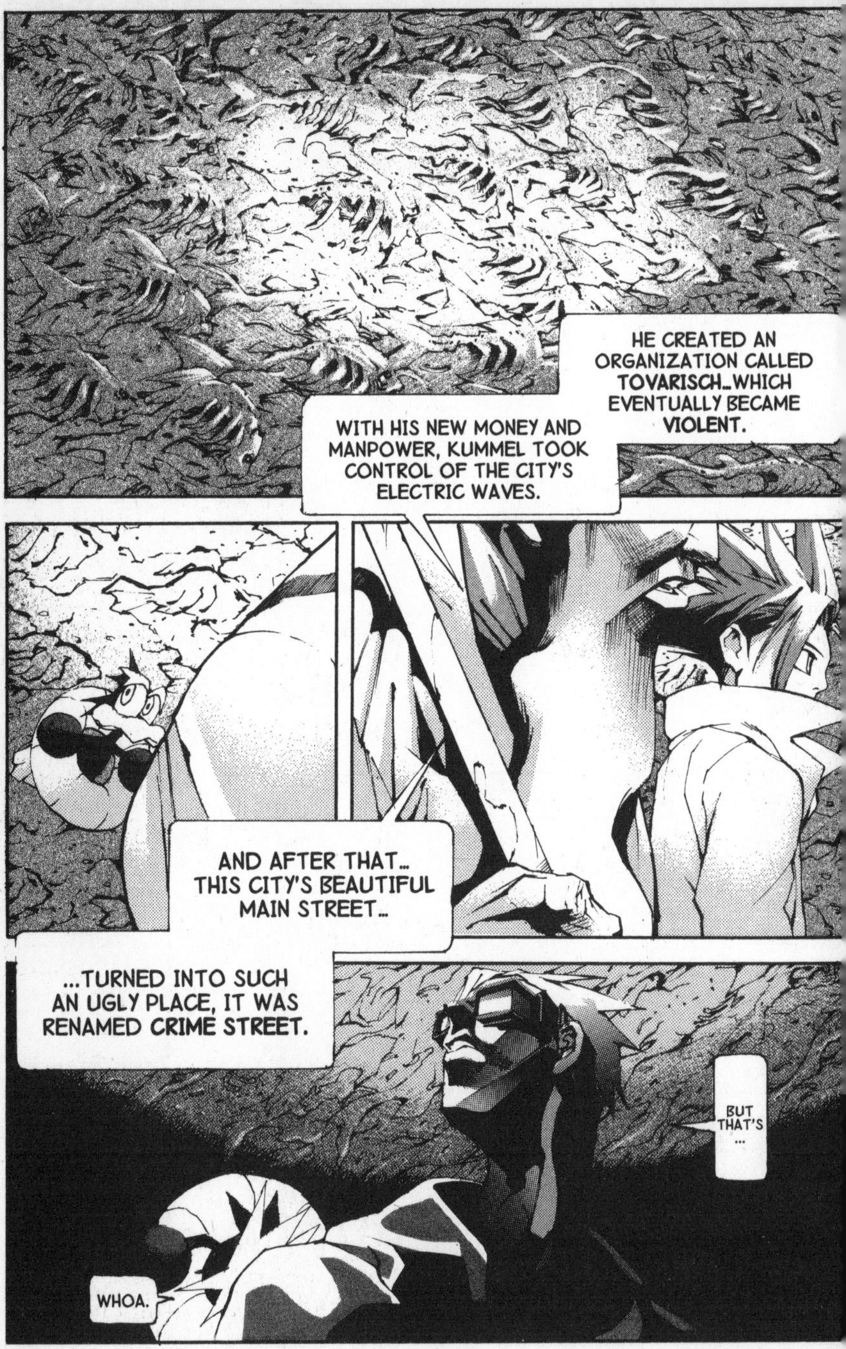
HE CREATED AN ORGANIZATION CALLED TOVARISCH...WHICH EVENTUALLY BECAME VIOLENT.
WITH HIS NEW MONEY AND MANPOWER, KUMMEL TOOK CONTROL OF THE CITY'S ELECTRIC WAVES.
AND AFTER THAT... THIS CITY'S BEAUTIFUL MAIN STREET...
...TURNED INTO SUCH AN UGLY PLACE, IT WAS RENAMED CRIME STREET.
BUT THAT'S ...
WHOA.

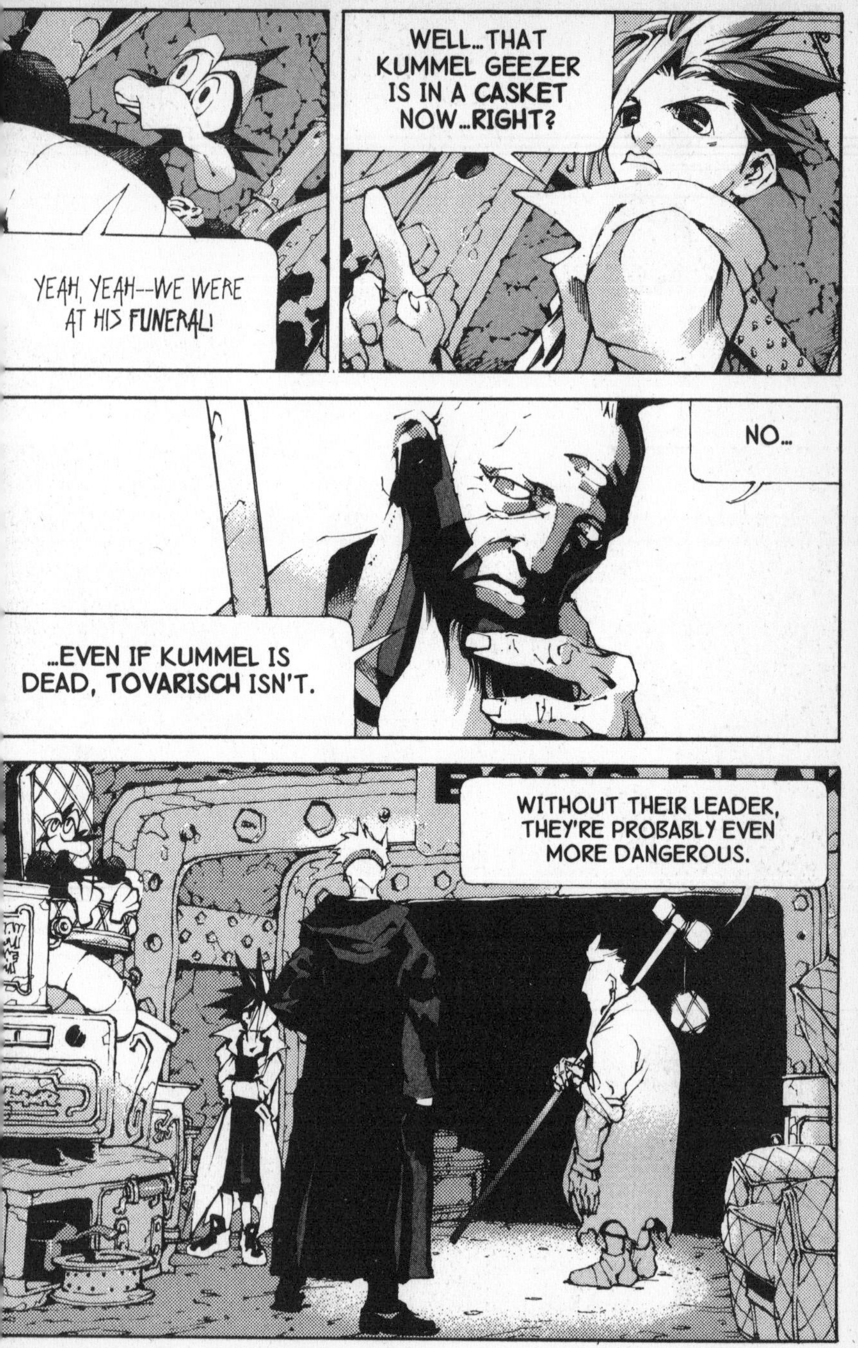
YEAH, YEAH--WE WERE AT HIS FUNERAL!
WELL...THAT KUMMEL GEEZER IS IN A CASKET NOW...RIGHT?
NO...
...EVEN IF KUMMEL IS DEAD, TOVARISCH ISN'T.
WITHOUT THEIR LEADER, THEY'RE PROBABLY EVEN MORE DANGEROUS.

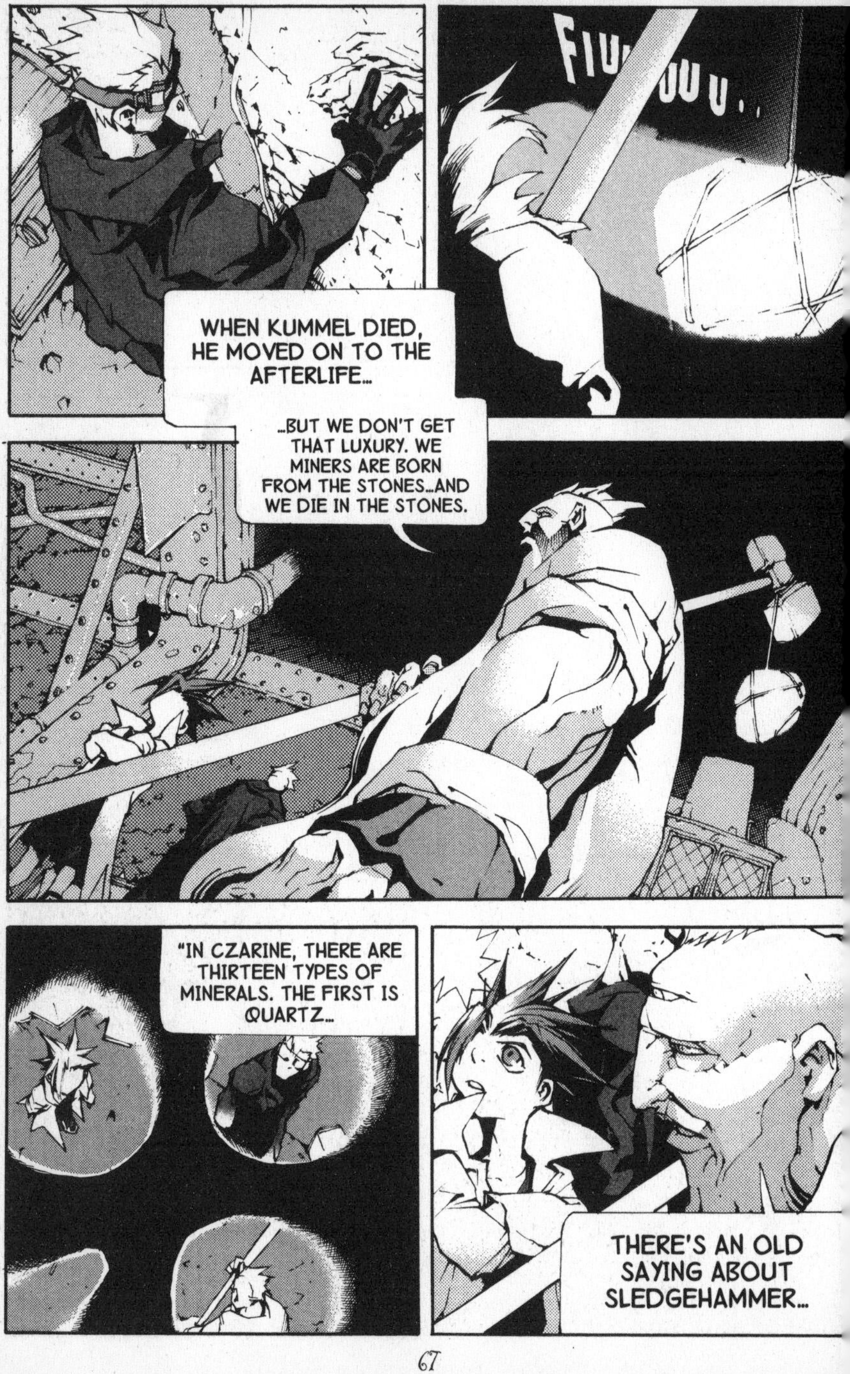
FIUUUU U..
WHEN KUMMEL DIED, HE MOVED ON TO THE AFTERLIFE...
...BUT WE DON'T GET THAT LUXURY. WE MINERS ARE BORN FROM THE STONES...AND WE DIE IN THE STONES.
"IN CZARINE, THERE ARE THIRTEEN TYPES OF MINERALS. THE FIRST IS QUARTZ...
THERE'S AN OLD SAYING ABOUT SLEDGEHAMMER...

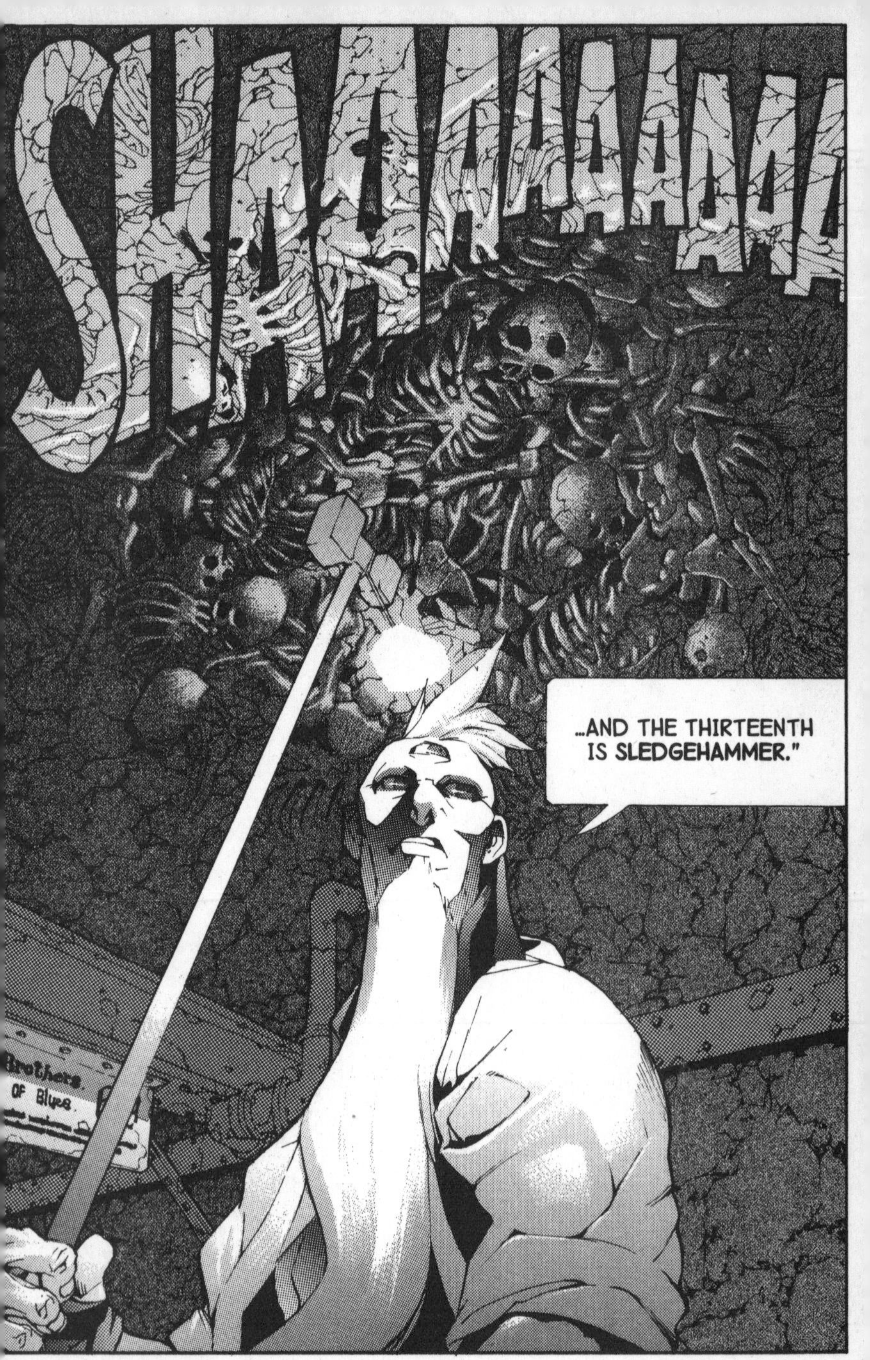
...AND THE THIRTEENTH IS SLEDGEHAMMER."

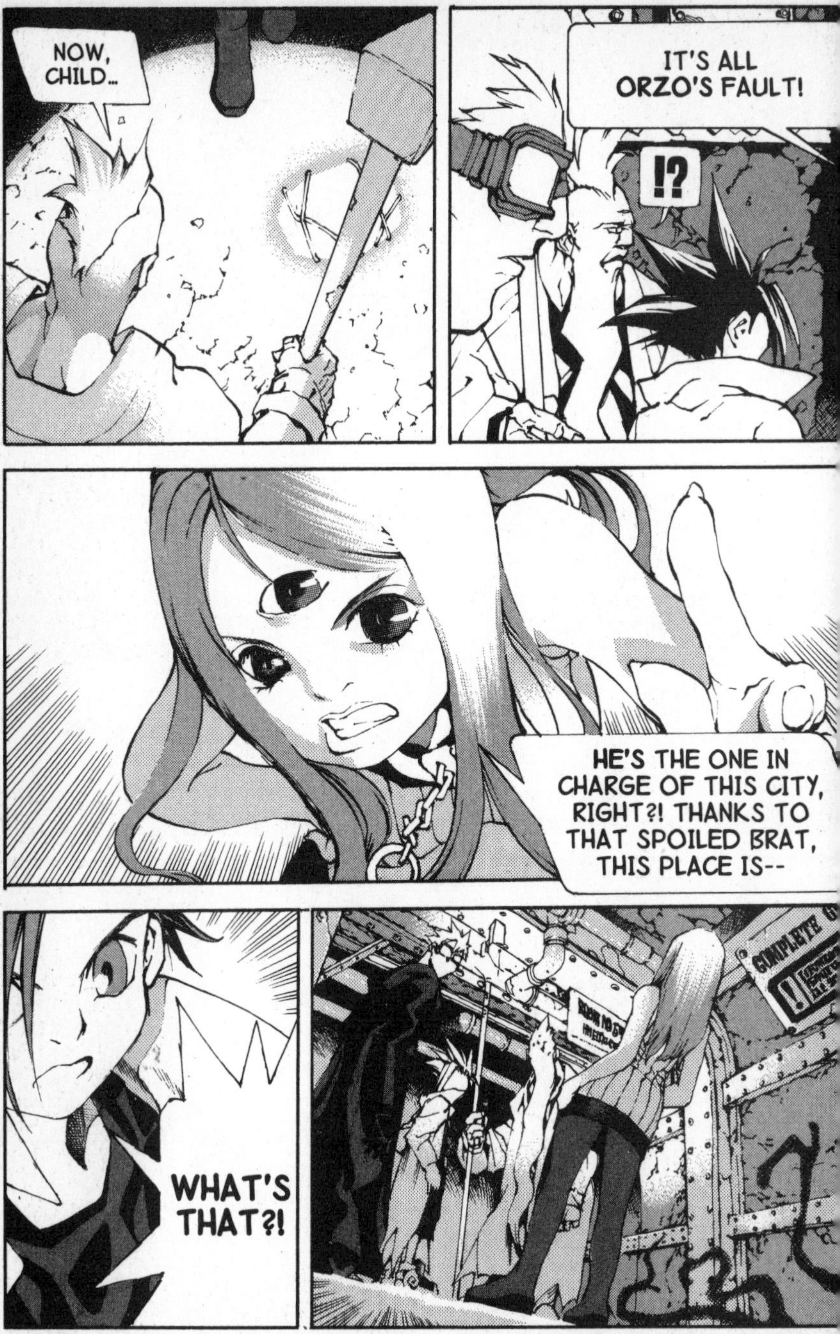

NOW, CHILD...
IT'S ALL ORZO'S FAULT!
!?
HE'S THE ONE IN CHARGE OF THIS CITY, RIGHT?! THANKS TO THAT SPOILED BRAT, THIS PLACE IS--
WHAT'S THAT?!

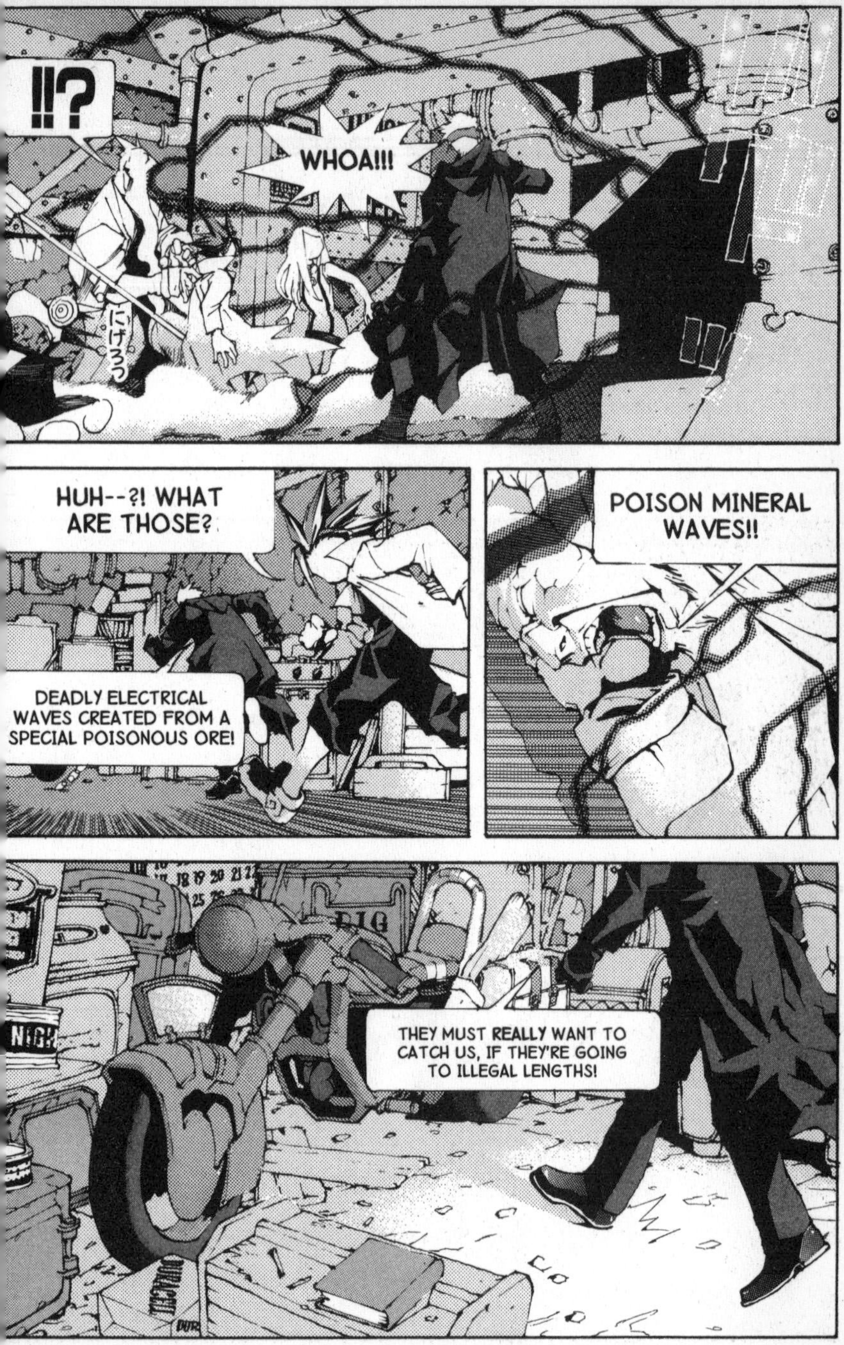
WHOA!!!
!!?
にげろっ
POISON MINERAL WAVES!!
HUH--?! WHAT ARE THOSE?
DEADLY ELECTRICAL WAVES CREATED FROM A SPECIAL POISONOUS ORE!
THEY MUST REALLY WANT TO CATCH US, IF THEY'RE GOING TO ILLEGAL LENGTHS!

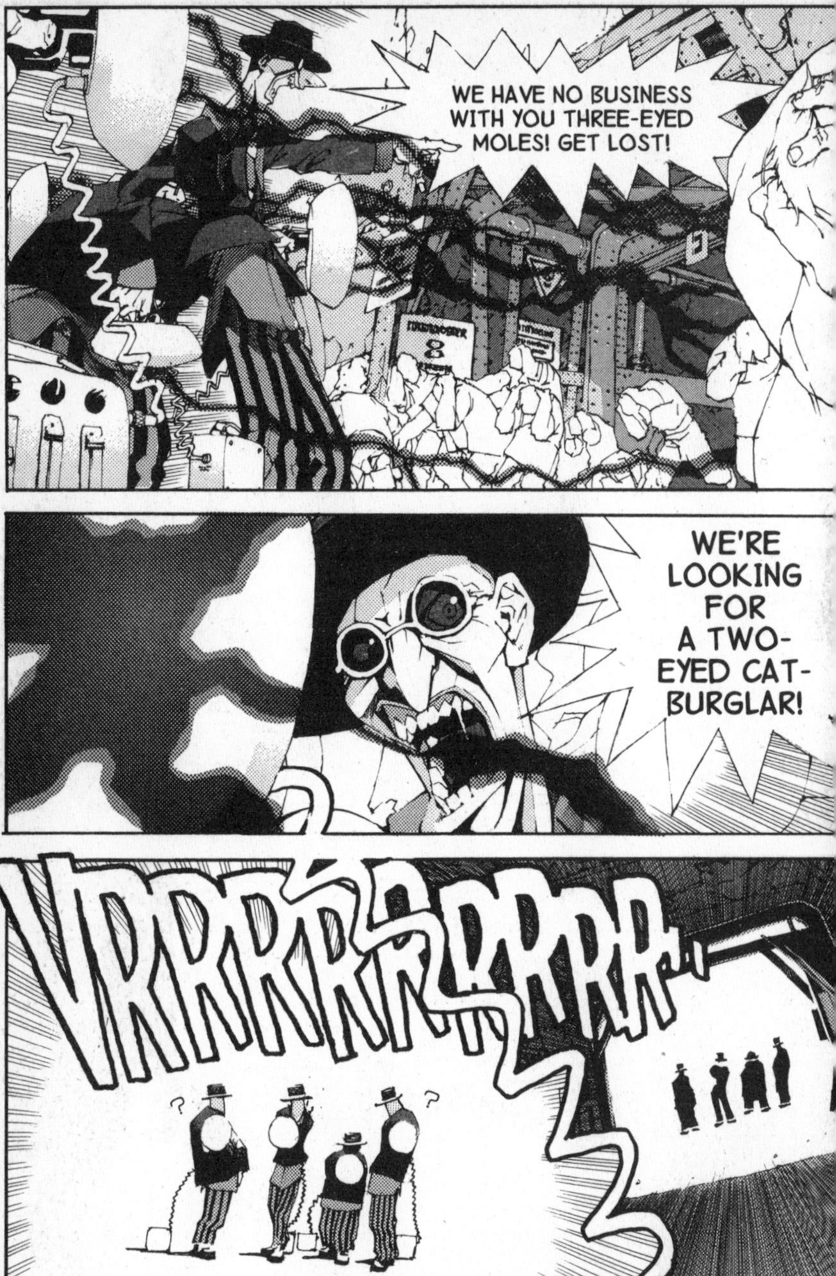
WE HAVE NO BUSINESS WITH YOU THREE-EYED MOLES! GET LOST!
WE'RE LOOKING FOR A TWO-EYED CAT-BURGLAR!

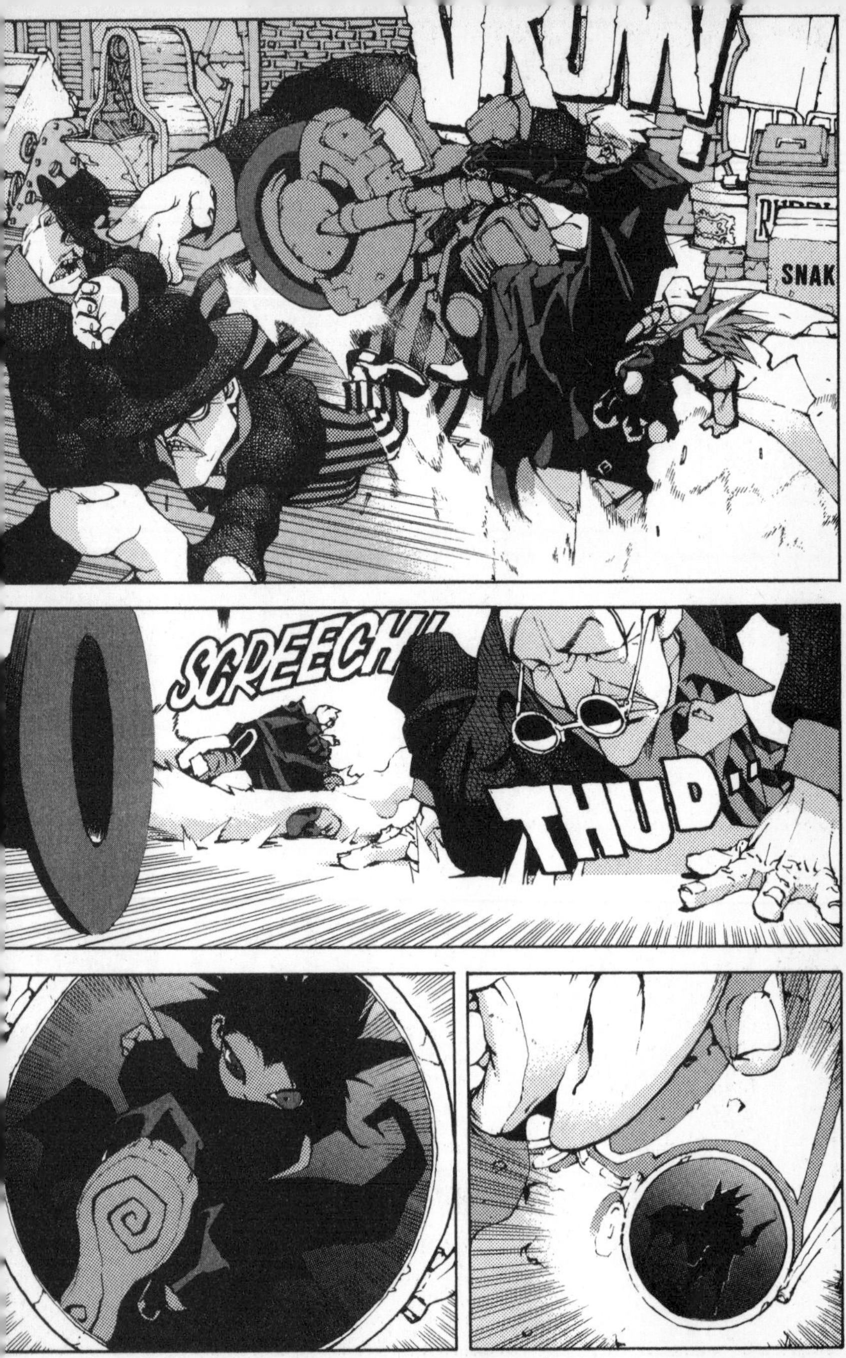
VROW!
SNAK
SCREEECH!!
THUD...

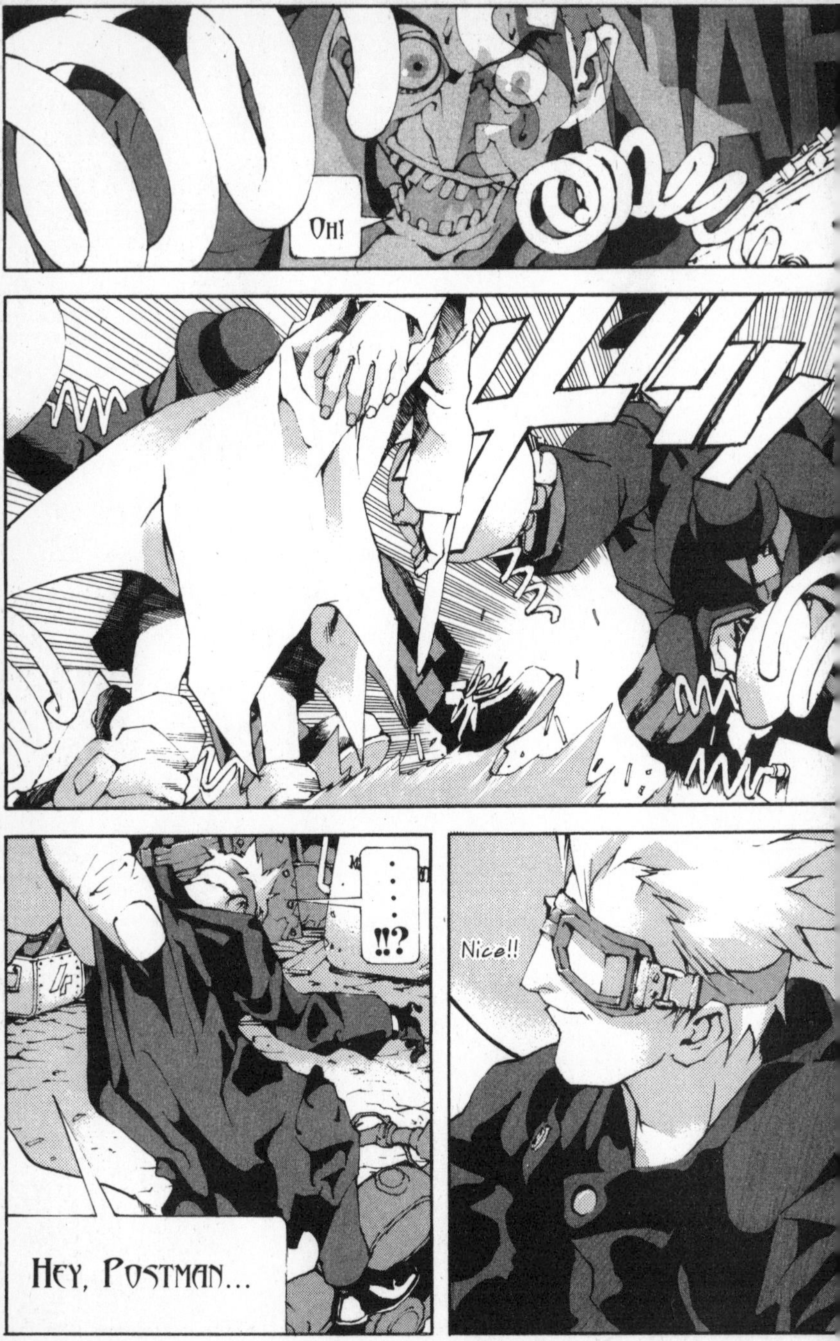

Oh!
.....
!!?
Hey, Postman...
Nice!!

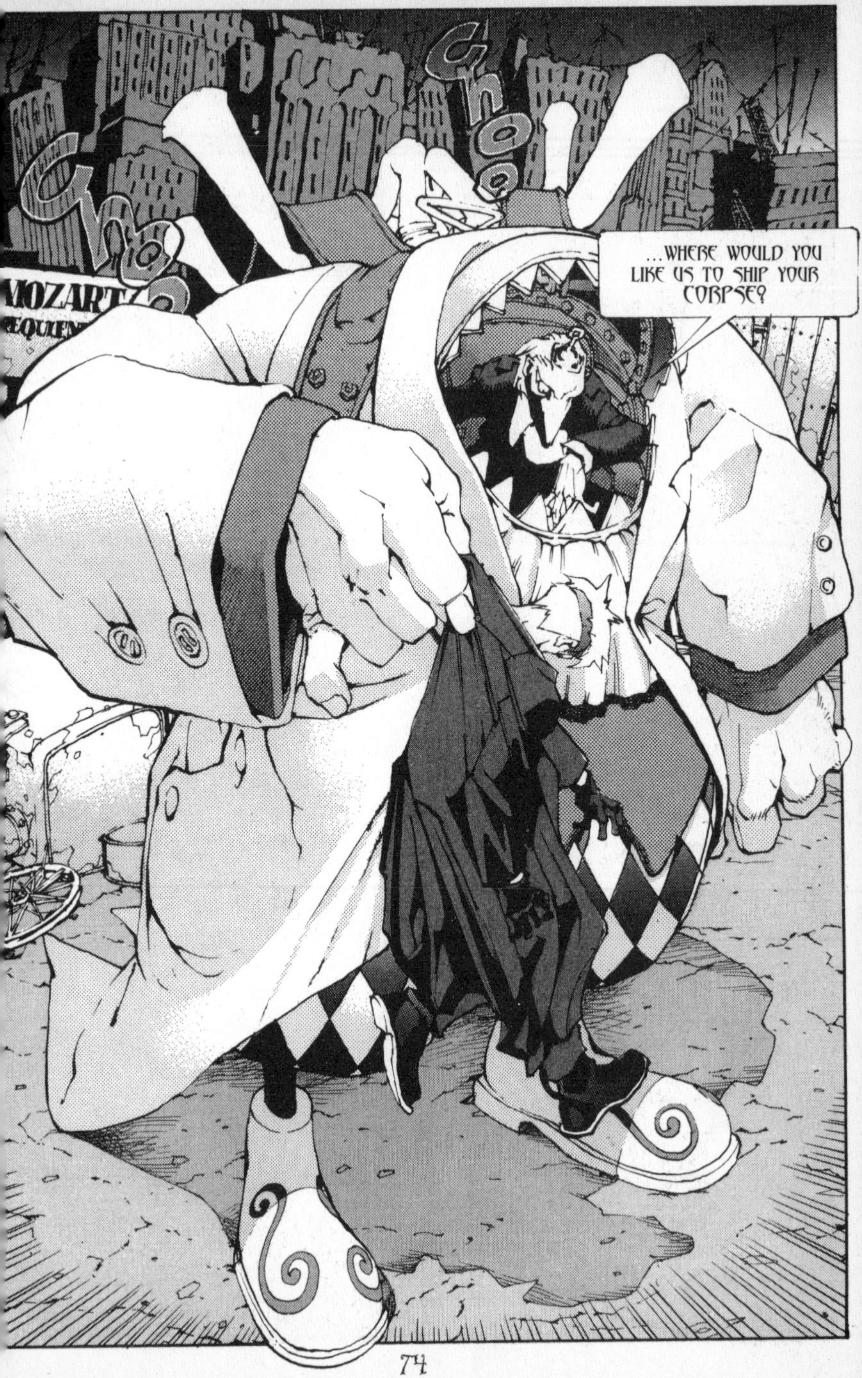
MOZART
...WHERE WOULD YOU LIKE US TO SHIP YOUR CORPSE?

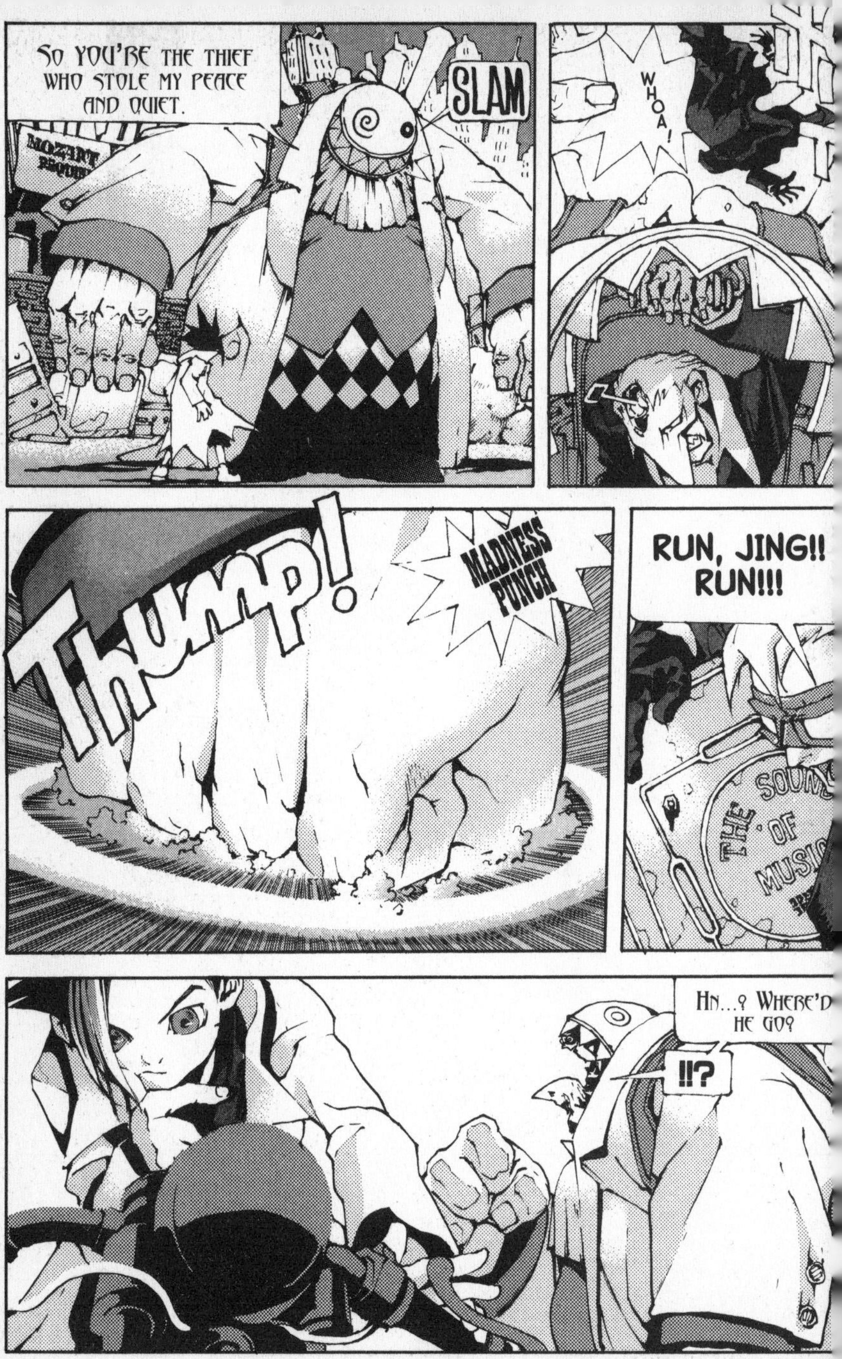
SO YOU'RE THE THIEF WHO STOLE MY PEACE AND QUIET.
SLAM
WHOA!
THUMP!
MADNESS PUNCH
RUN, JING!! RUN!!!
HN...? WHERE'D HE GO?
!!?

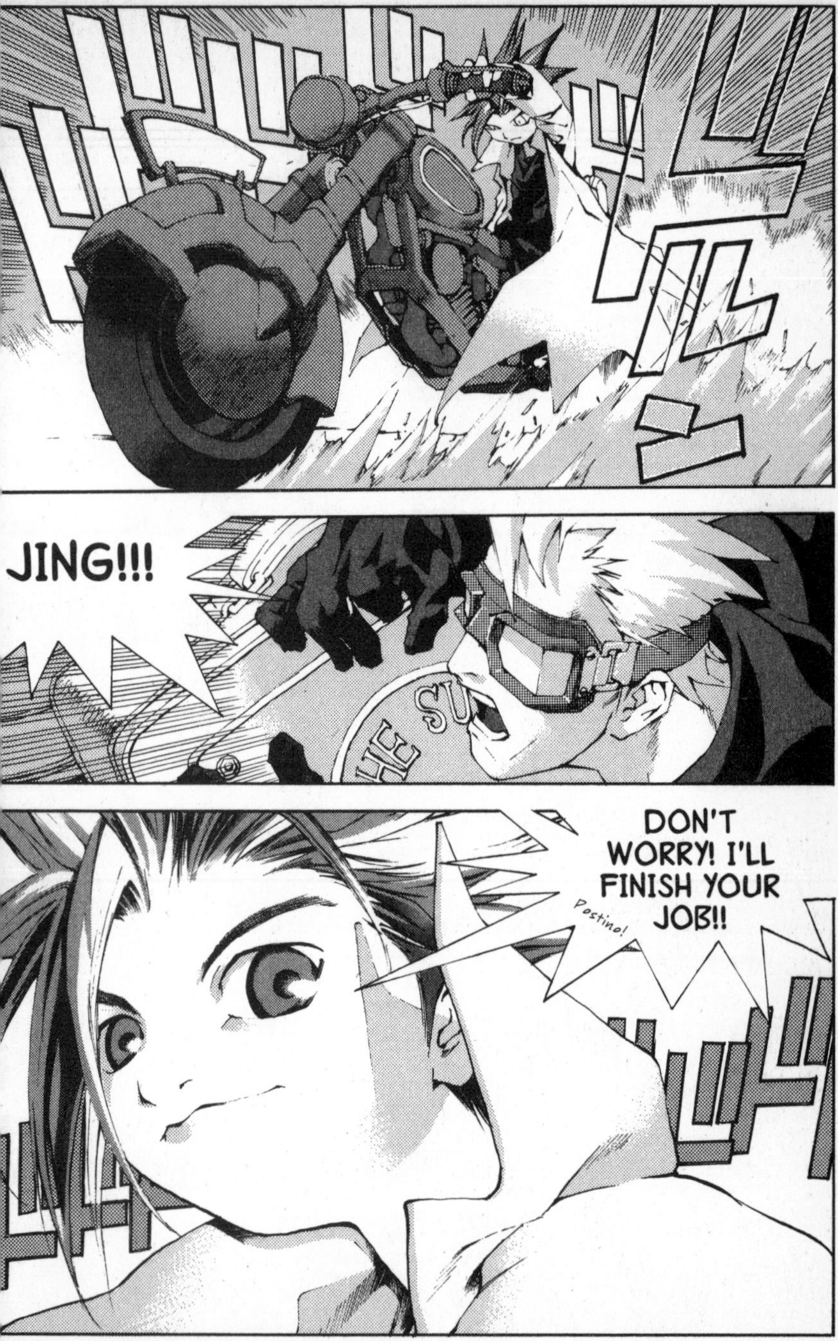
JING!!!
DON'T WORRY! I'LL FINISH YOUR JOB!!
Postino!

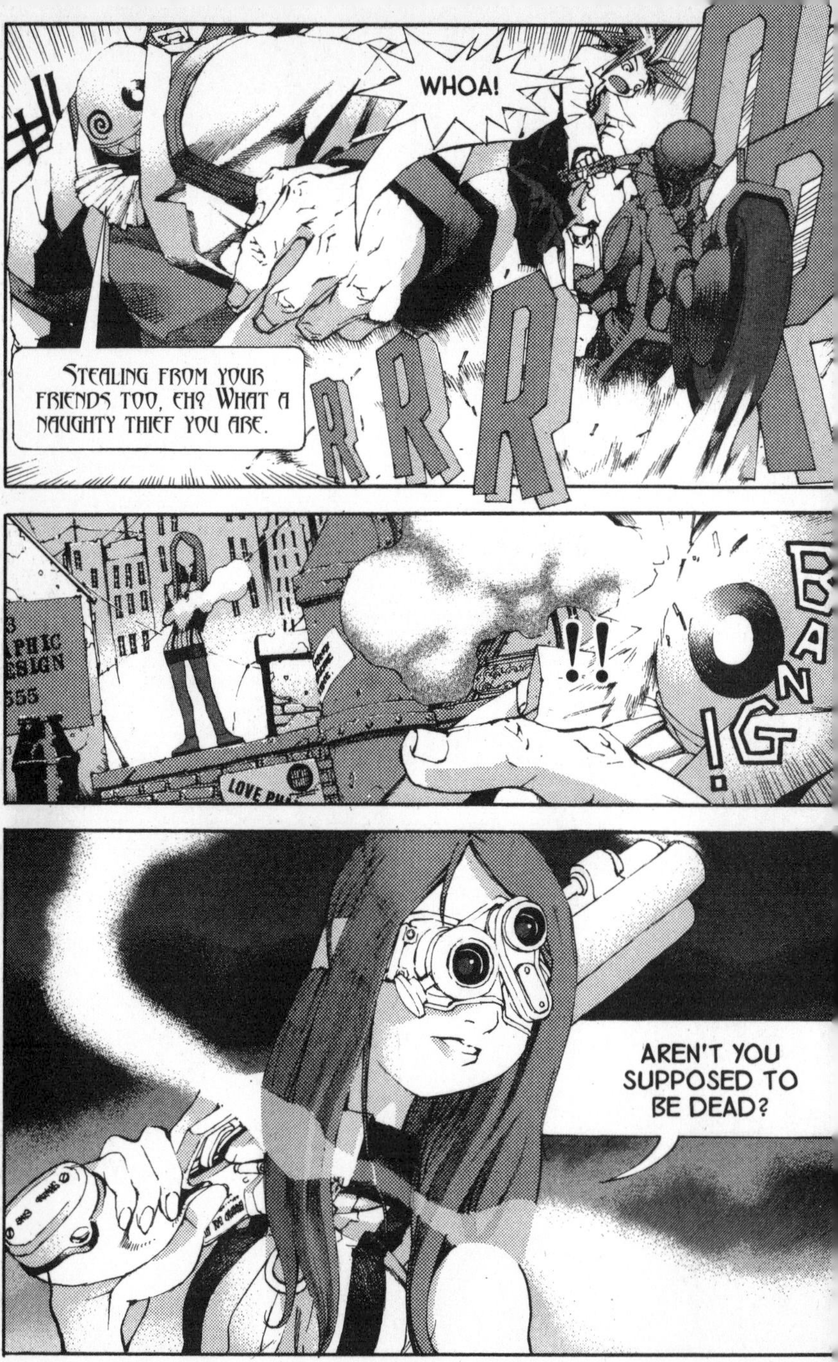
WHOA!
STEALING FROM YOUR FRIENDS TOO, EH? WHAT A NAUGHTY THIEF YOU ARE.
RRRR
!!
BANG!
AREN'T YOU SUPPOSED TO BE DEAD?

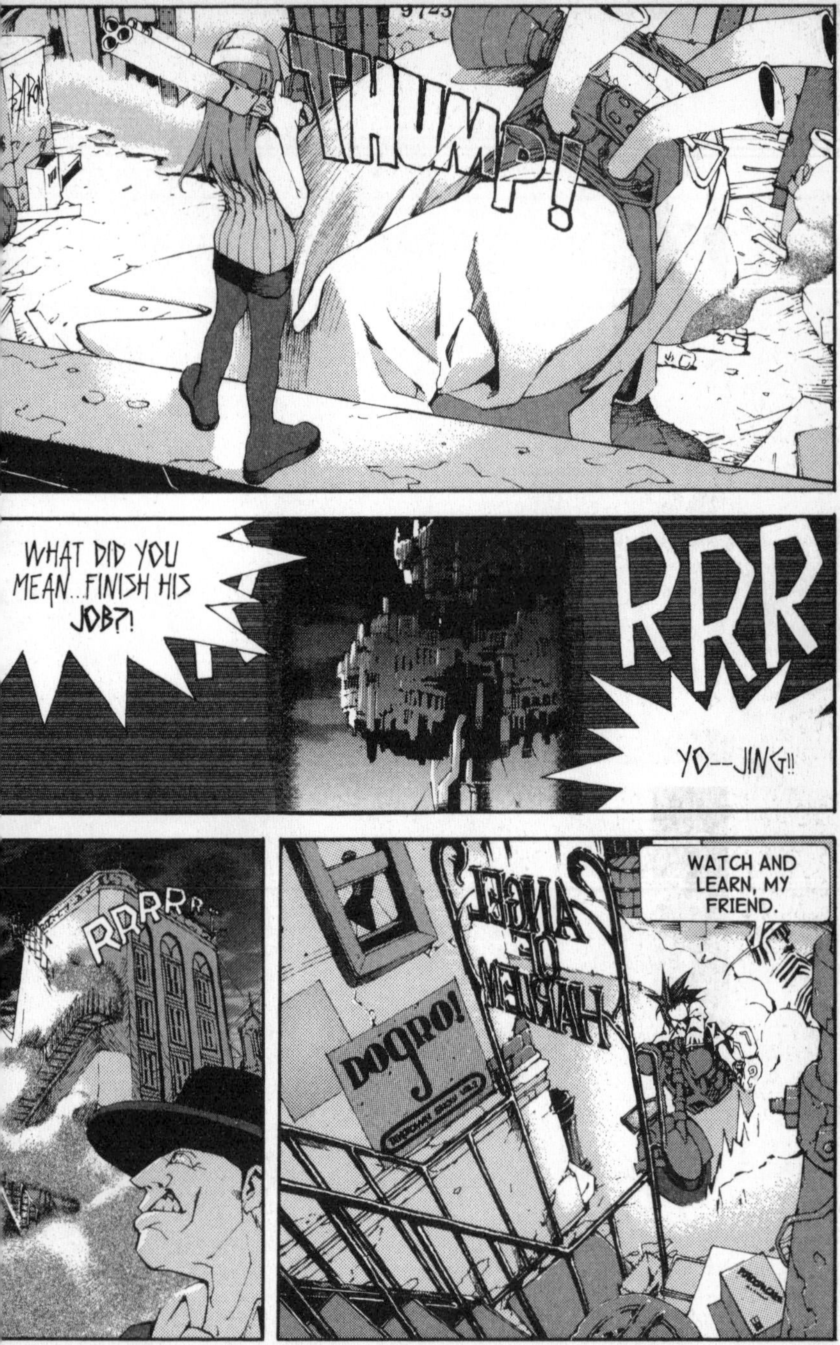
THUMP!
WHAT DID YOU MEAN...FINISH HIS JOB?!
RRR
YO--JING!!
RRRRR...
WATCH AND LEARN, MY FRIEND.

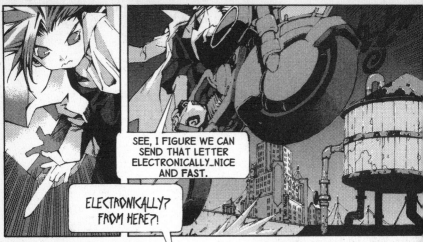

SEE, I FIGURE WE CAN SEND THAT LETTER ELECTRONICALLY...NICE AND FAST.

ELECTRONICALLY? FROM HERE?!

WELL, WE'D BE USING ELECTRIC LINES, ANYWAY...

VROOM!

VRRRI

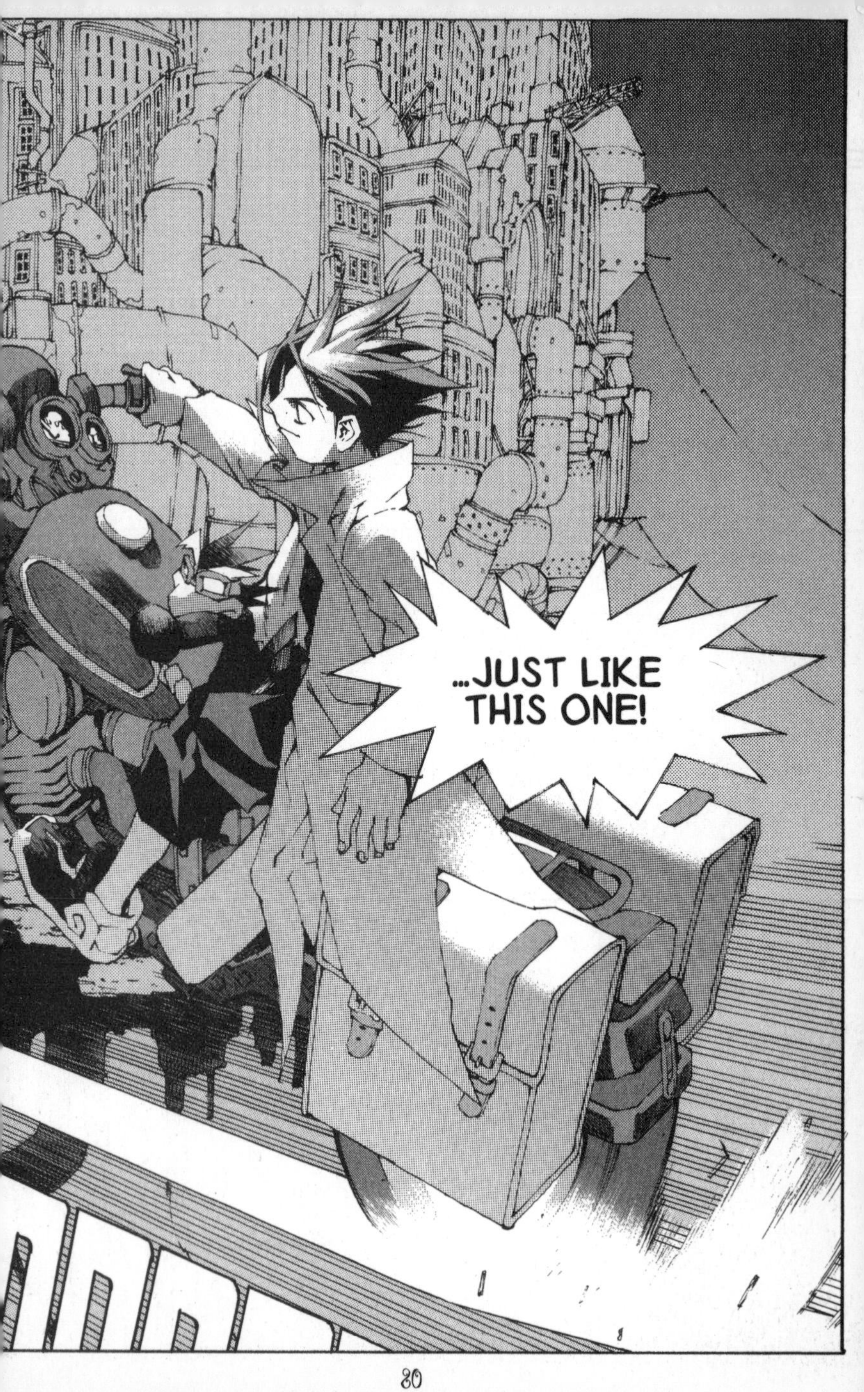
...JUST LIKE
THIS ONE!

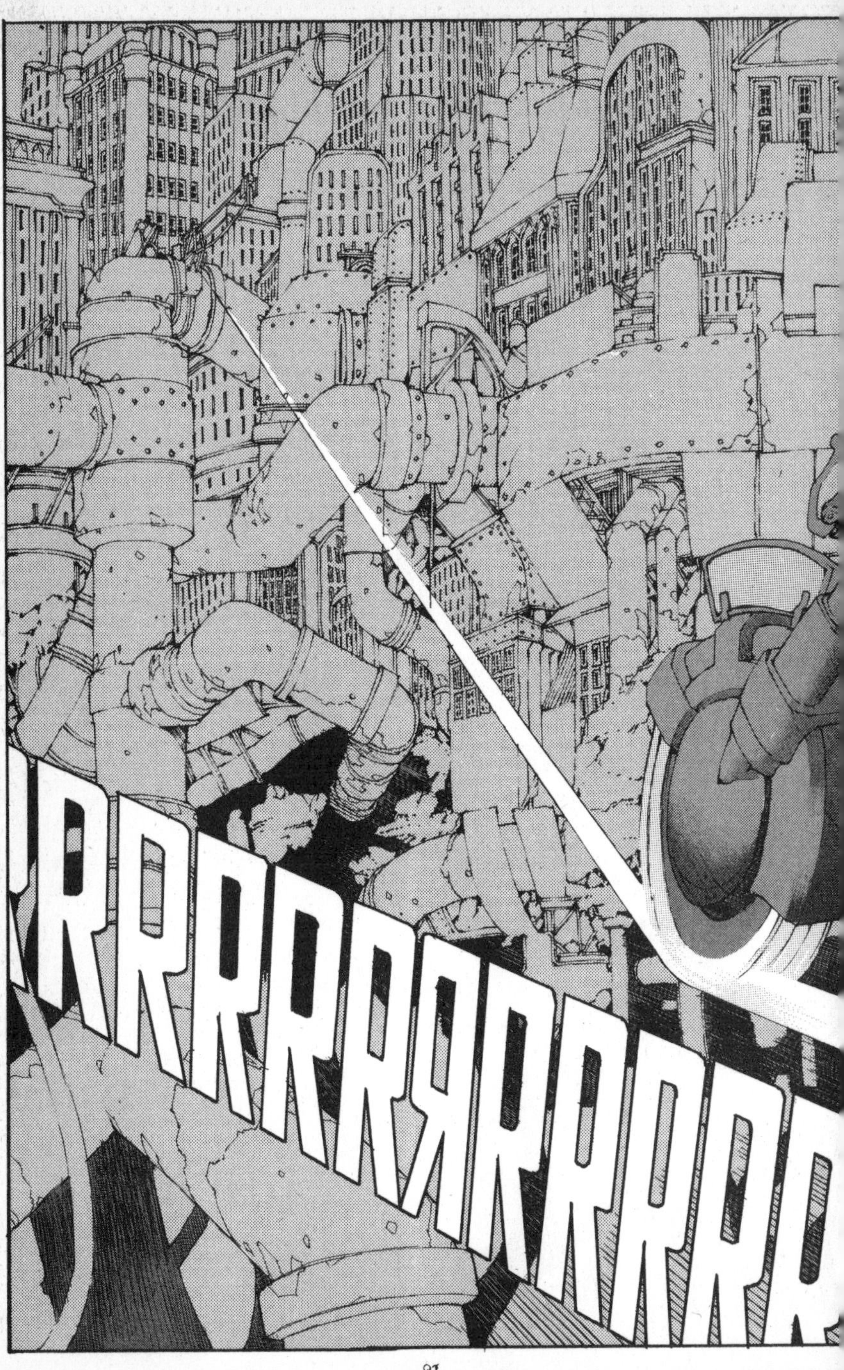
RRRRRRRRRRRR

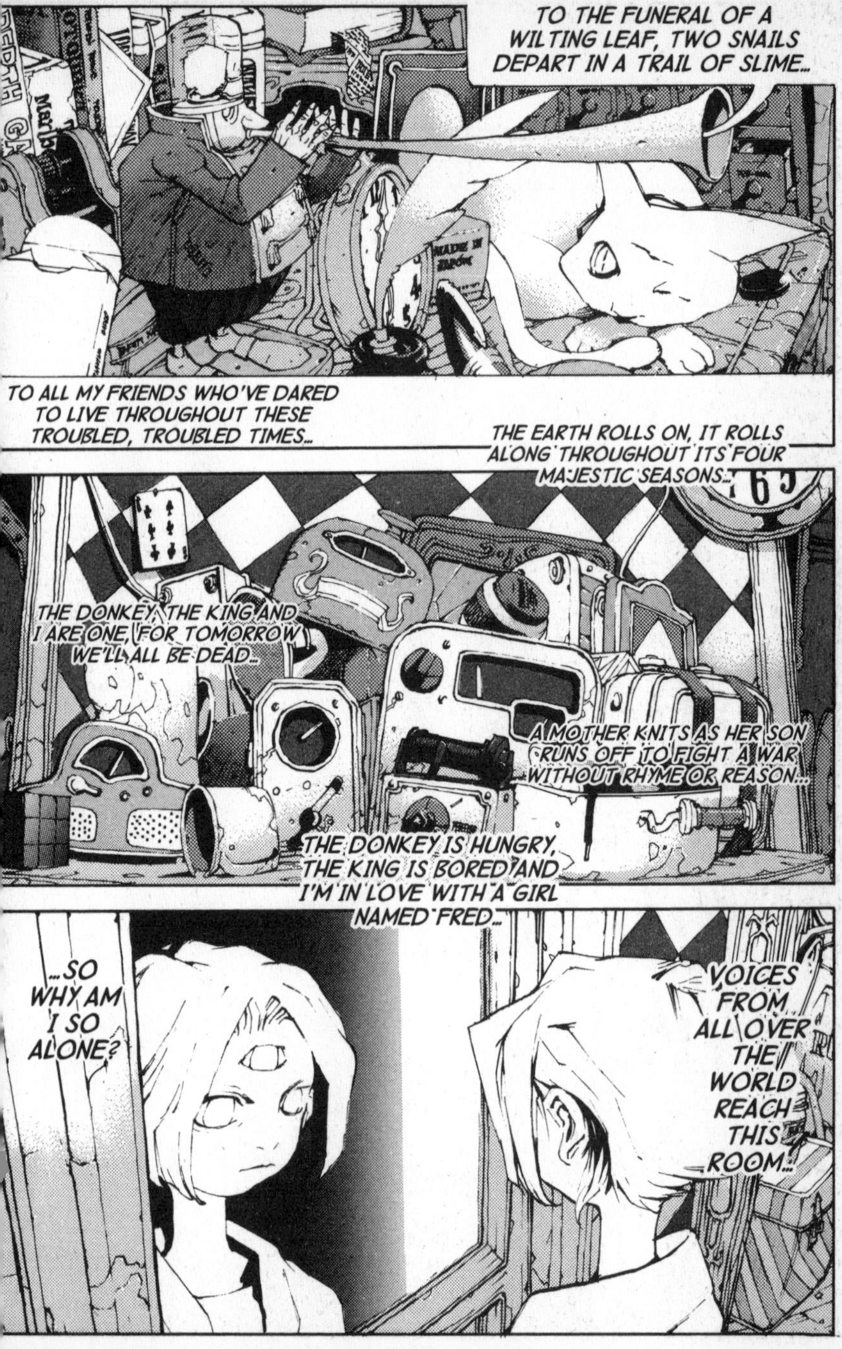
TO THE FUNERAL OF A WILTING LEAF, TWO SNAILS DEPART IN A TRAIL OF SLIME...
TO ALL MY FRIENDS WHO'VE DARED TO LIVE THROUGHOUT THESE TROUBLED, TROUBLED TIMES...
THE EARTH ROLLS ON, IT ROLLS ALONG THROUGHOUT ITS FOUR MAJESTIC SEASONS...
A MOTHER KNITS AS HER SON RUNS OFF TO FIGHT A WAR WITHOUT RHYME OR REASON...
THE DONKEY, THE KING AND I ARE ONE, FOR TOMORROW WE'LL ALL BE DEAD...
THE DONKEY IS HUNGRY, THE KING IS BORED AND I'M IN LOVE WITH A GIRL NAMED FRED...
...SO WHY AM I SO ALONE?
VOICES FROM ALL OVER THE WORLD REACH THIS ROOM...
MADE IN JAPAN

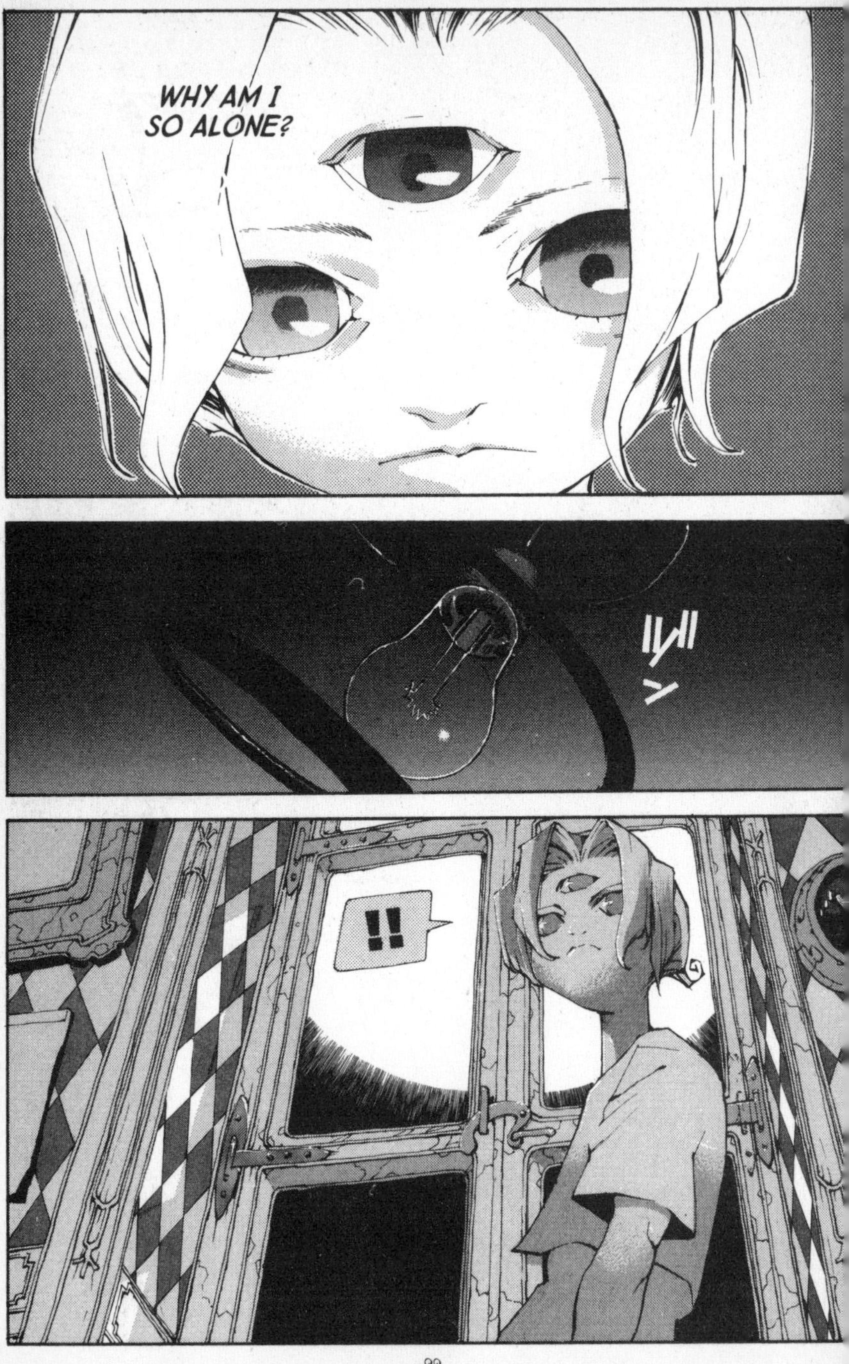
WHY AM I SO ALONE?
!!

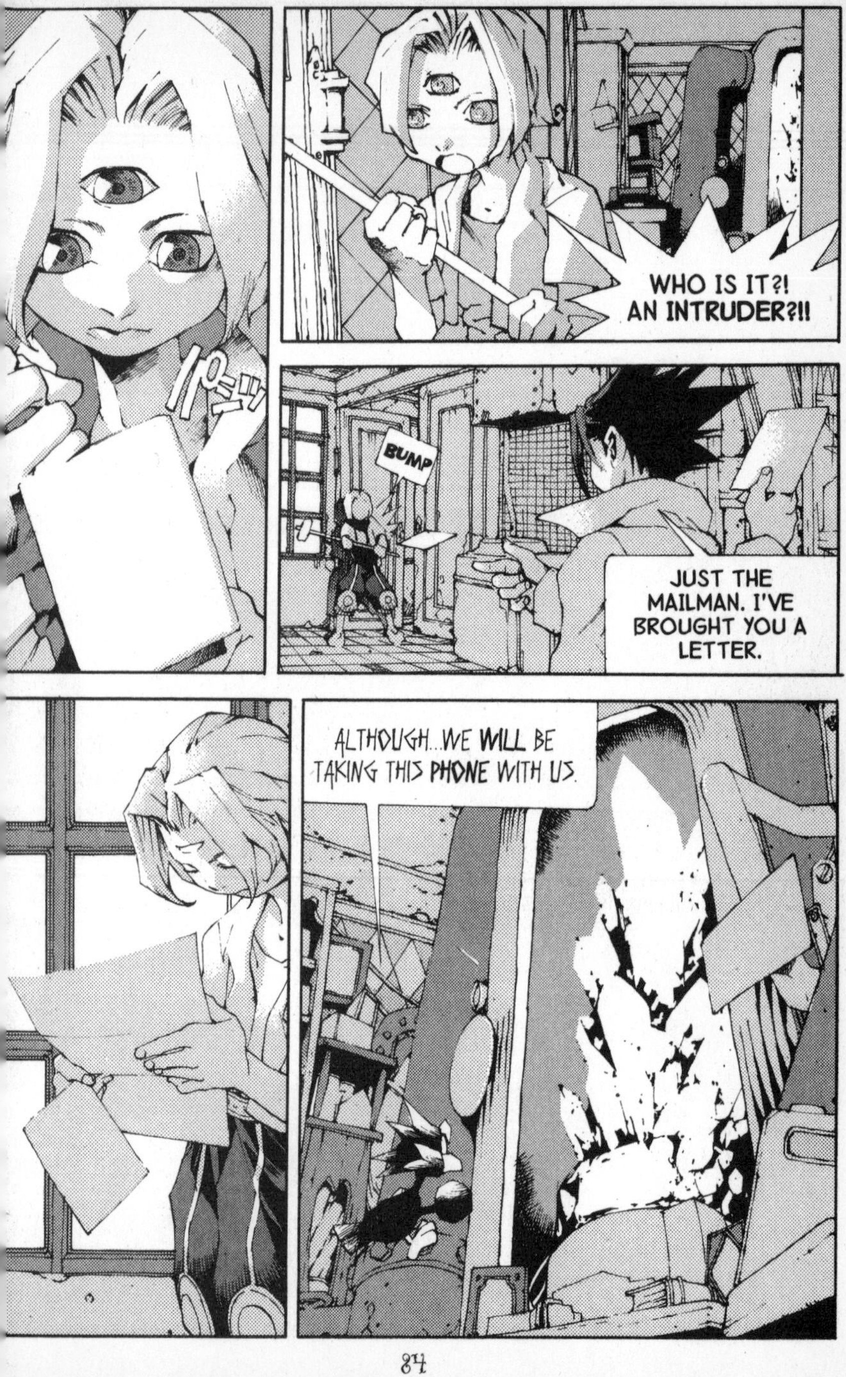
WHO IS IT?! AN INTRUDER?!!
BUMP
JUST THE MAILMAN. I'VE BROUGHT YOU A LETTER.
ALTHOUGH...WE WILL BE TAKING THIS PHONE WITH US.

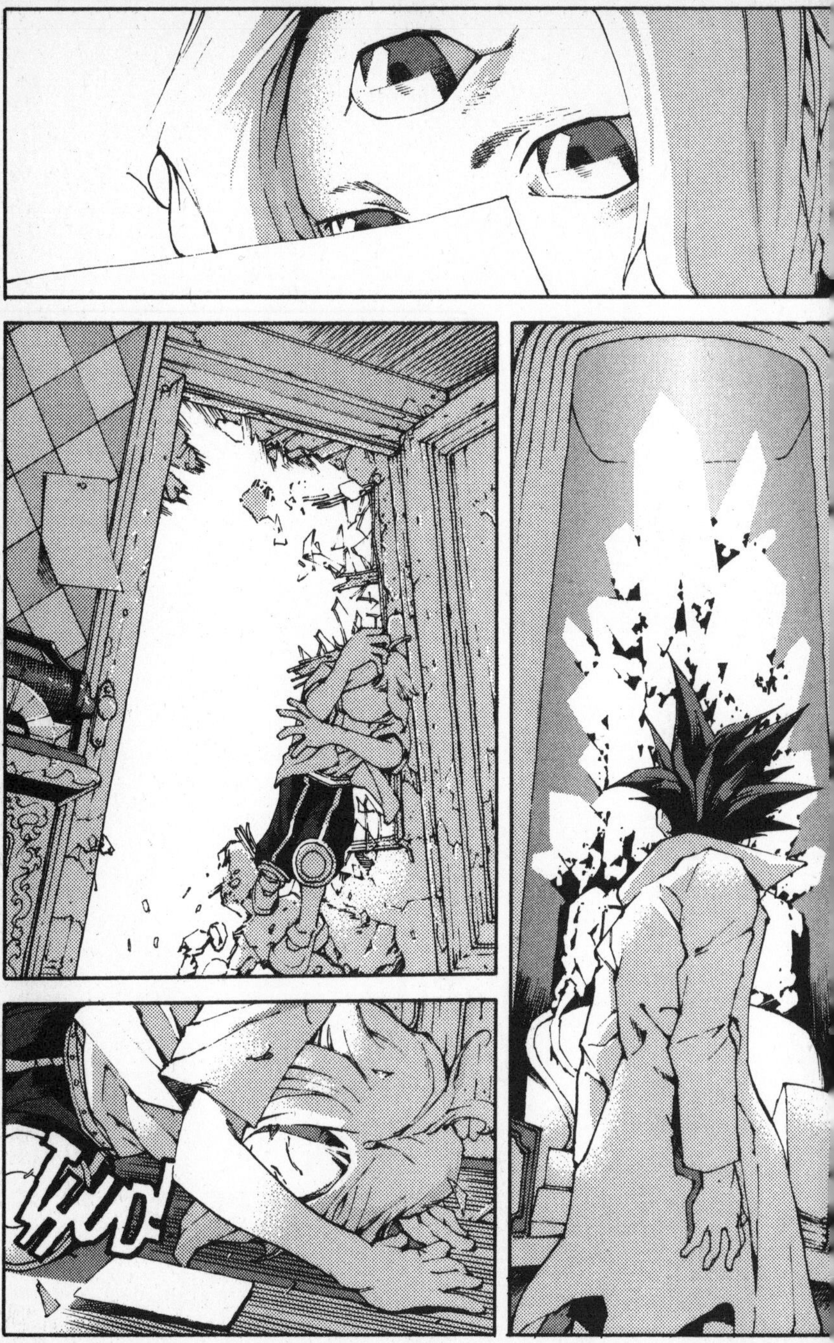
THUD

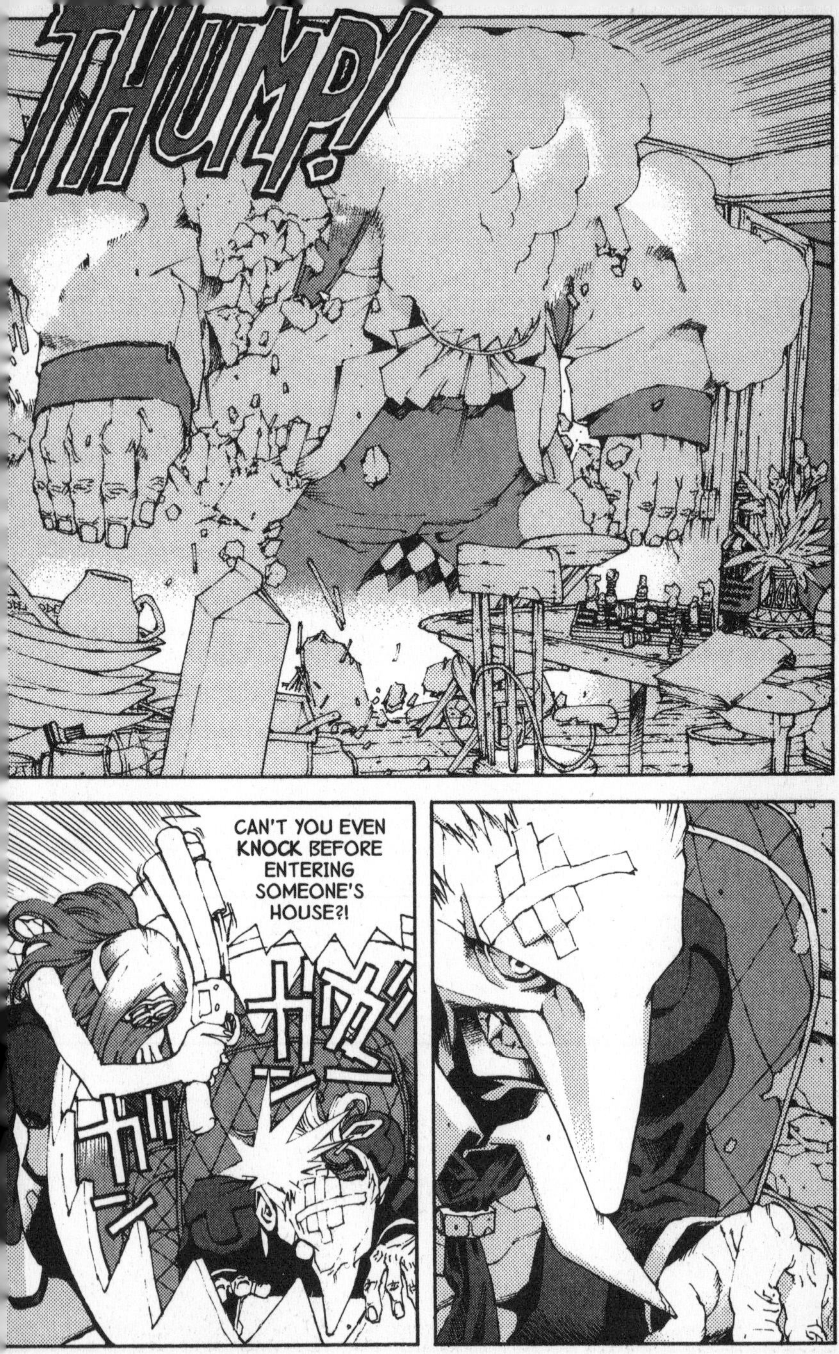
THUMP!
CAN'T YOU EVEN KNOCK BEFORE ENTERING SOMEONE'S HOUSE?!

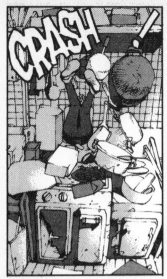

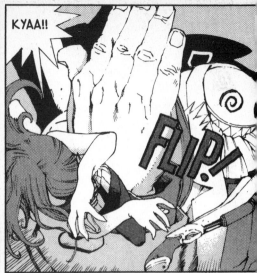

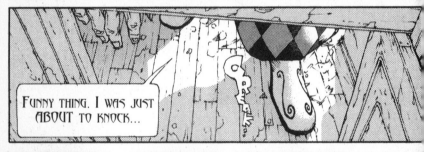

KYAA!!
FLIP!
CRASH
CREAK...
FUNNY THING. I WAS JUST ABOUT TO KNOCK...
CREAK
...KNOCK YOU OUT PERMANENTLY.

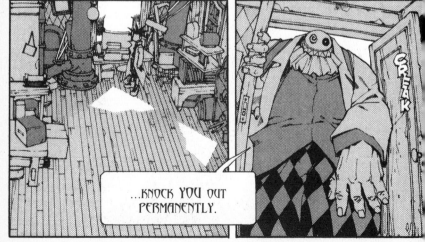

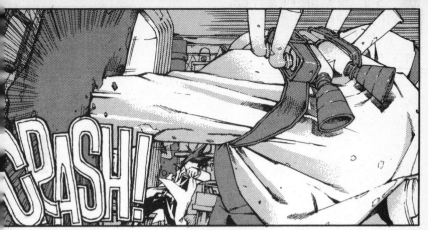

TO THROW SUCH AN EXCITING FUTURE TO THE WIND--WHAT A STRANGE CHILD YOU ARE.

ZRISH!

KIIIIIR!!

AH...THE SUNLIGHT...!

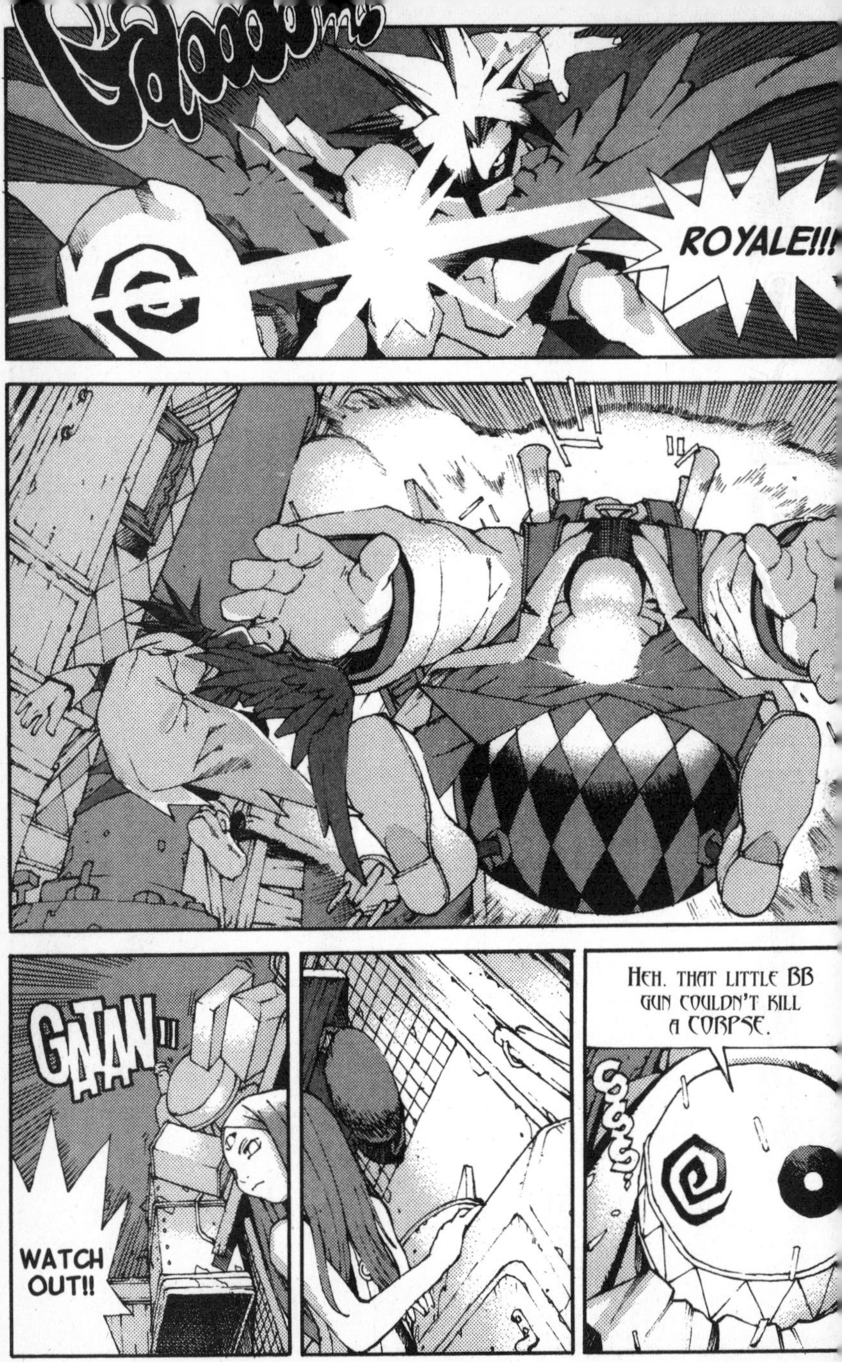
ROYALE!!!
HEH. THAT LITTLE BB GUN COULDN'T KILL A CORPSE.
GATAN!!
WATCH OUT!!

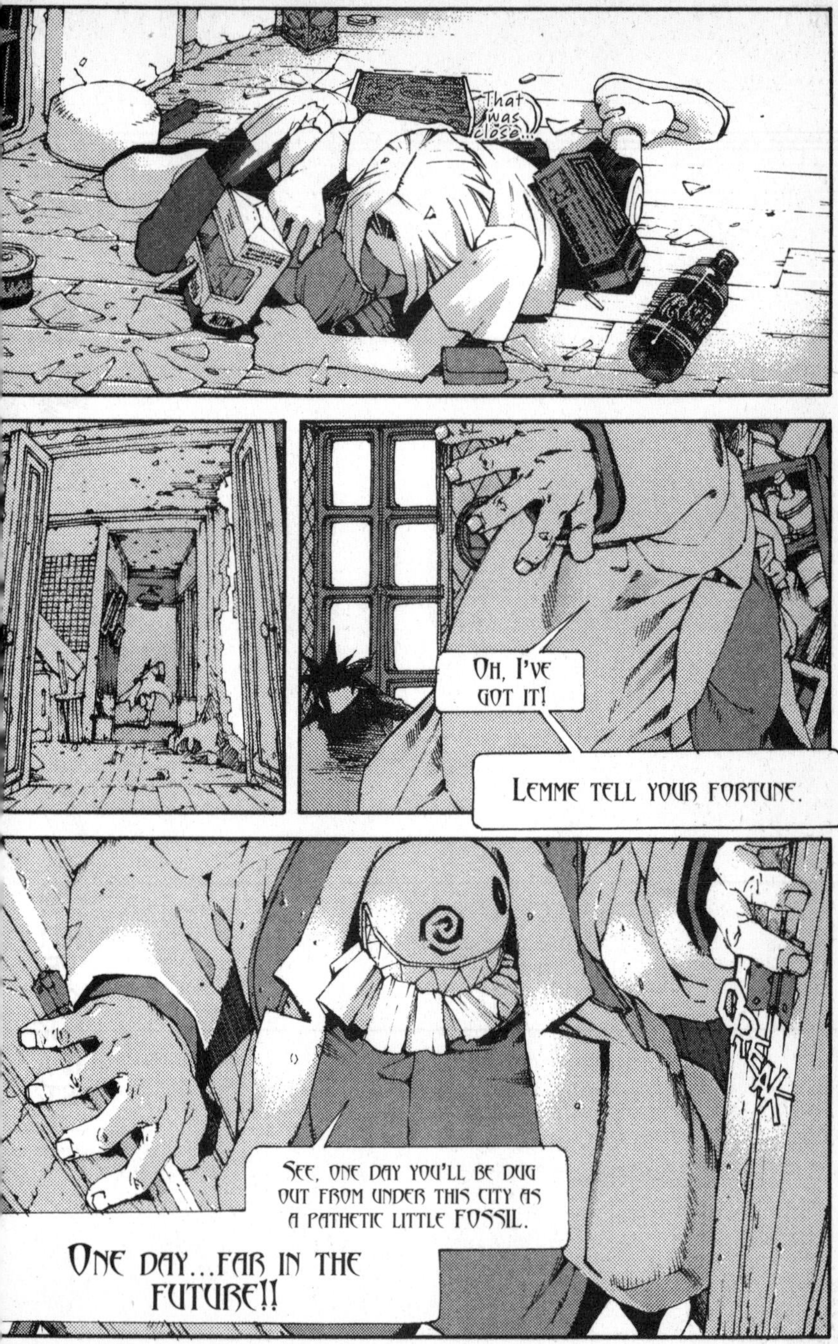
That was close...
Oh, I've got it!
Lemme tell your fortune.
CREAK
See, one day you'll be dug out from under this city as a pathetic little FOSSIL.
One day...far in the future!!

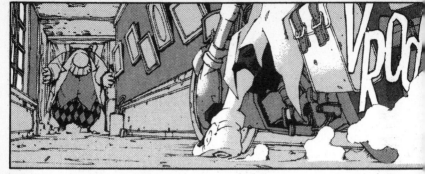

I MAY BE YOUNG...

DON'T TRY AND FORCE YOUR FUTURE ON ME JUST 'CUZ I'M A KID.

THUD!!

...BUT I'VE GOT ENOUGH OF A PAST...

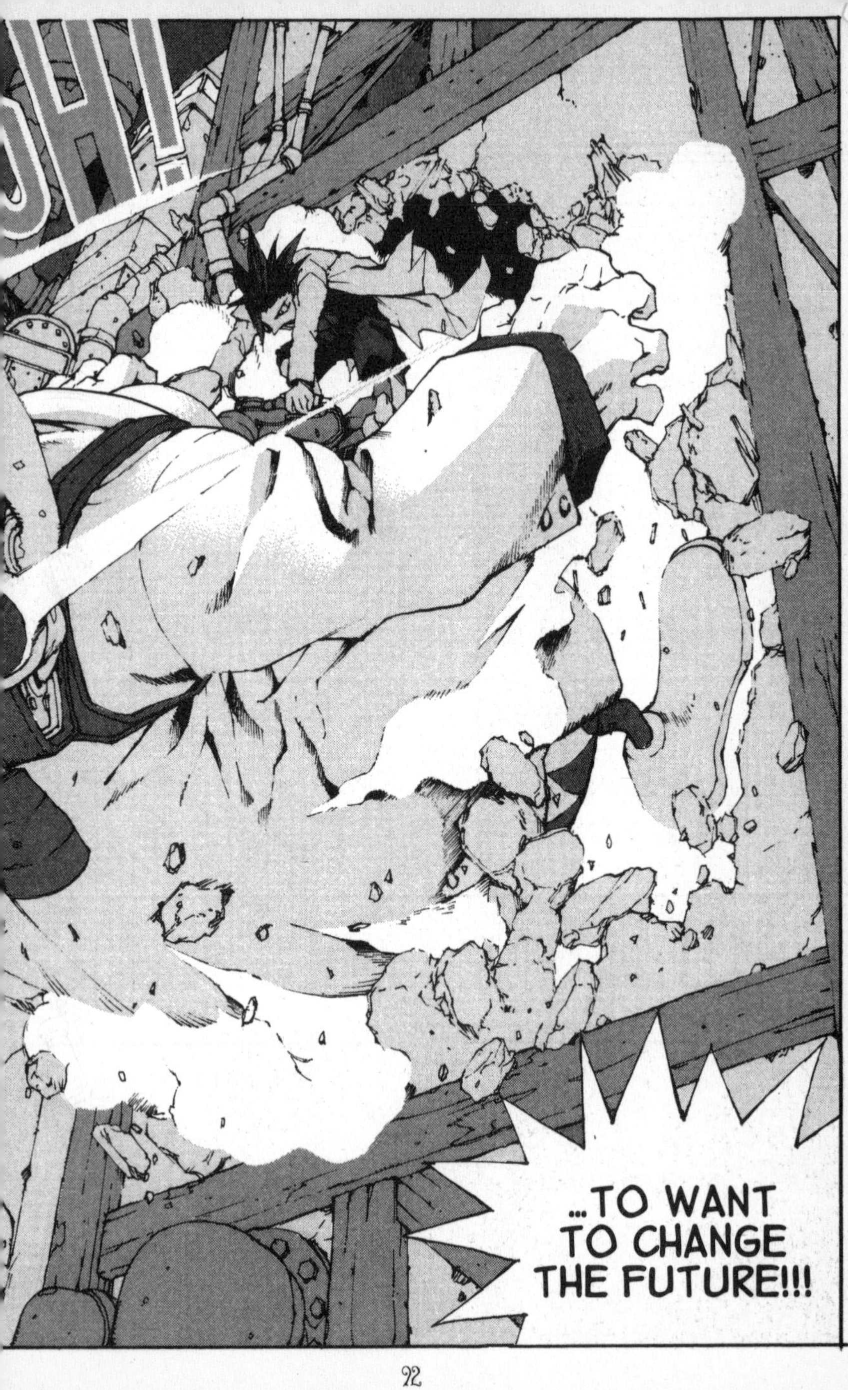
...TO WANT
TO CHANGE
THE FUTURE!!!

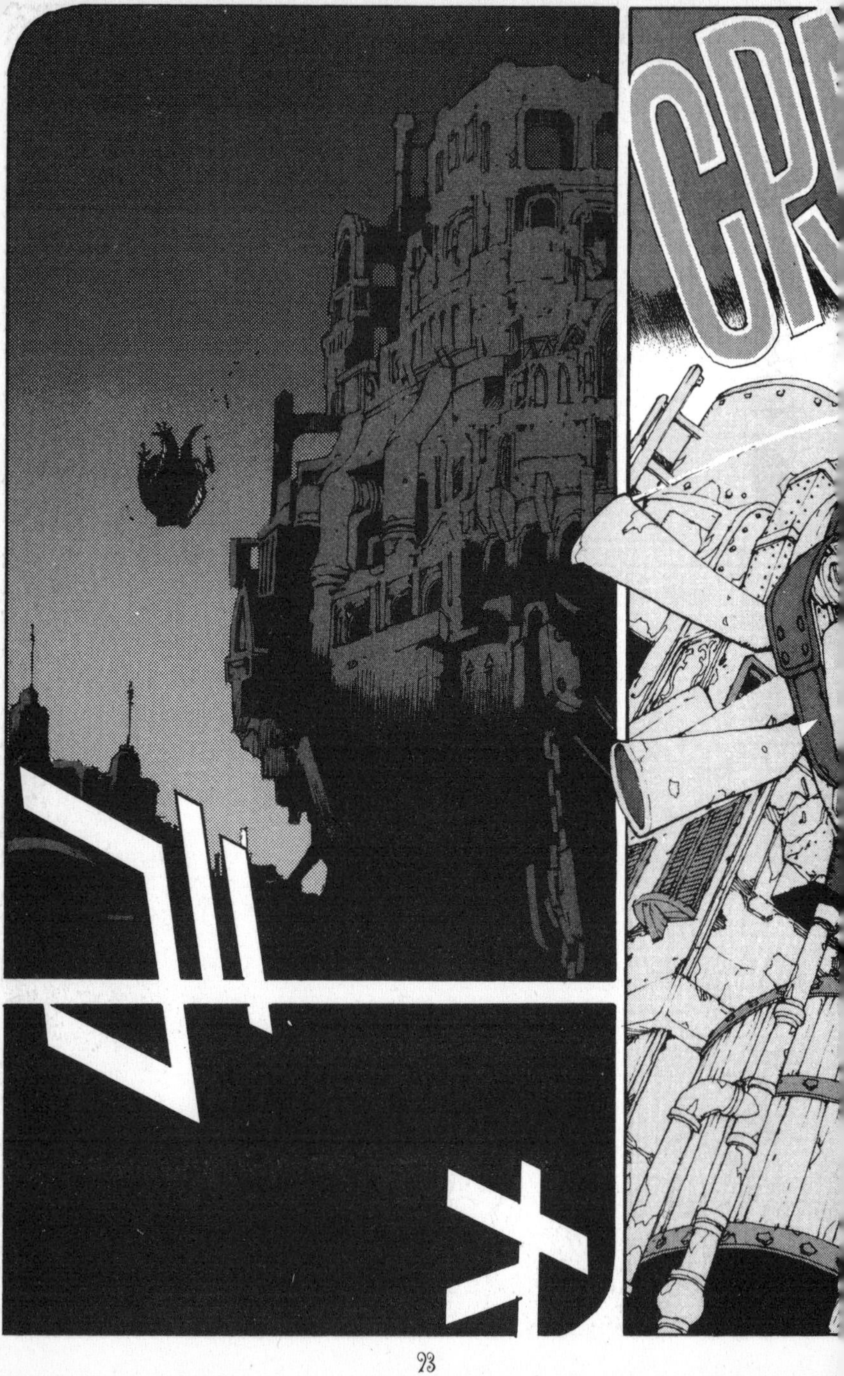

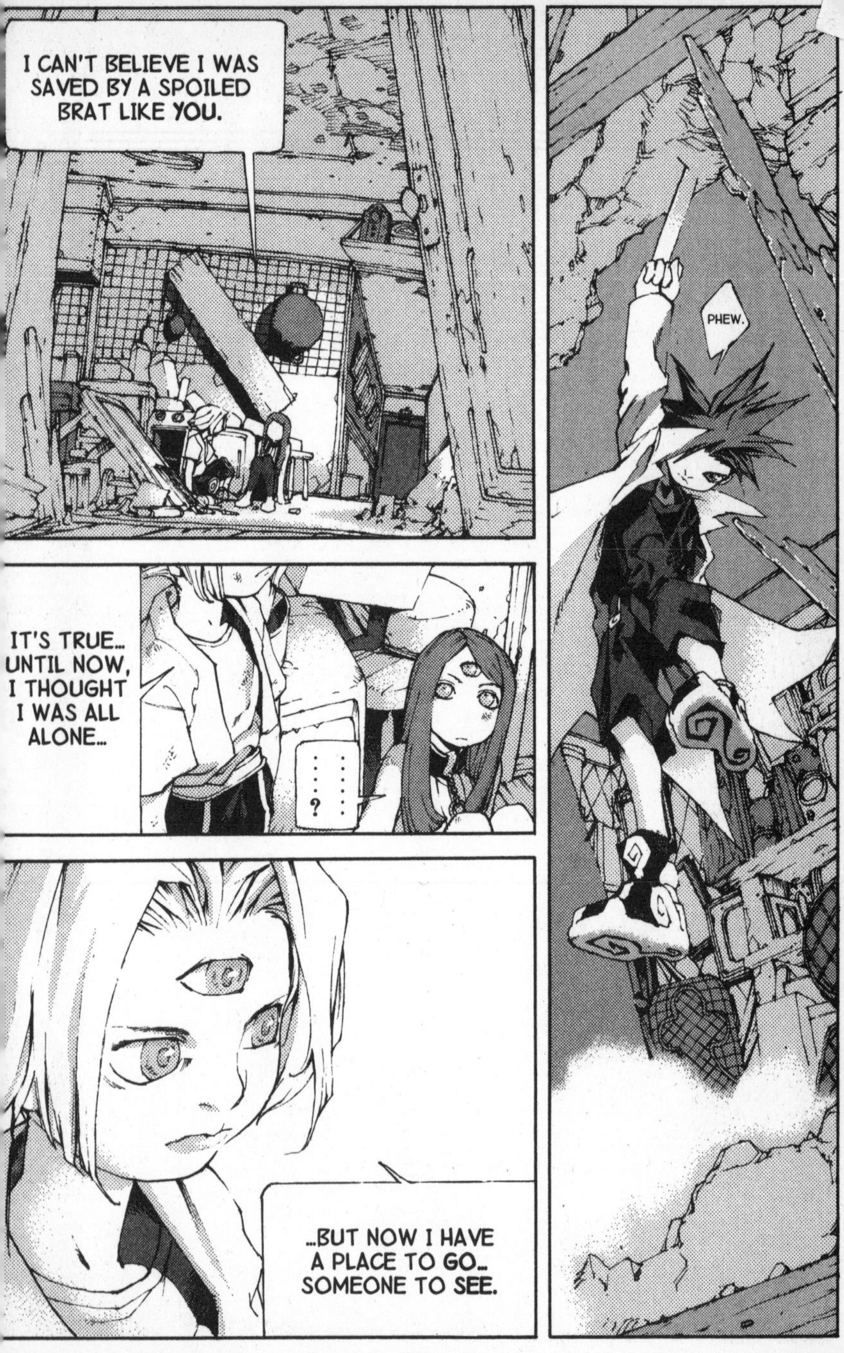
PHEW.
I CAN'T BELIEVE I WAS SAVED BY A SPOILED BRAT LIKE YOU.
IT'S TRUE... UNTIL NOW, I THOUGHT I WAS ALL ALONE...
......?
...BUT NOW I HAVE A PLACE TO GO... SOMEONE TO SEE.

THANKS FOR THE LETTER.

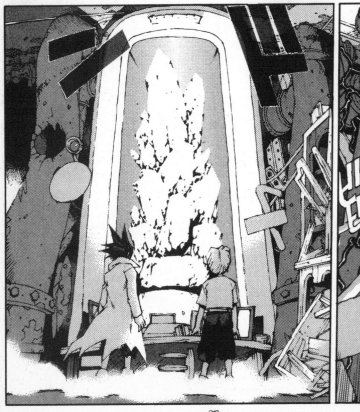

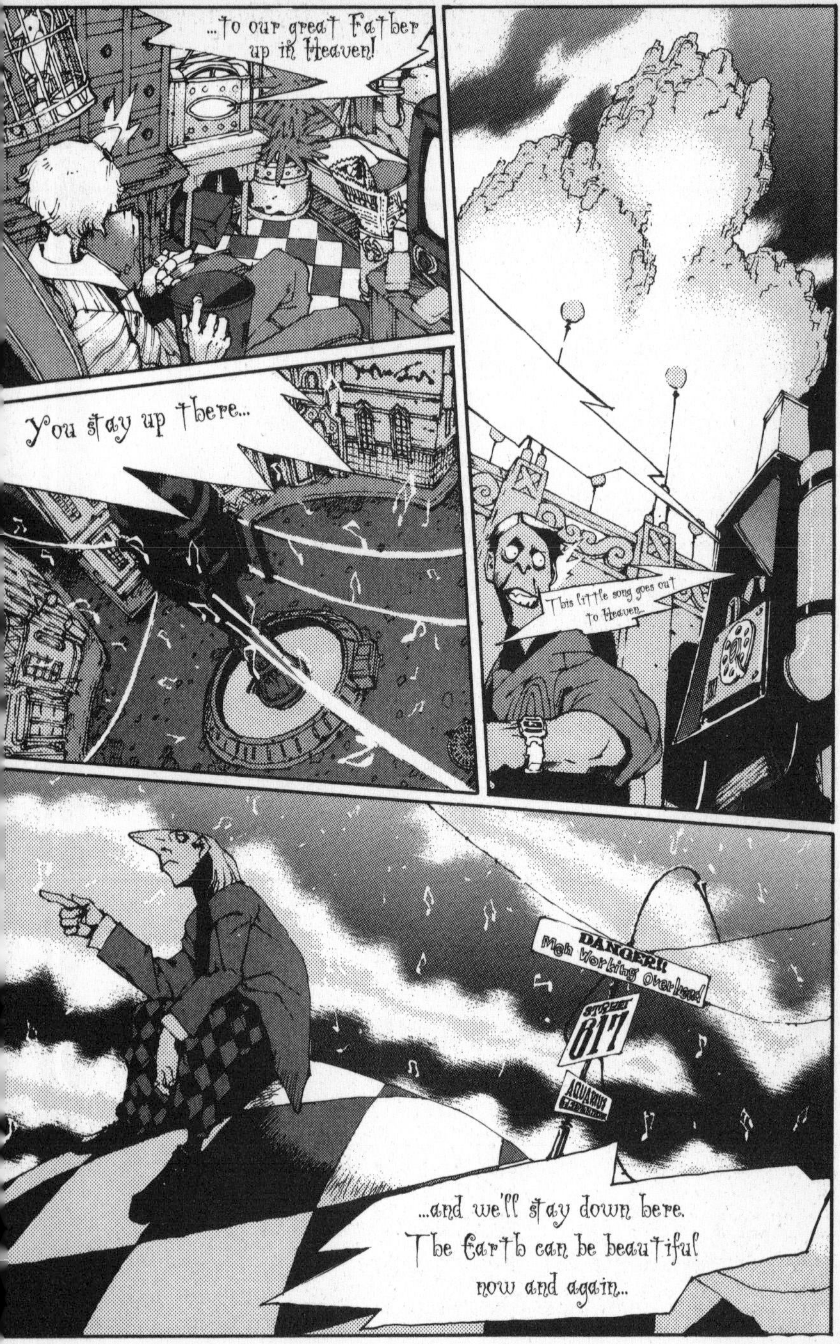

...to our great Father up in Heaven!
This little song goes out to Heaven...
You stay up there...
DANGER!! Men Working Overhead!
817
AQUARIUS
...and we'll stay down here. The Earth can be beautiful now and again...

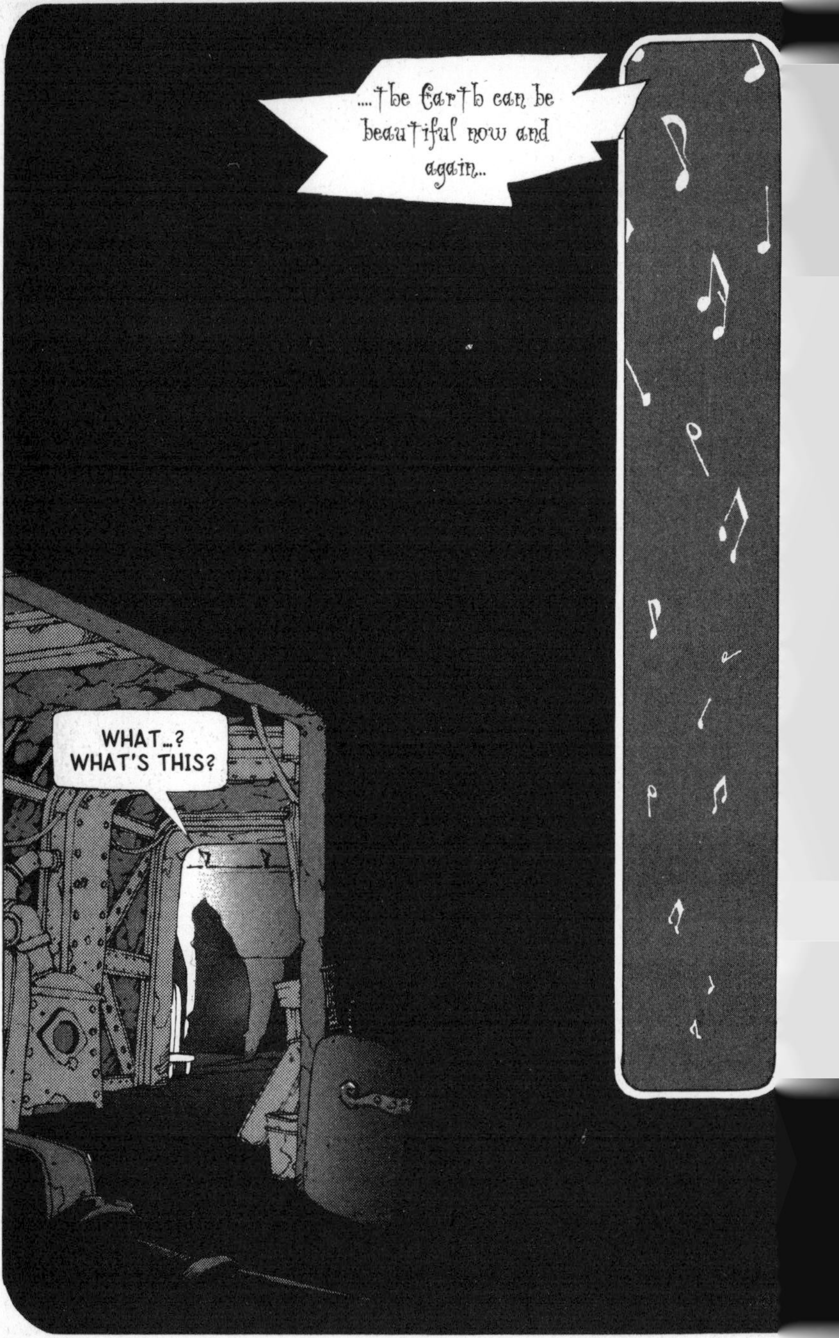
...The Earth can be beautiful now and again...
WHAT...? WHAT'S THIS?

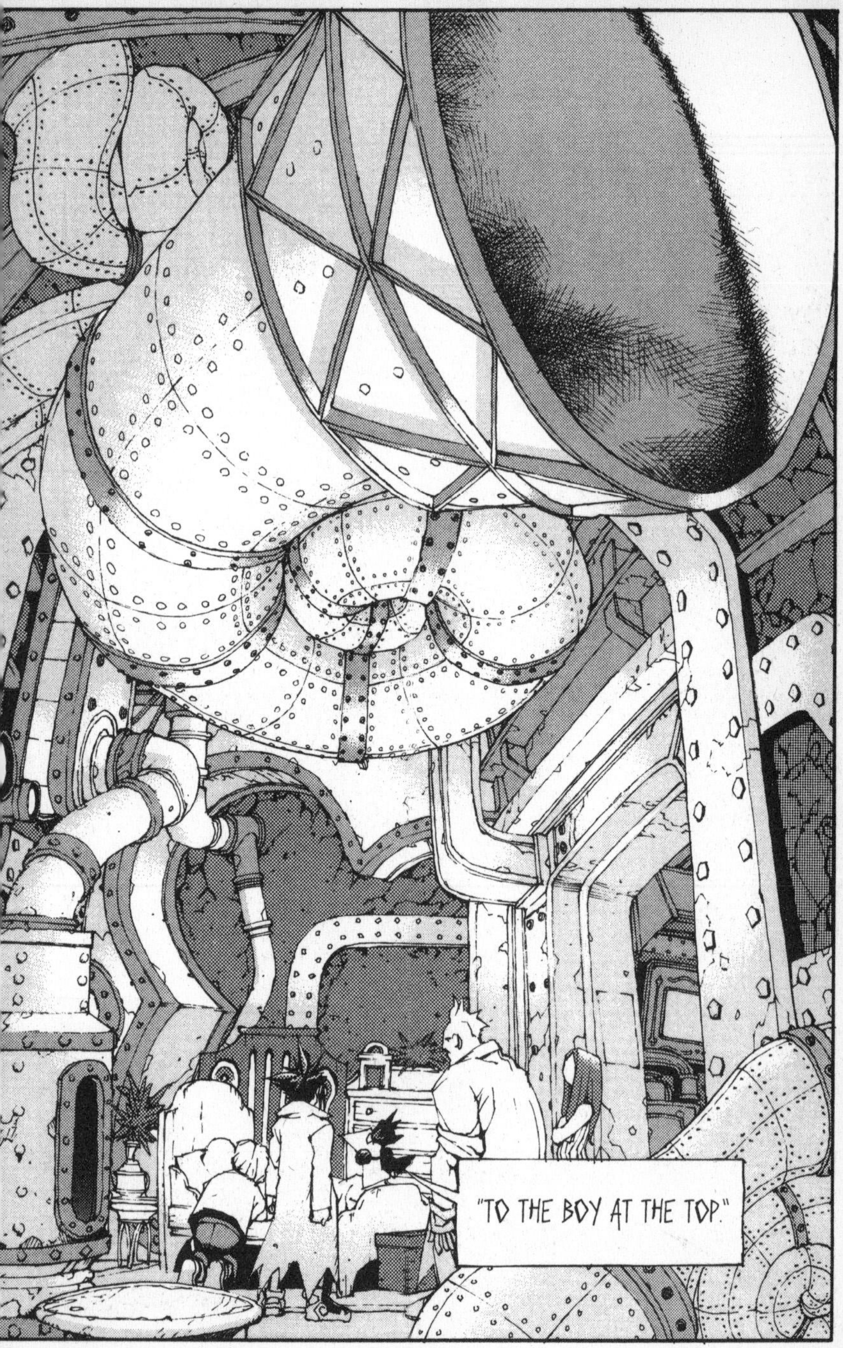
"TO THE BOY AT THE TOP."

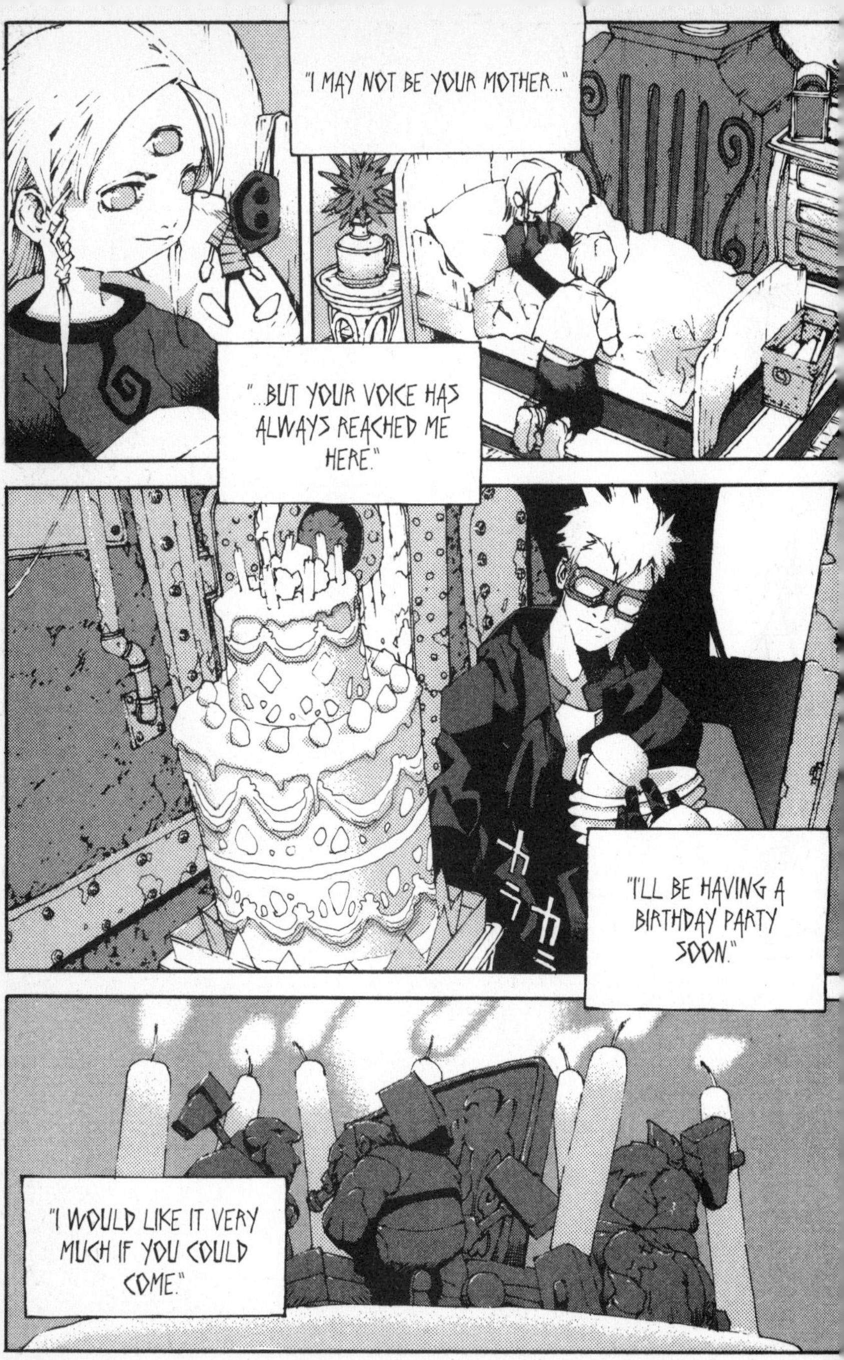
"I MAY NOT BE YOUR MOTHER..."
"...BUT YOUR VOICE HAS ALWAYS REACHED ME HERE."
"I'LL BE HAVING A BIRTHDAY PARTY SOON."
"I WOULD LIKE IT VERY MUCH IF YOU COULD COME."

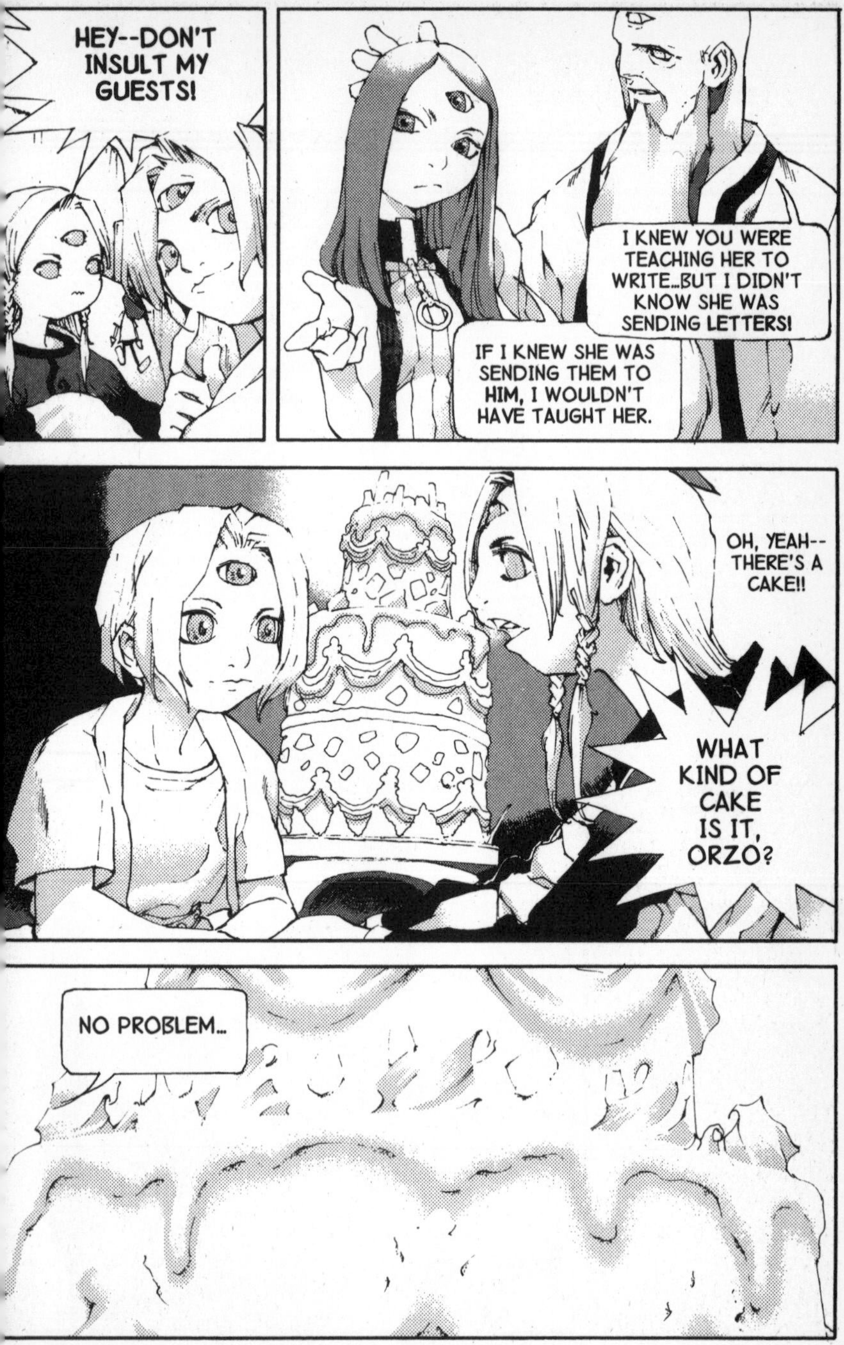
HEY--DON'T INSULT MY GUESTS!
I KNEW YOU WERE TEACHING HER TO WRITE...BUT I DIDN'T KNOW SHE WAS SENDING LETTERS!
IF I KNEW SHE WAS SENDING THEM TO HIM, I WOULDN'T HAVE TAUGHT HER.
OH, YEAH--THERE'S A CAKE!!
WHAT KIND OF CAKE IS IT, ORZO?
NO PROBLEM...

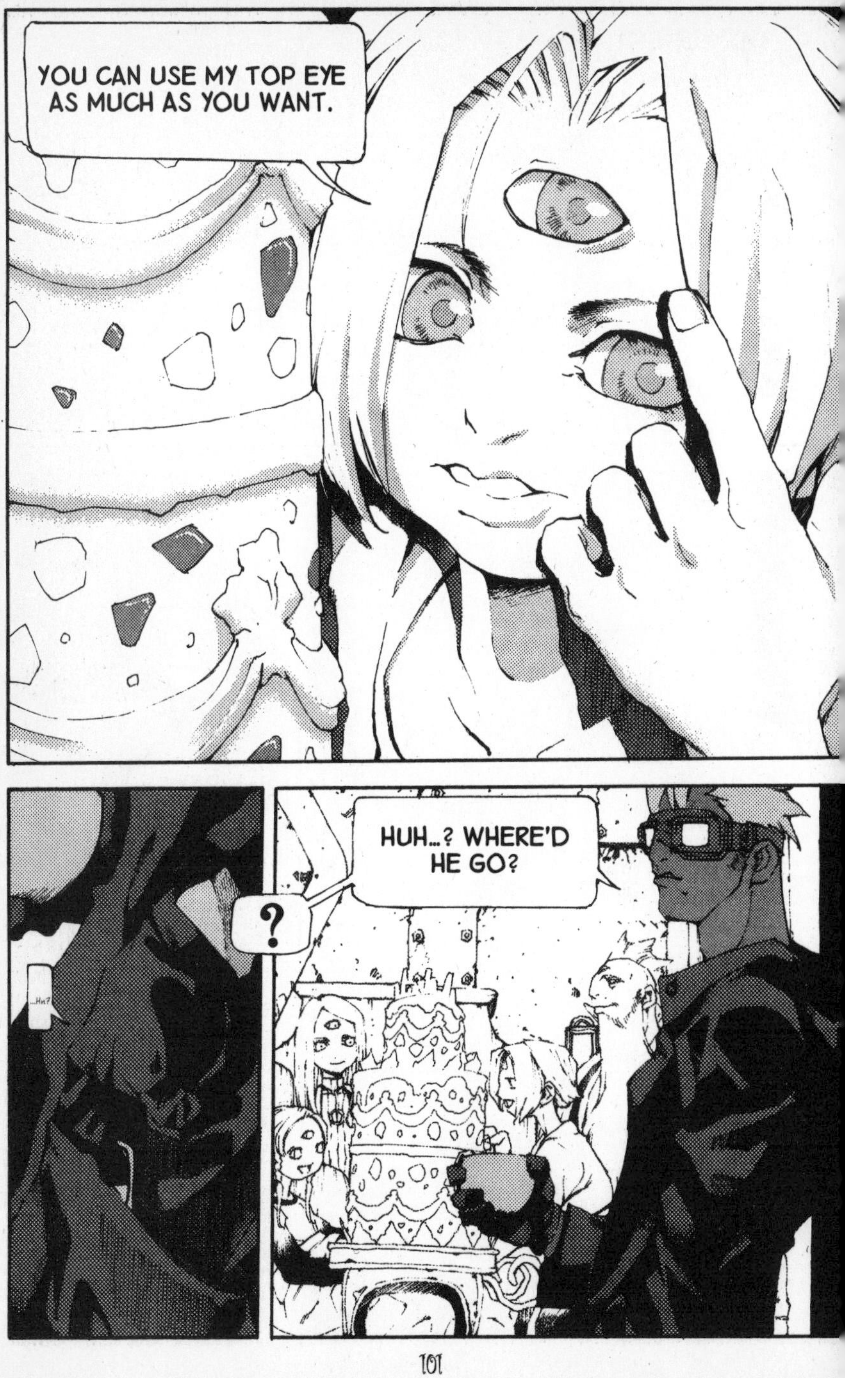
YOU CAN USE MY TOP EYE AS MUCH AS YOU WANT.
HUH...? WHERE'D HE GO?
?
...Hn?

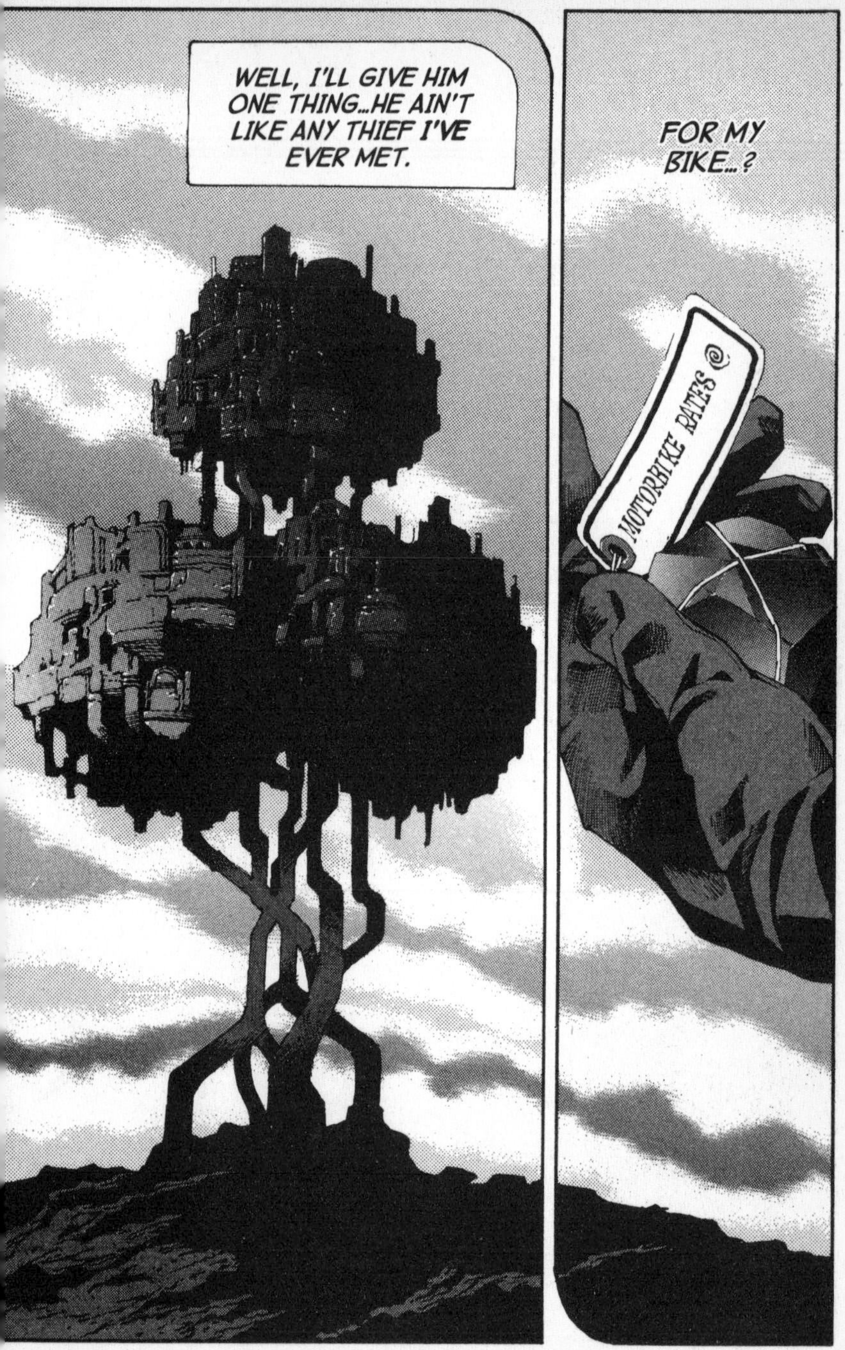
WELL, I'LL GIVE HIM ONE THING...HE AIN'T LIKE ANY THIEF I'VE EVER MET.
FOR MY BIKE...?
MOTORBIKE RATES

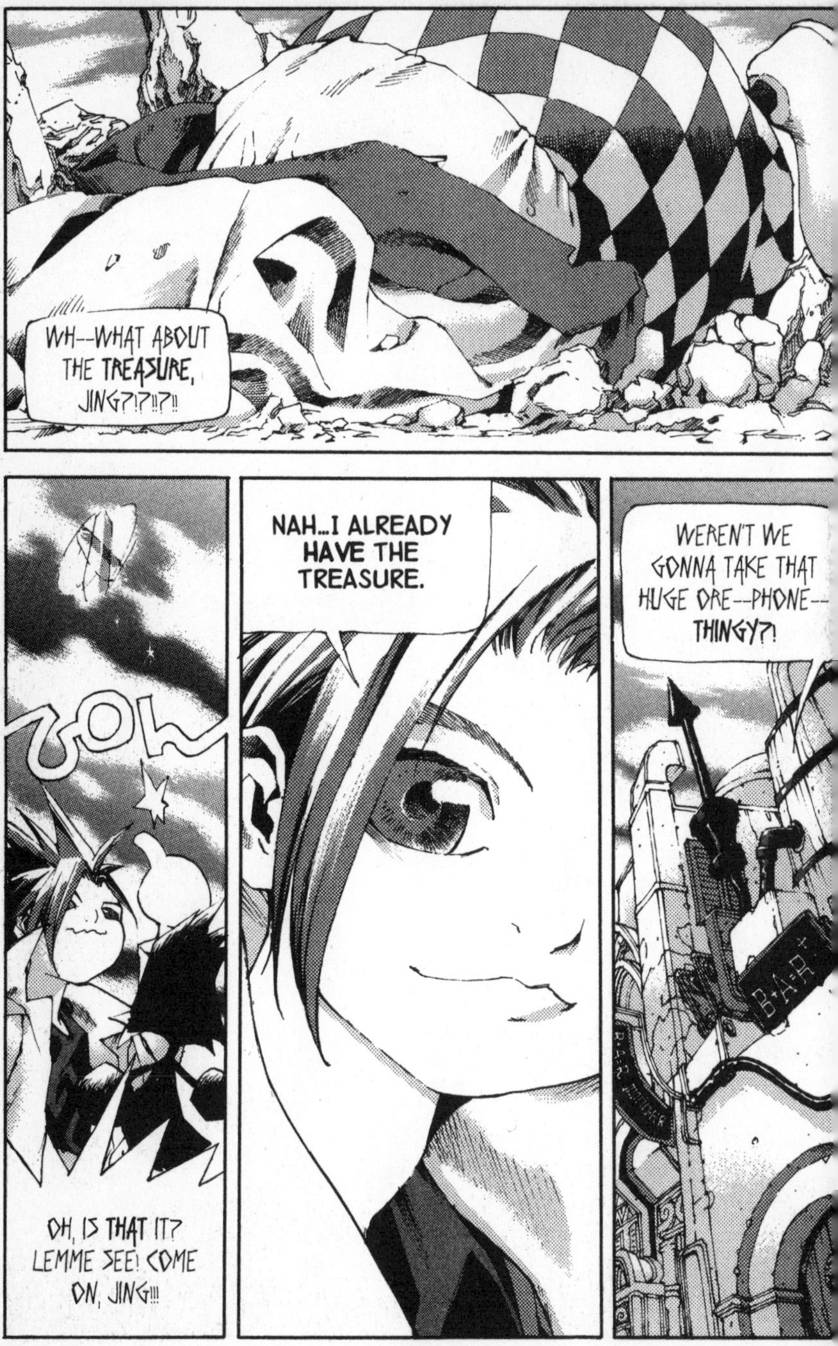
WH--WHAT ABOUT THE TREASURE, JING?!?!!?!!
WEREN'T WE GONNA TAKE THAT HUGE ORE--PHONE--THINGY?!
NAH...I ALREADY HAVE THE TREASURE.
OH, IS THAT IT? LEMME SEE! COME ON, JING!!!
B·A·R

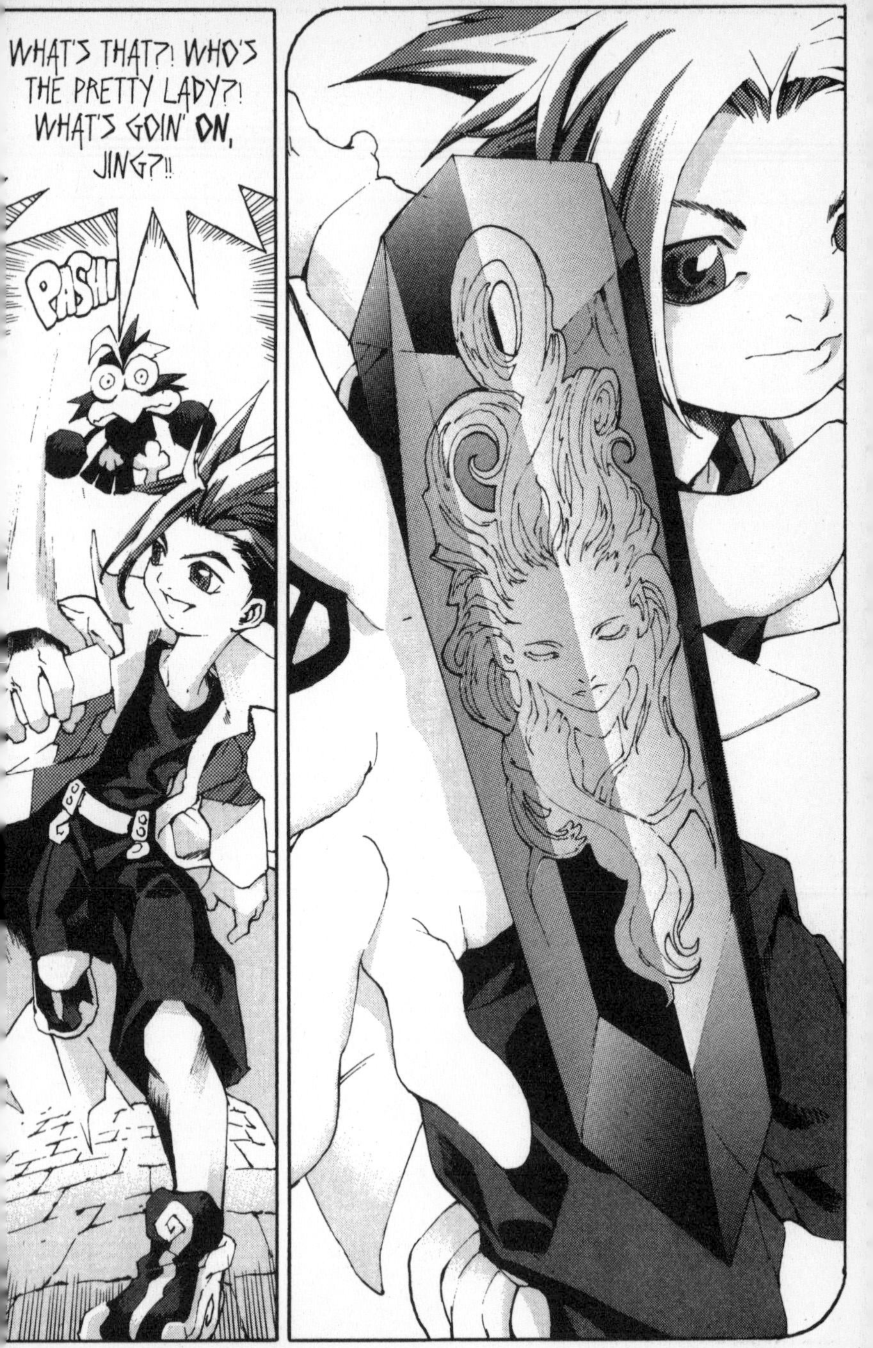
WHAT'S THAT?! WHO'S THE PRETTY LADY?! WHAT'S GOIN' ON, JING?!!
PASH

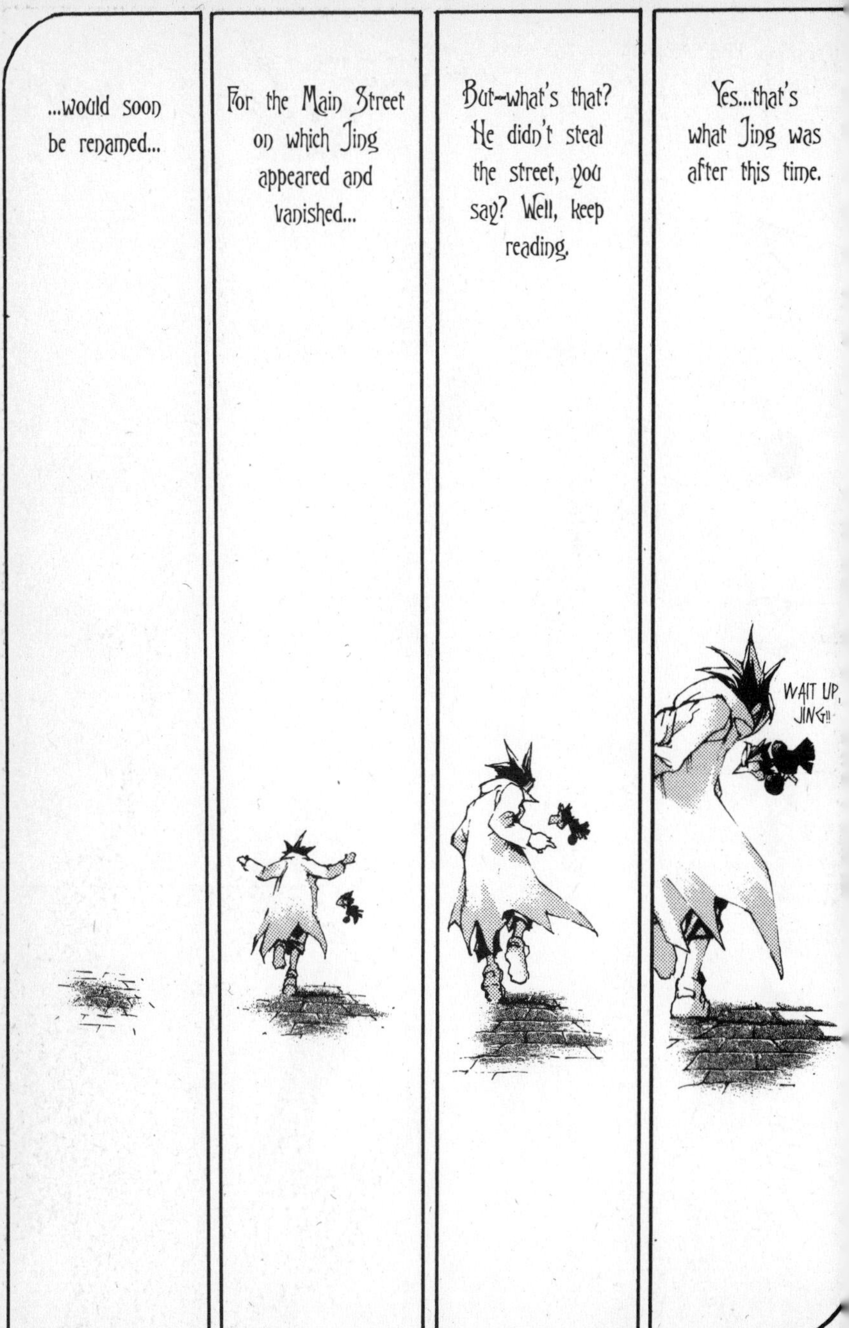
...would soon be renamed...
For the Main Street on which Jing appeared and vanished...
But--what's that? He didn't steal the street, you say? Well, keep reading.
Yes...that's what Jing was after this time.
WAIT UP, JING!!

Rue de Jing...
"King of Crime Street."

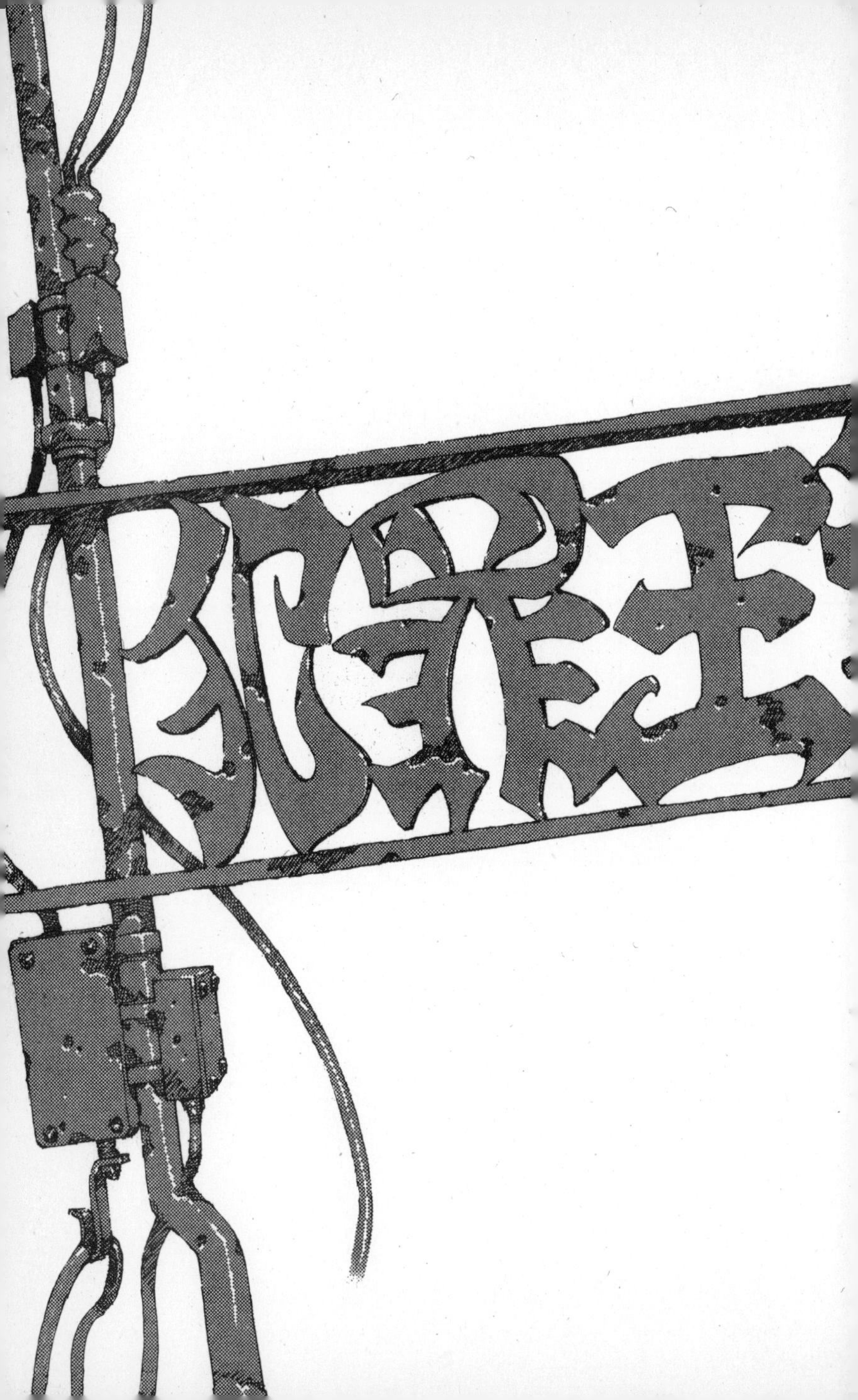

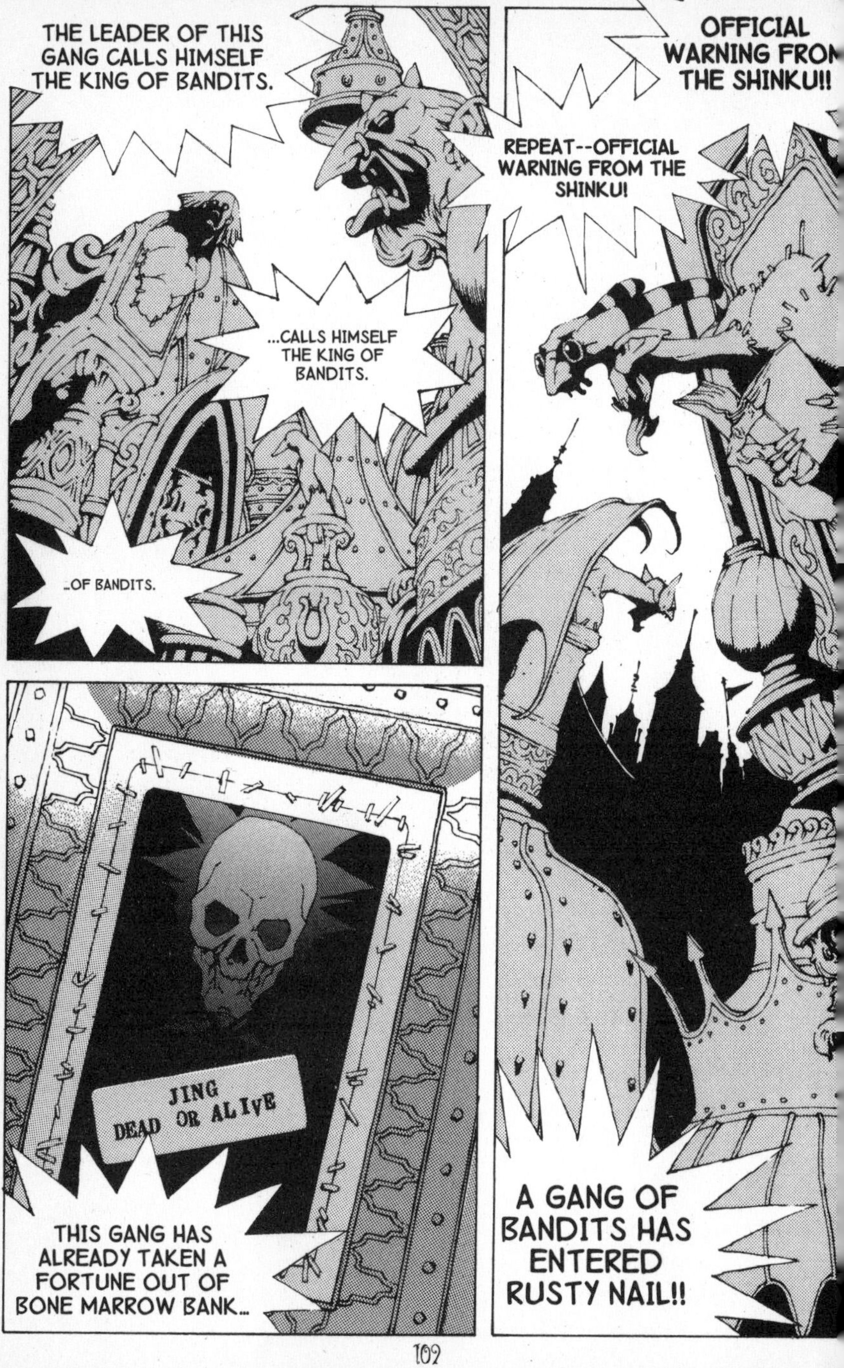
OFFICIAL WARNING FROM THE SHINKU!!
REPEAT--OFFICIAL WARNING FROM THE SHINKU!
A GANG OF BANDITS HAS ENTERED RUSTY NAIL!!
THE LEADER OF THIS GANG CALLS HIMSELF THE KING OF BANDITS.
...CALLS HIMSELF THE KING OF BANDITS.
...OF BANDITS.
JING
DEAD OR ALIvE
THIS GANG HAS ALREADY TAKEN A FORTUNE OUT OF BONE MARROW BANK...

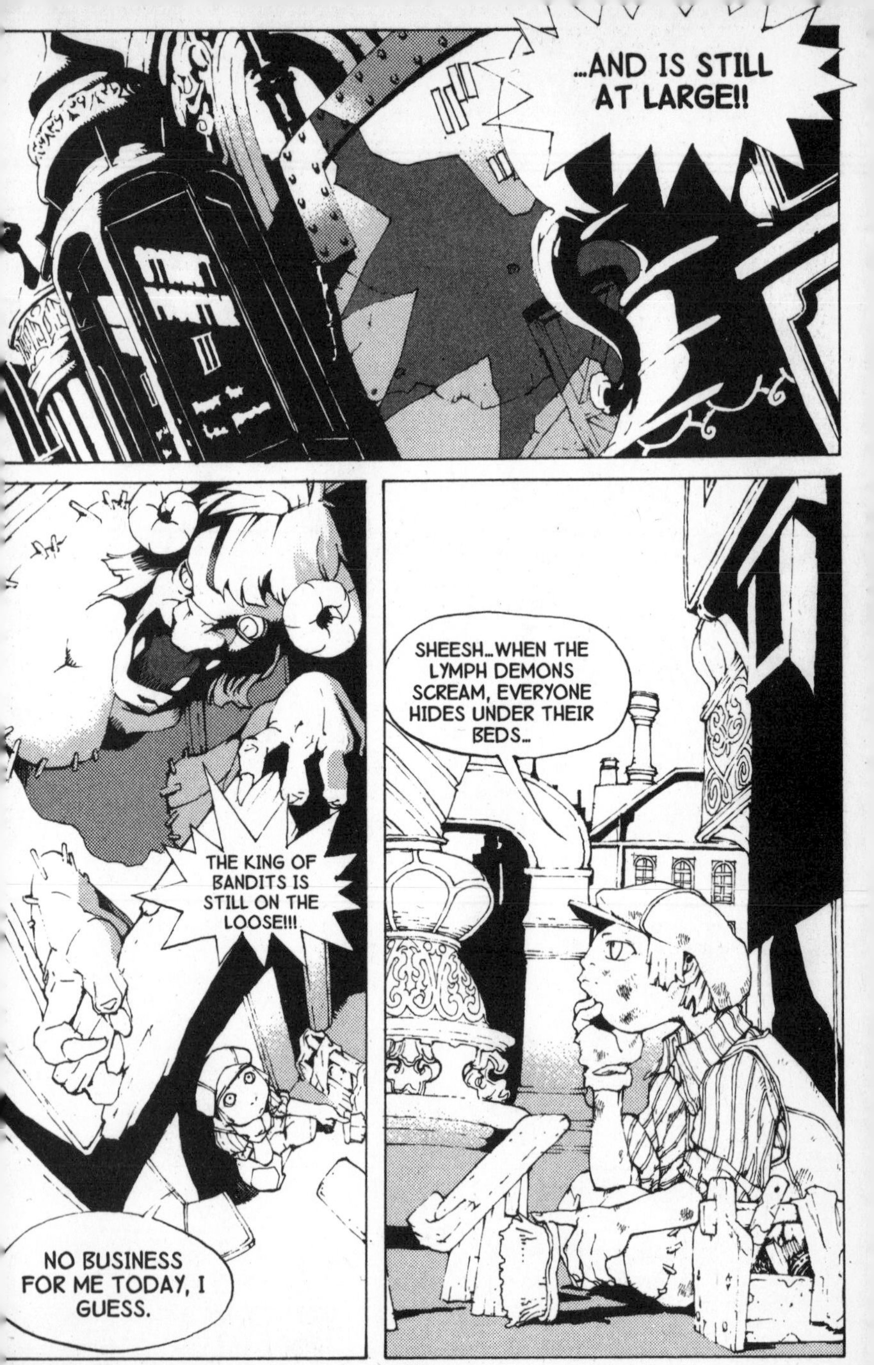
...AND IS STILL AT LARGE!!
THE KING OF BANDITS IS STILL ON THE LOOSE!!!
NO BUSINESS FOR ME TODAY, I GUESS.
SHEESH...WHEN THE LYMPH DEMONS SCREAM, EVERYONE HIDES UNDER THEIR BEDS...

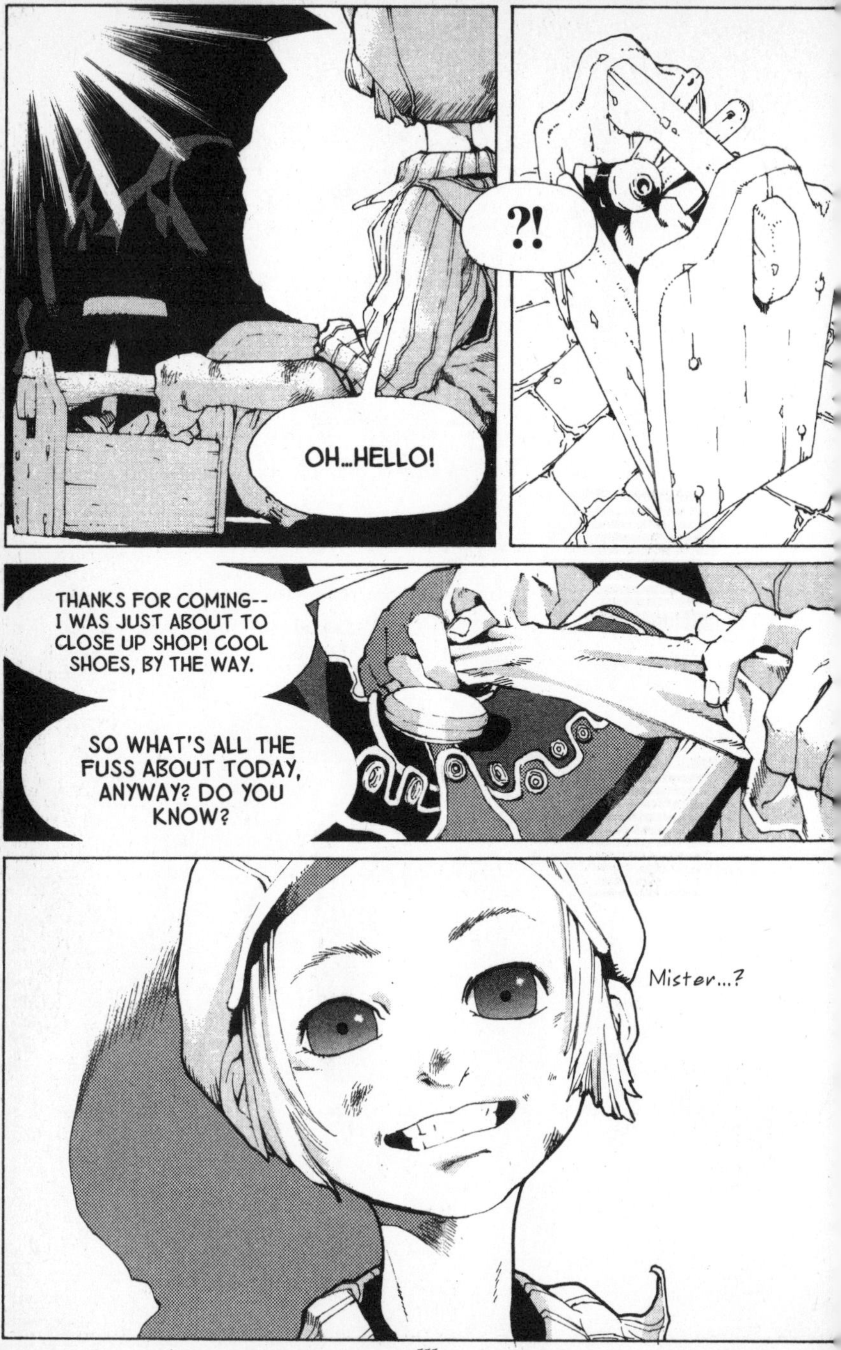
?!
OH...HELLO!
THANKS FOR COMING-- I WAS JUST ABOUT TO CLOSE UP SHOP! COOL SHOES, BY THE WAY.
SO WHAT'S ALL THE FUSS ABOUT TODAY, ANYWAY? DO YOU KNOW?
Mister...?

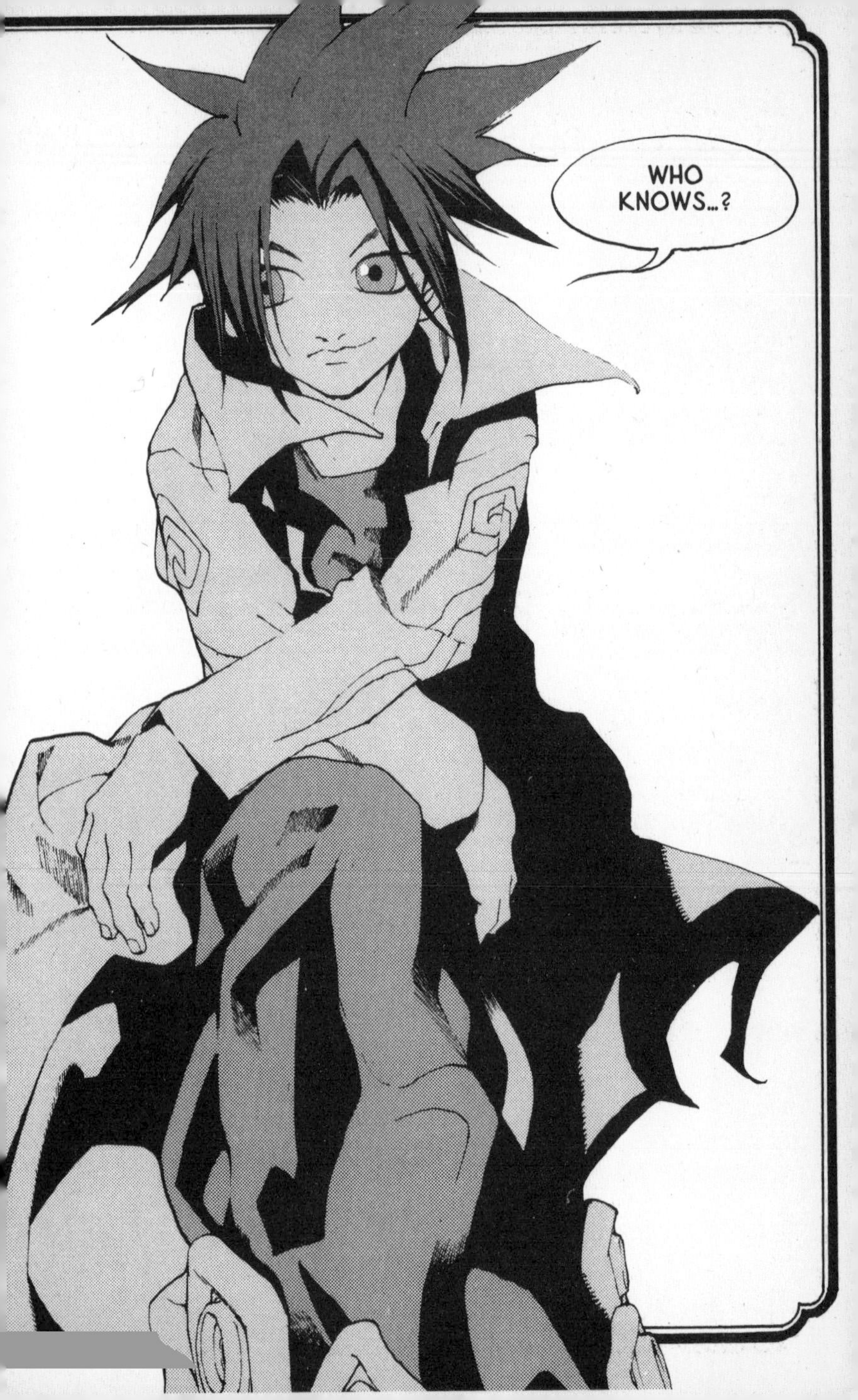
WHO KNOWS...?

The Saga of Rusty Nail--Home of the Holy Brain

3rd Shot - The Patchwork City

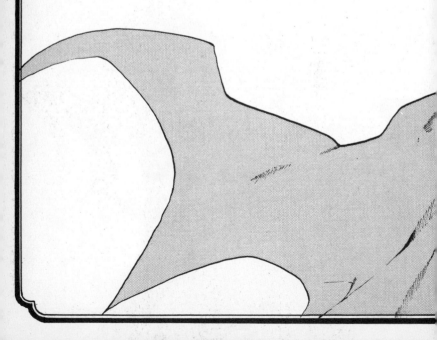

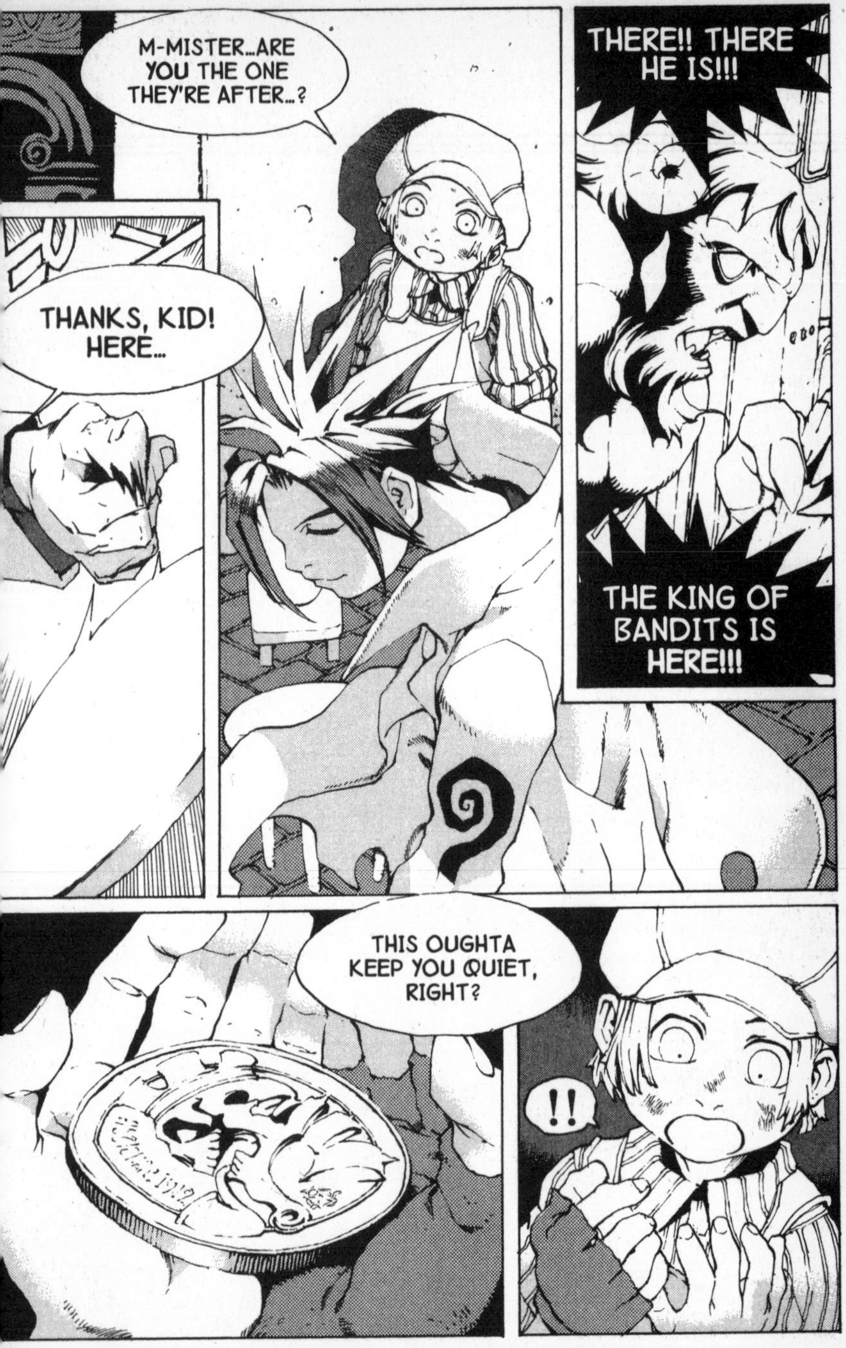
M-MISTER...ARE YOU THE ONE THEY'RE AFTER...?
THERE!! THERE HE IS!!!
THE KING OF BANDITS IS HERE!!!
THANKS, KID! HERE...
THIS OUGHTA KEEP YOU QUIET, RIGHT?
!!

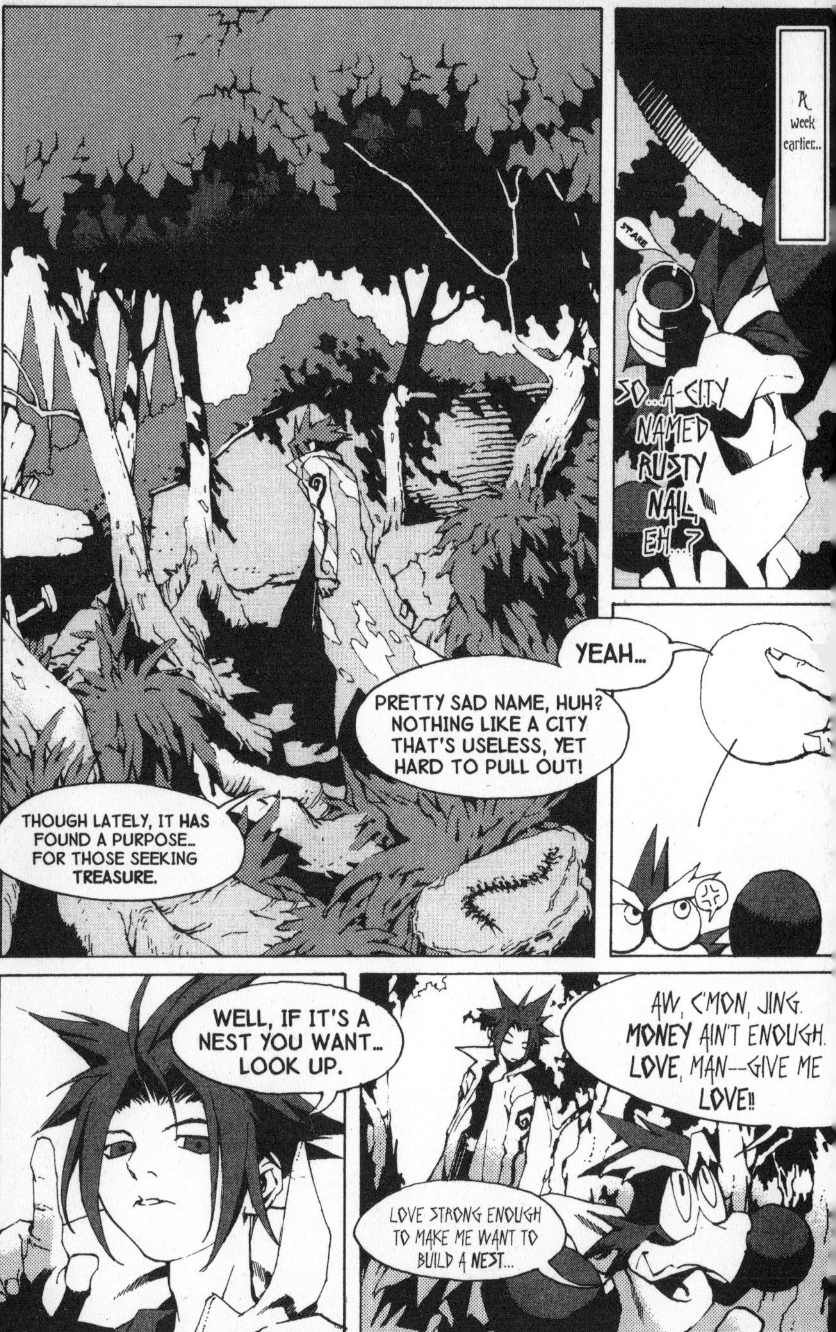
A week earlier...
STARE
SO...A CITY NAMED RUSTY NAIL, EH...?
YEAH...
PRETTY SAD NAME, HUH? NOTHING LIKE A CITY THAT'S USELESS, YET HARD TO PULL OUT!
THOUGH LATELY, IT HAS FOUND A PURPOSE... FOR THOSE SEEKING TREASURE.
AW, C'MON, JING. MONEY AIN'T ENOUGH. LOVE, MAN--GIVE ME LOVE!!
LOVE STRONG ENOUGH TO MAKE ME WANT TO BUILD A NEST...
WELL, IF IT'S A NEST YOU WANT... LOOK UP.

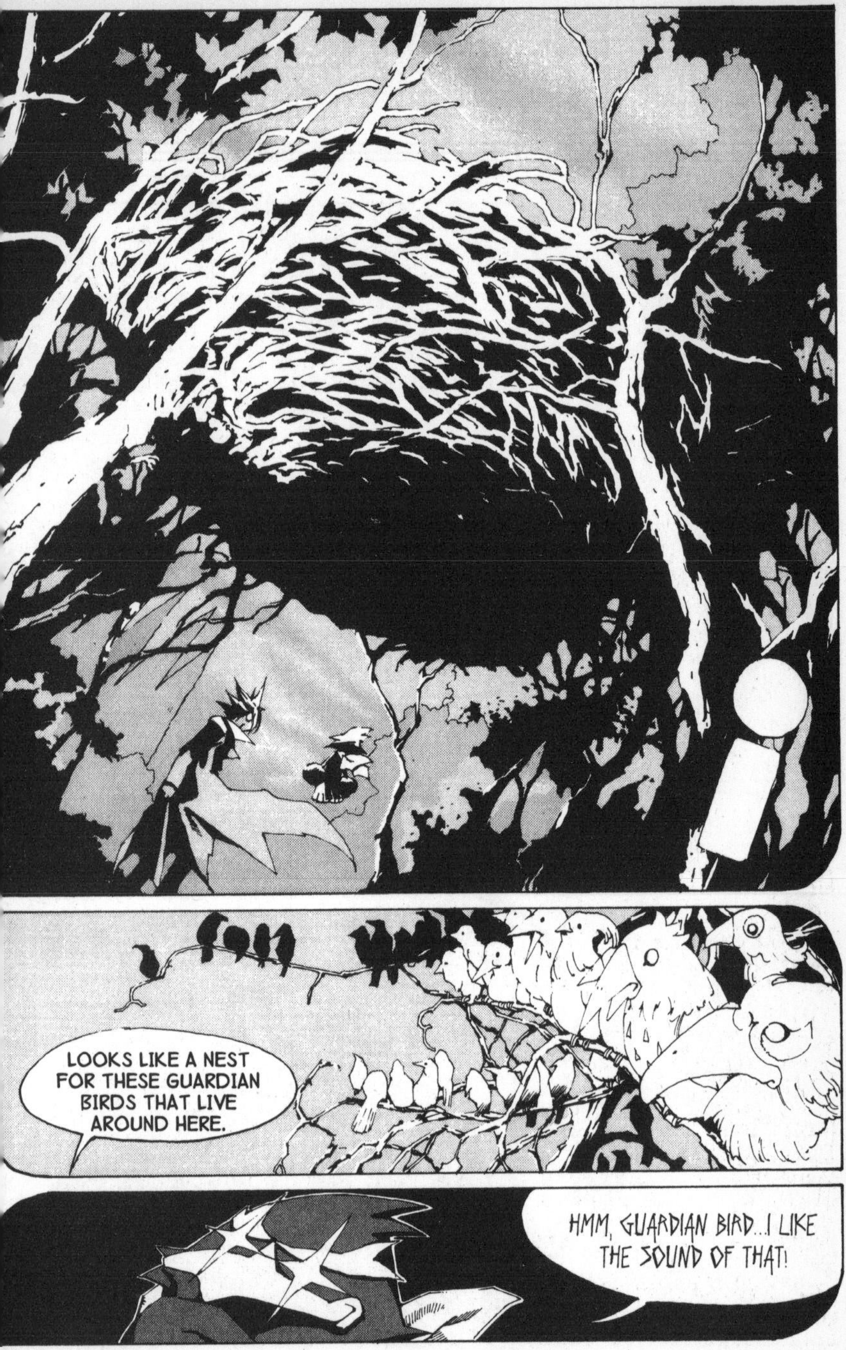
LOOKS LIKE A NEST FOR THESE GUARDIAN BIRDS THAT LIVE AROUND HERE.
HMM, GUARDIAN BIRD...I LIKE THE SOUND OF THAT!

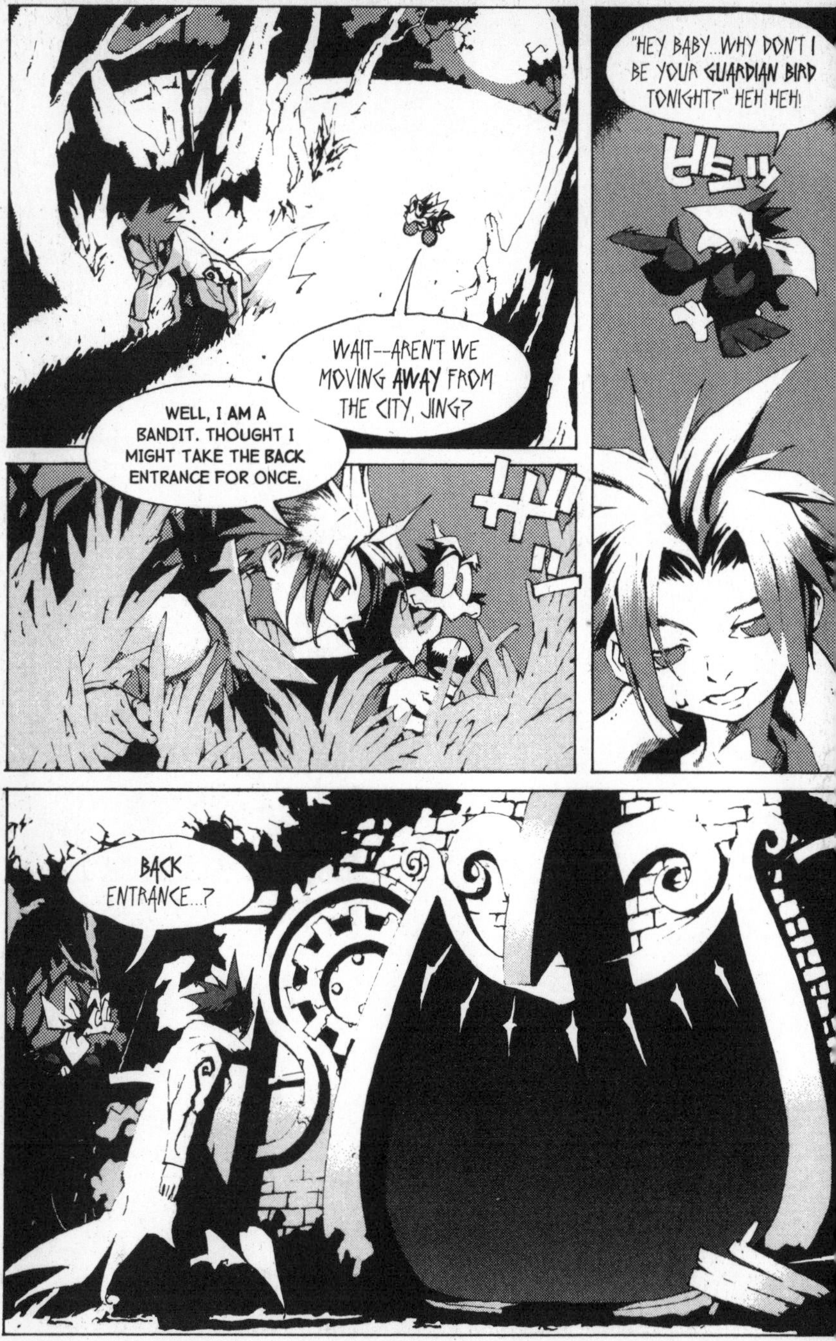
WAIT--AREN'T WE MOVING AWAY FROM THE CITY, JING?
WELL, I AM A BANDIT. THOUGHT I MIGHT TAKE THE BACK ENTRANCE FOR ONCE.
"HEY BABY...WHY DON'T I BE YOUR GUARDIAN BIRD TONIGHT?" HEH HEH!
BACK ENTRANCE...?

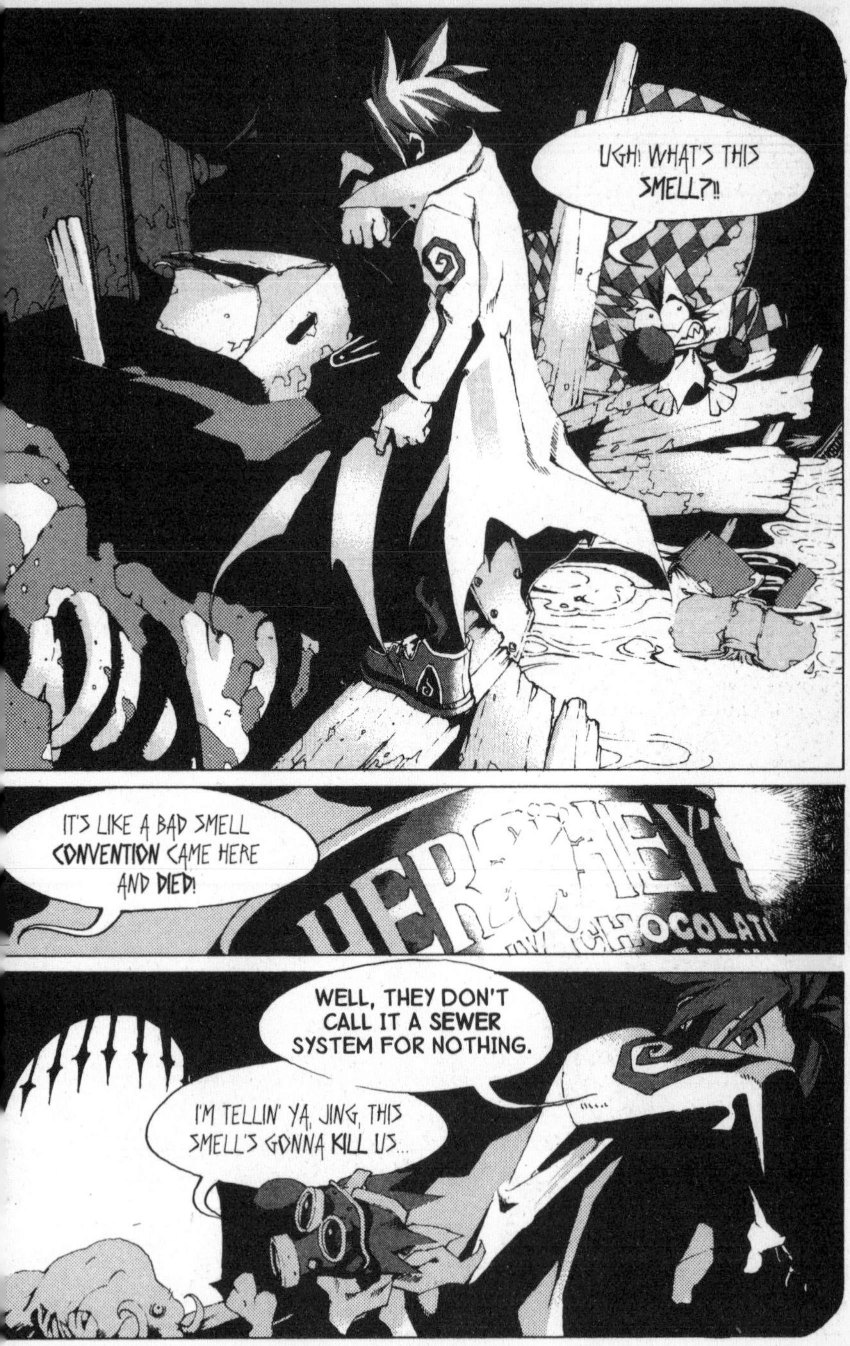
UGH! WHAT'S THIS SMELL?!!
IT'S LIKE A BAD SMELL CONVENTION CAME HERE AND DIED!
WELL, THEY DON'T CALL IT A SEWER SYSTEM FOR NOTHING.
I'M TELLIN' YA, JING, THIS SMELL'S GONNA KILL US...

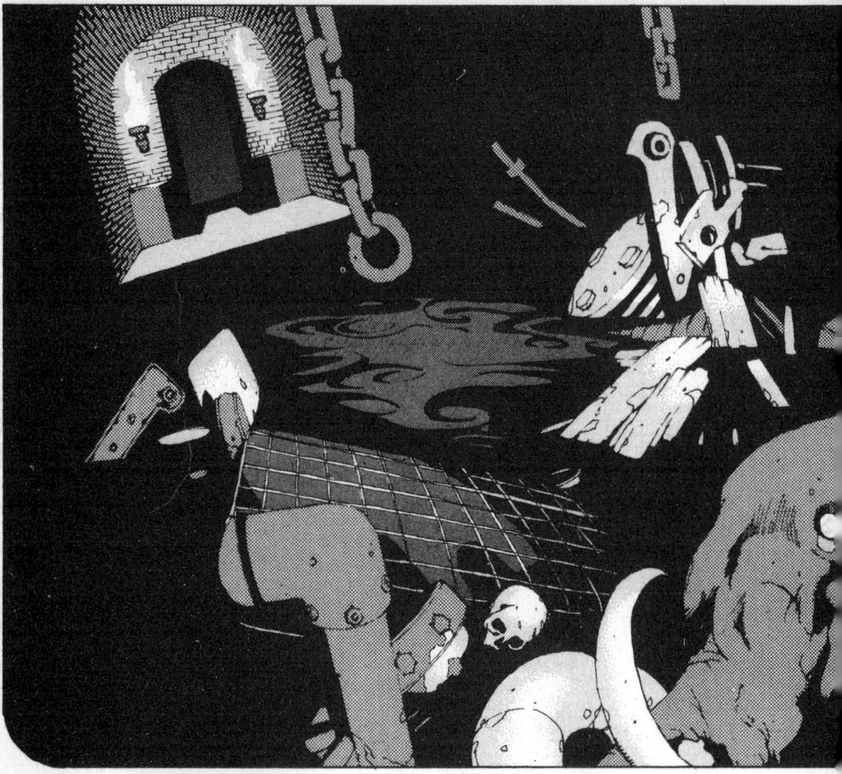

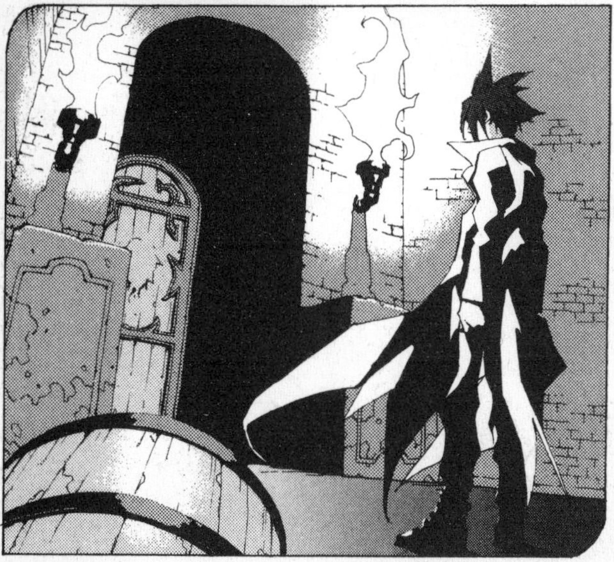

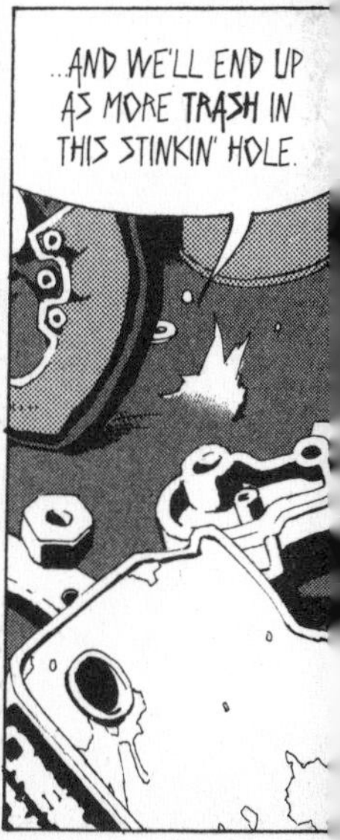
...AND WE'LL END UP AS MORE TRASH IN THIS STINKIN' HOLE.

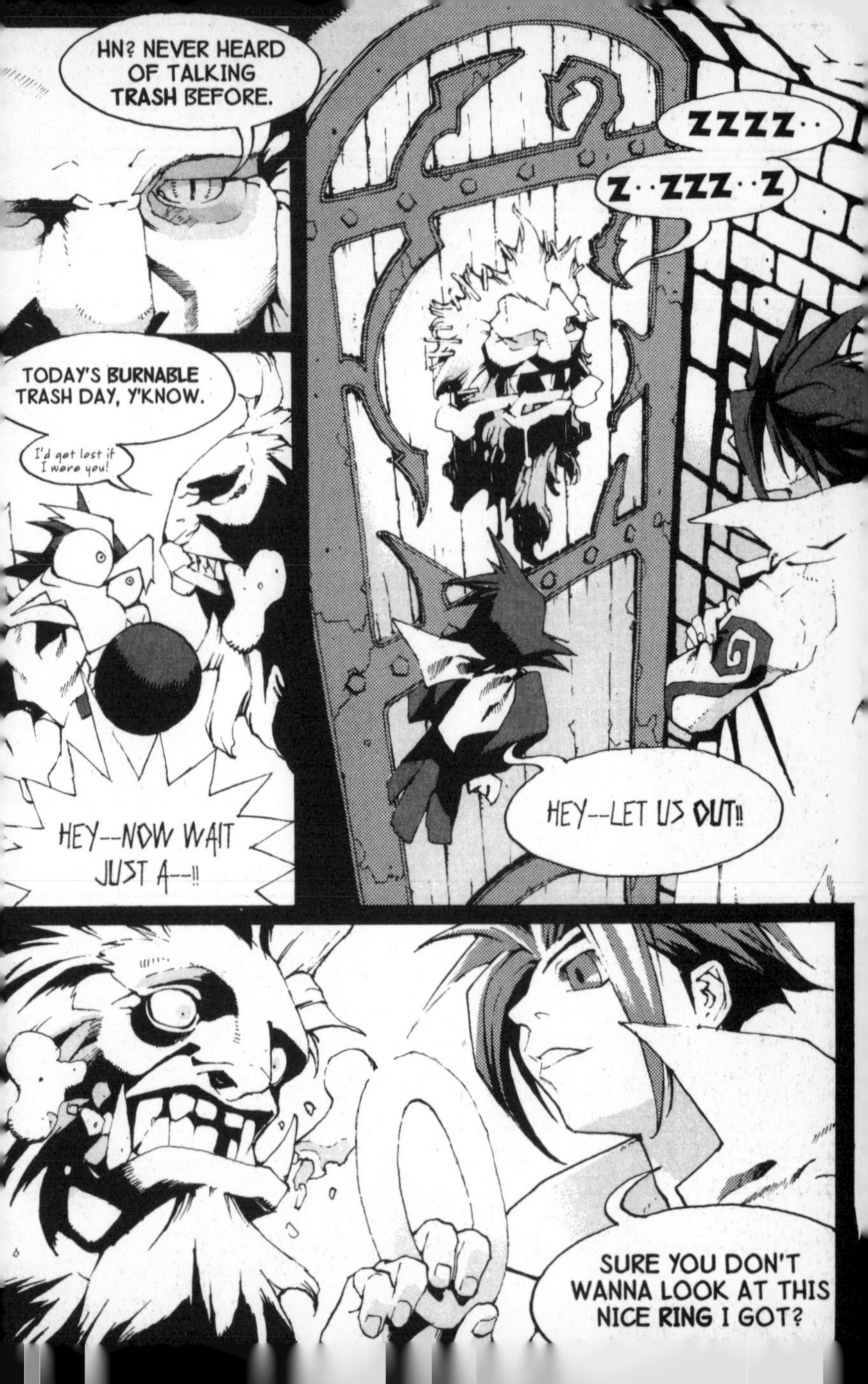
HN? NEVER HEARD OF TALKING TRASH BEFORE.
ZZZZ..
Z..ZZZ..Z
TODAY'S BURNABLE TRASH DAY, Y'KNOW.
I'd get lost if I were you!
HEY--NOW WAIT JUST A--!!
HEY--LET US OUT!!
SURE YOU DON'T WANNA LOOK AT THIS NICE RING I GOT?

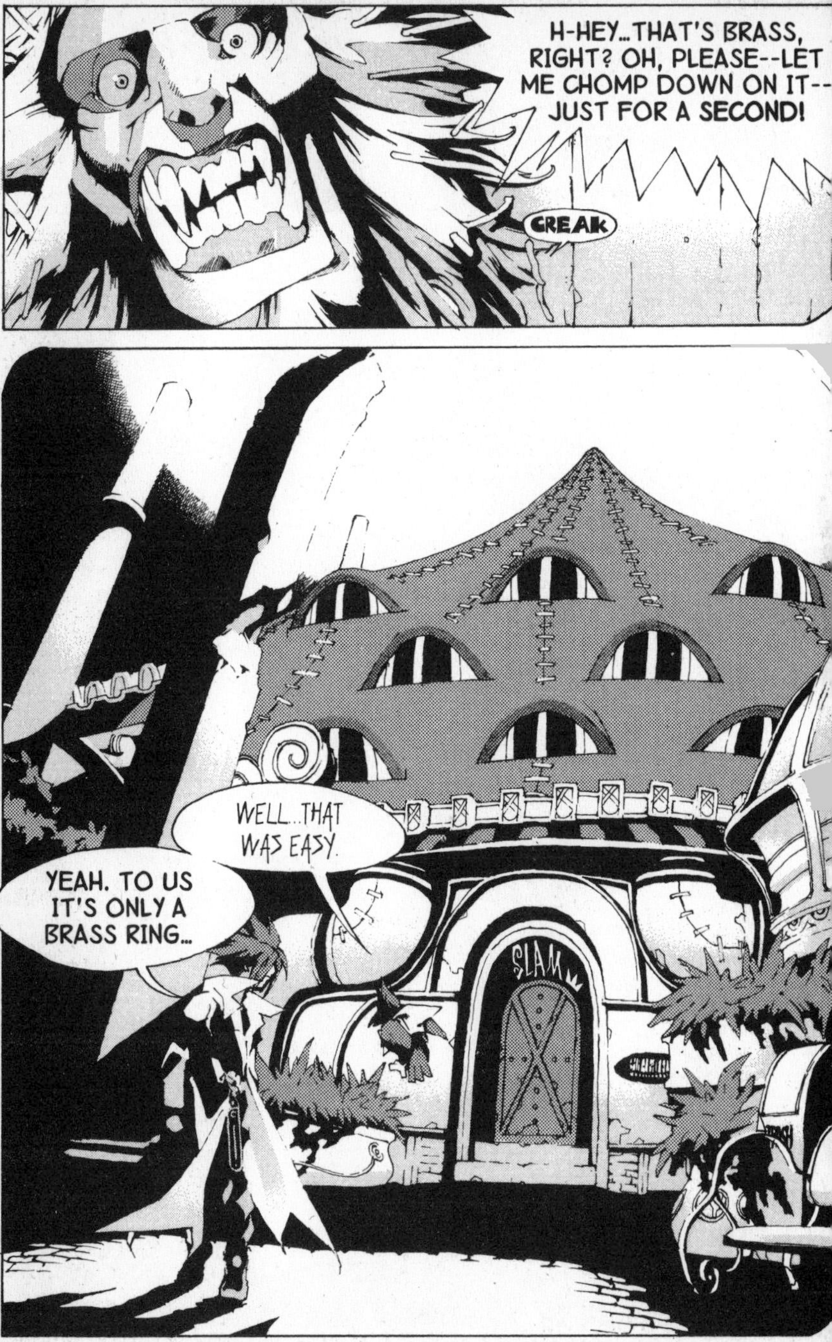
H-HEY...THAT'S BRASS, RIGHT? OH, PLEASE--LET ME CHOMP DOWN ON IT--JUST FOR A SECOND!
CREAK
WELL...THAT WAS EASY.
YEAH. TO US IT'S ONLY A BRASS RING...
SLAM

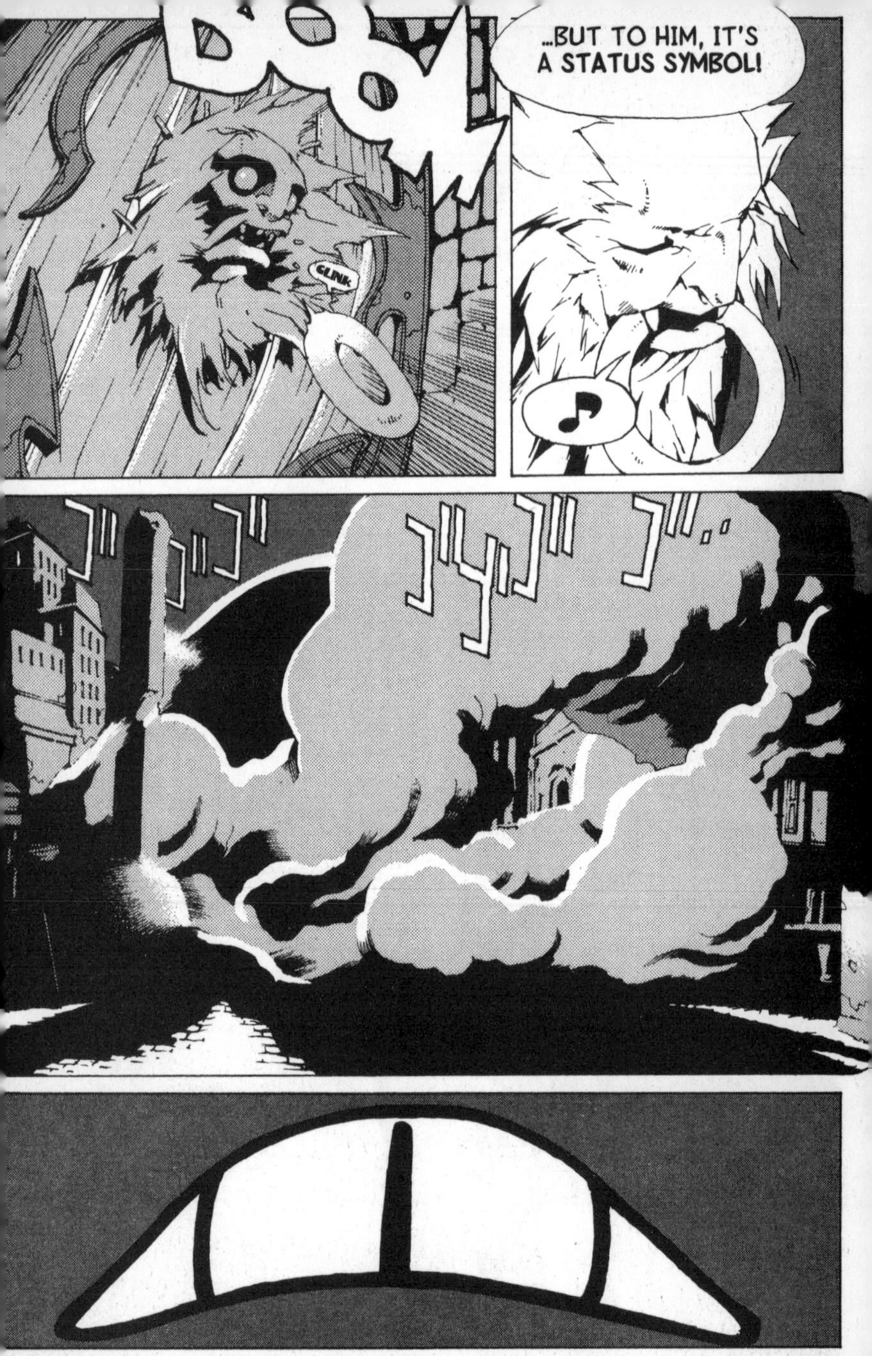
...BUT TO HIM, IT'S A STATUS SYMBOL!
CLINK

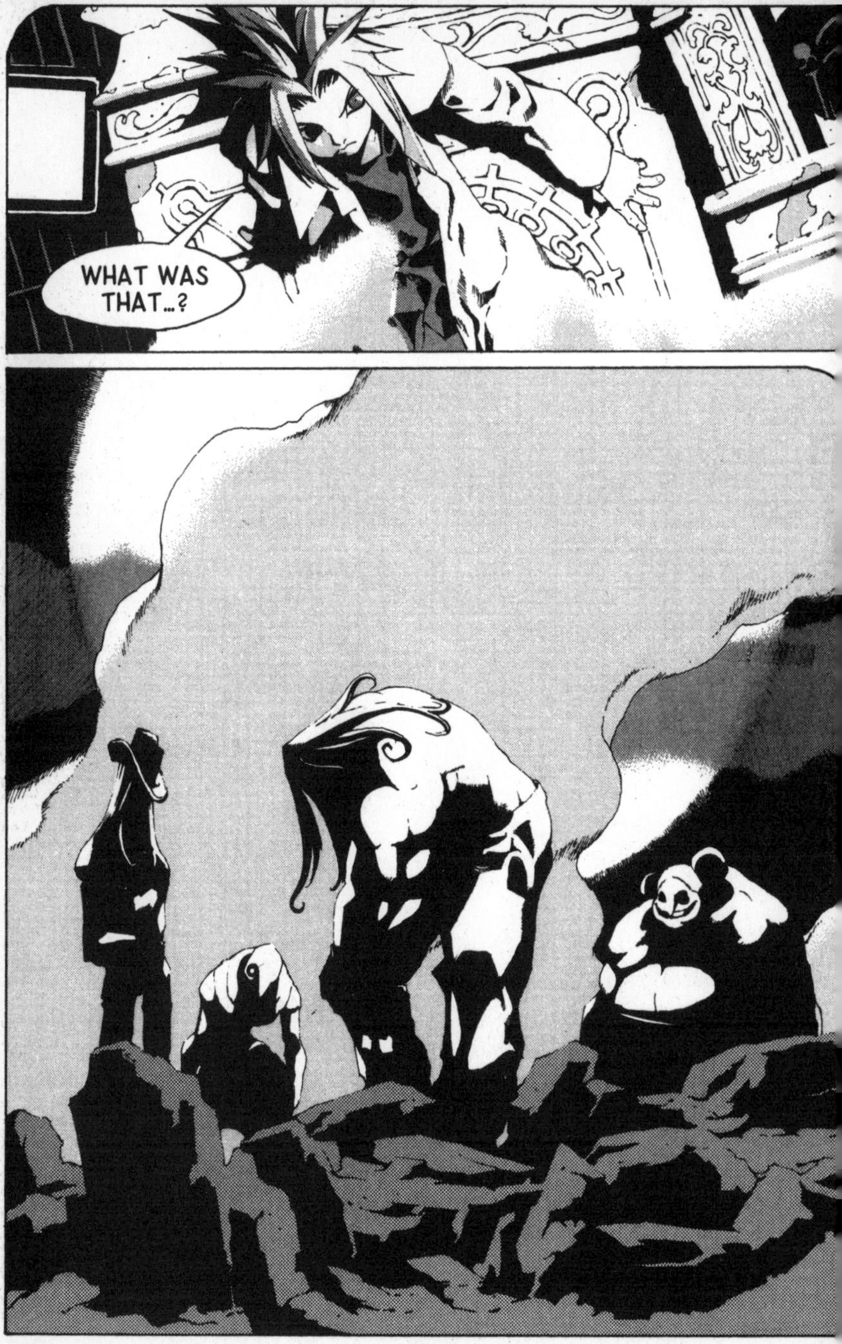
WHAT WAS THAT...?

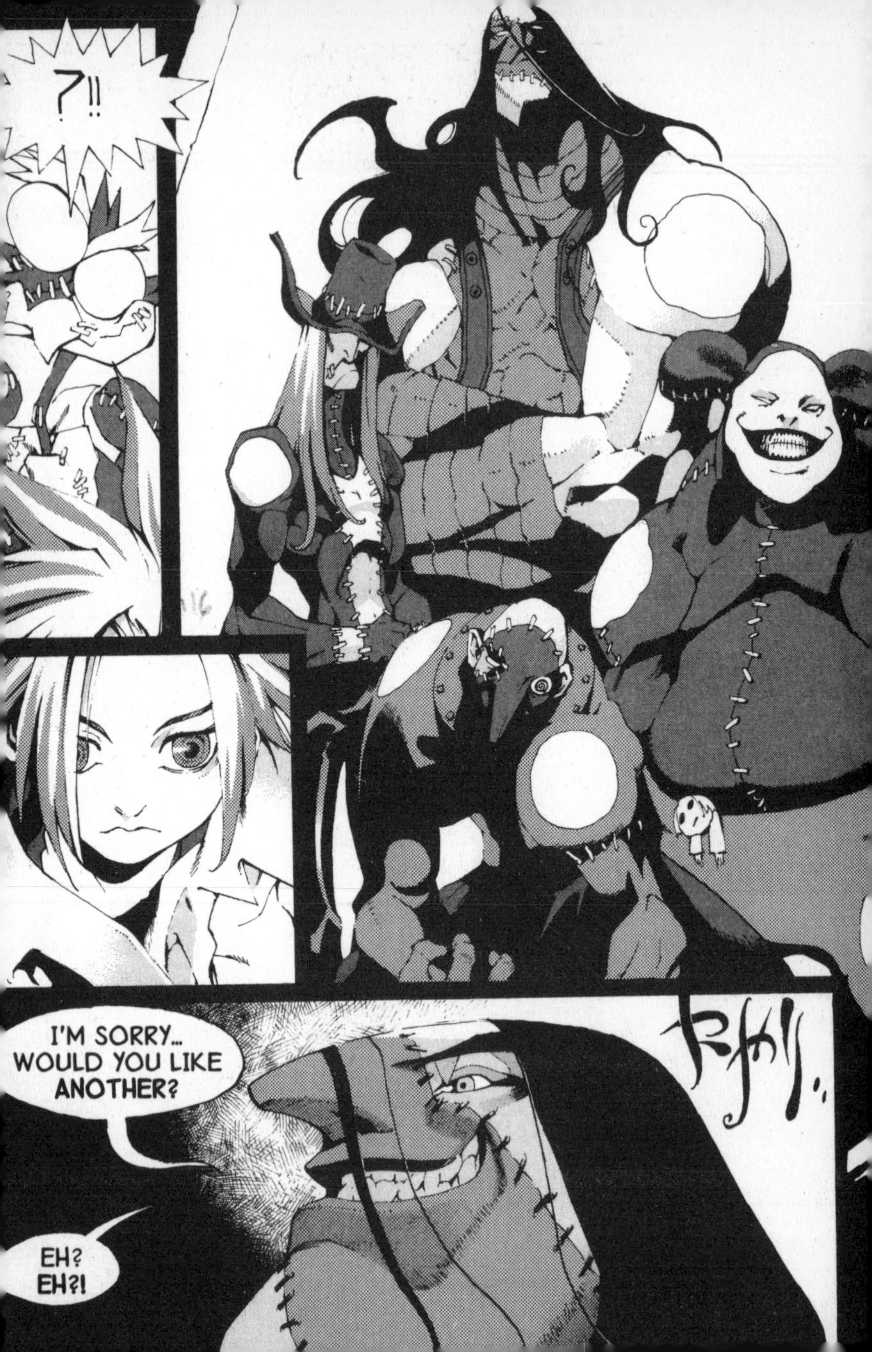
?!!
I'M SORRY...
WOULD YOU LIKE
ANOTHER?
EH?
EH?!

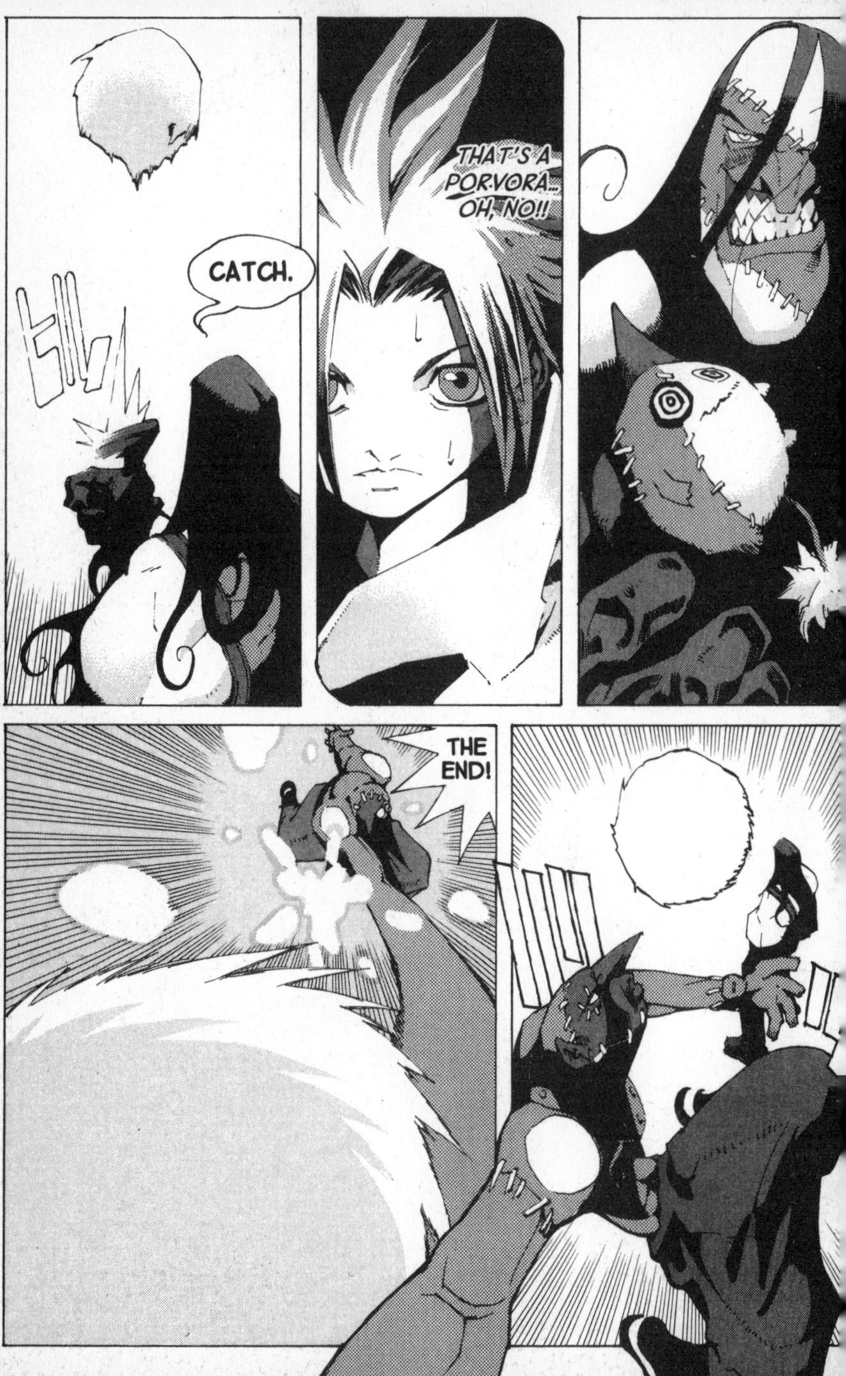
THAT'S A PORVORA... OH, NO!!
CATCH.
THE END!

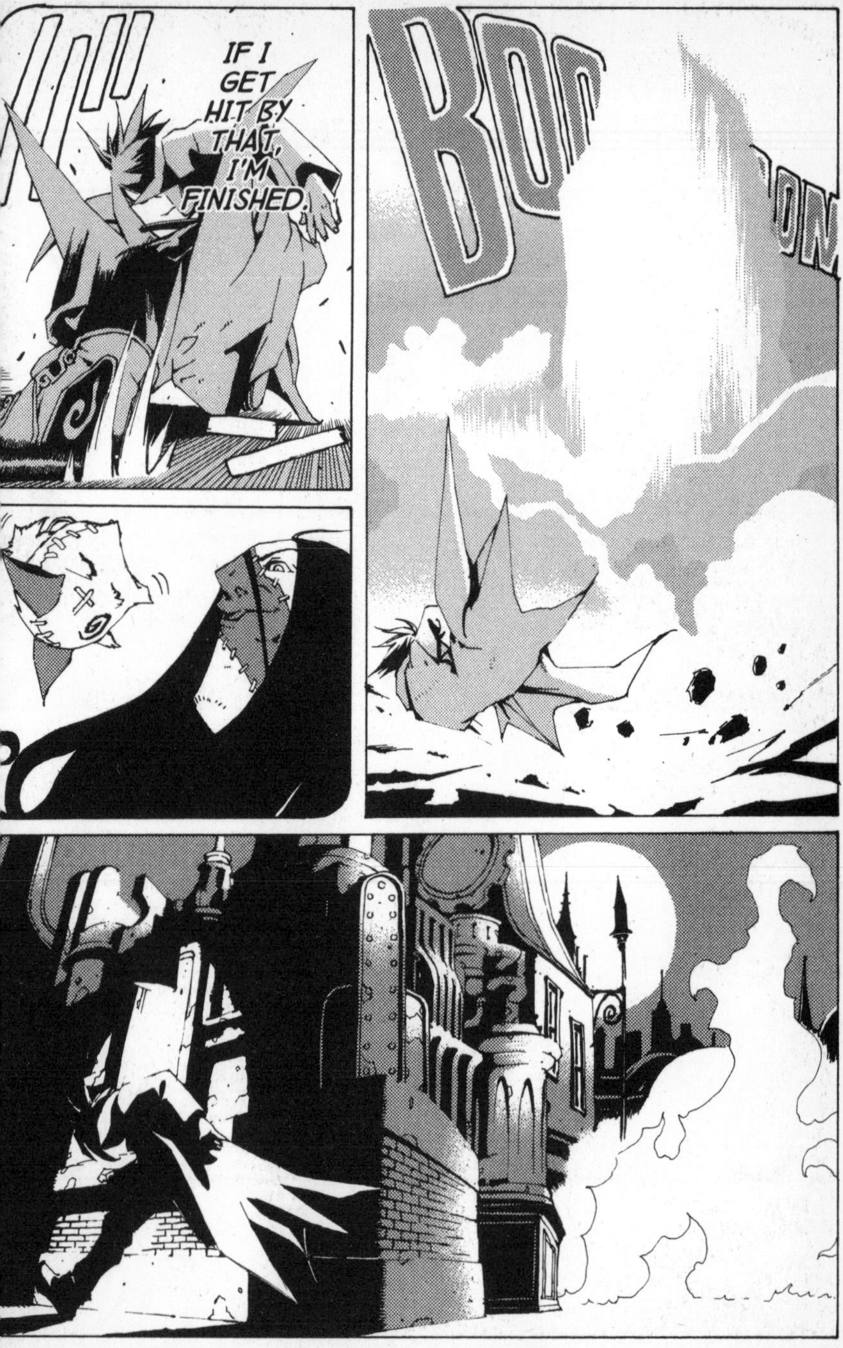
IF I GET HIT BY THAT, I'M FINISHED.

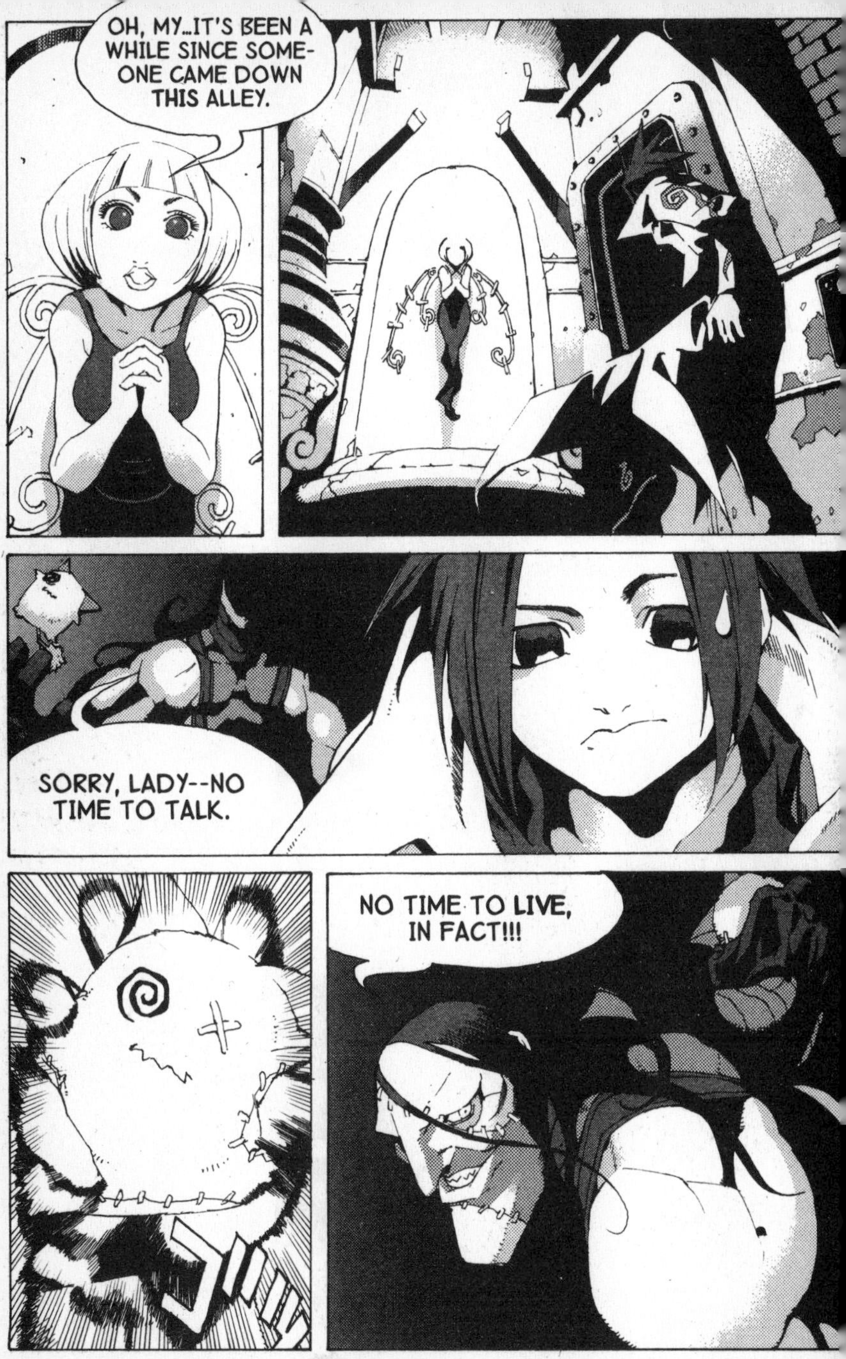
OH, MY...IT'S BEEN A WHILE SINCE SOME-ONE CAME DOWN THIS ALLEY.
SORRY, LADY--NO TIME TO TALK.
NO TIME TO LIVE, IN FACT!!!

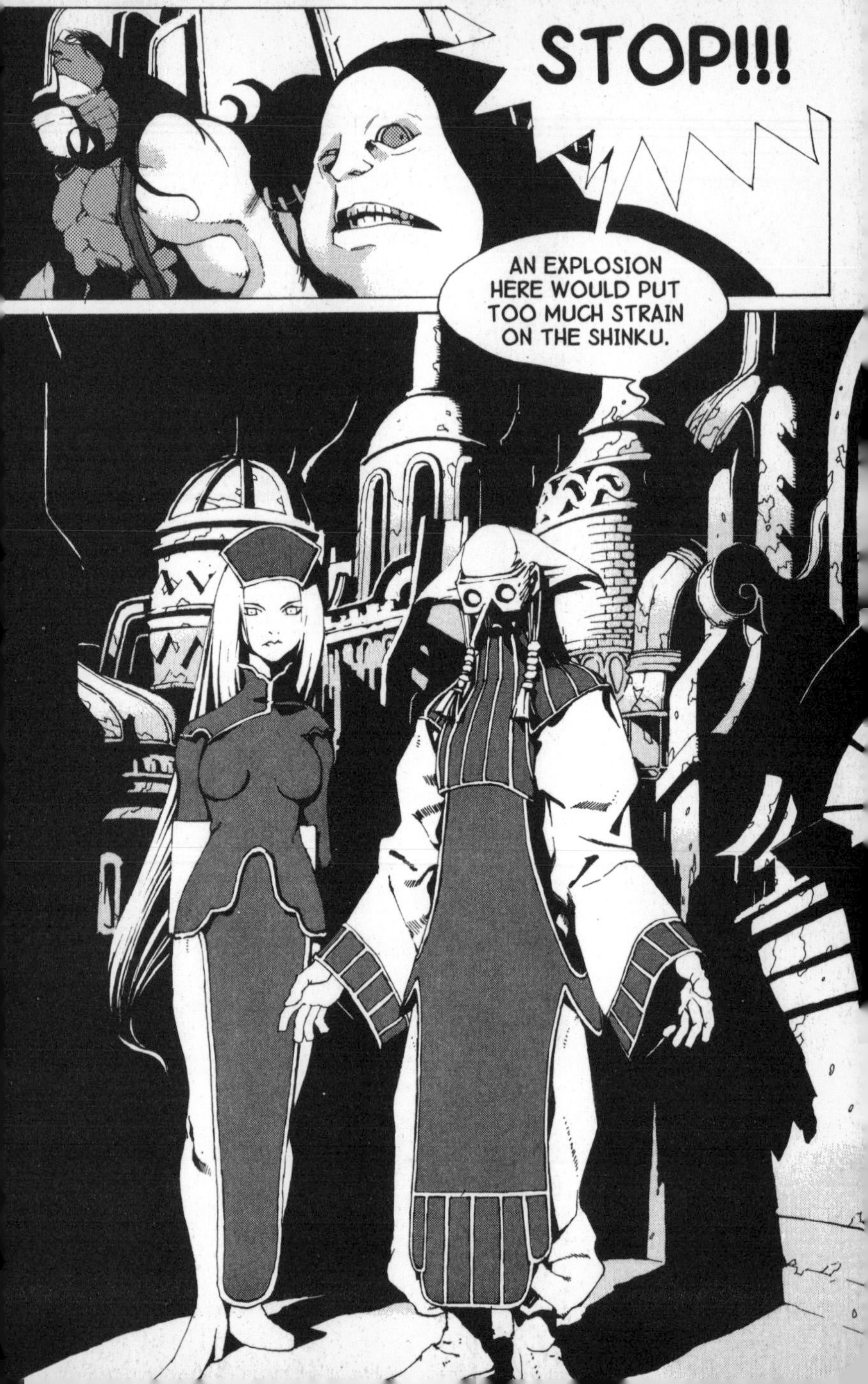
STOP!!!
AN EXPLOSION HERE WOULD PUT TOO MUCH STRAIN ON THE SHINKU.

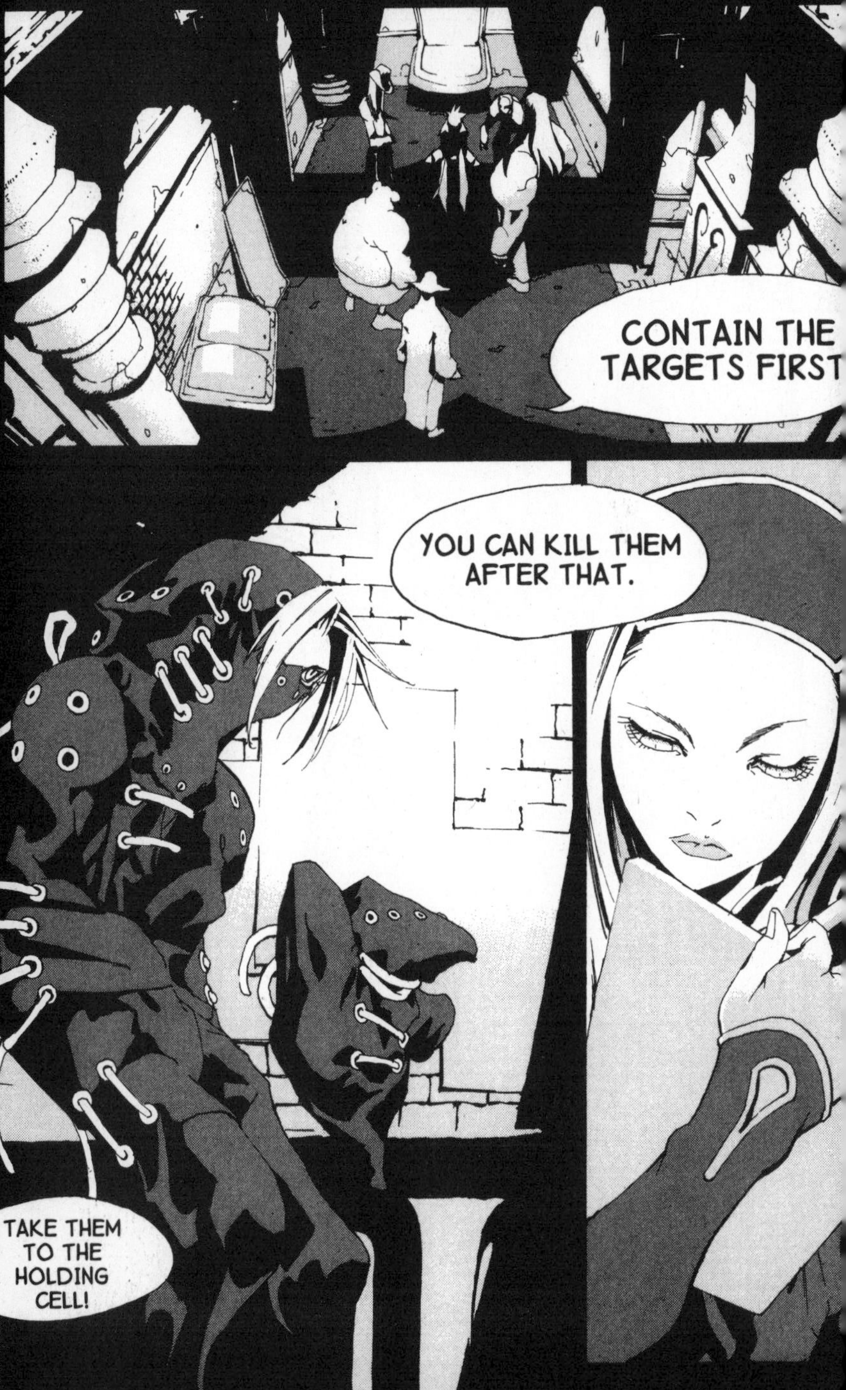
CONTAIN THE TARGETS FIRST
YOU CAN KILL THEM AFTER THAT.
TAKE THEM TO THE HOLDING CELL!

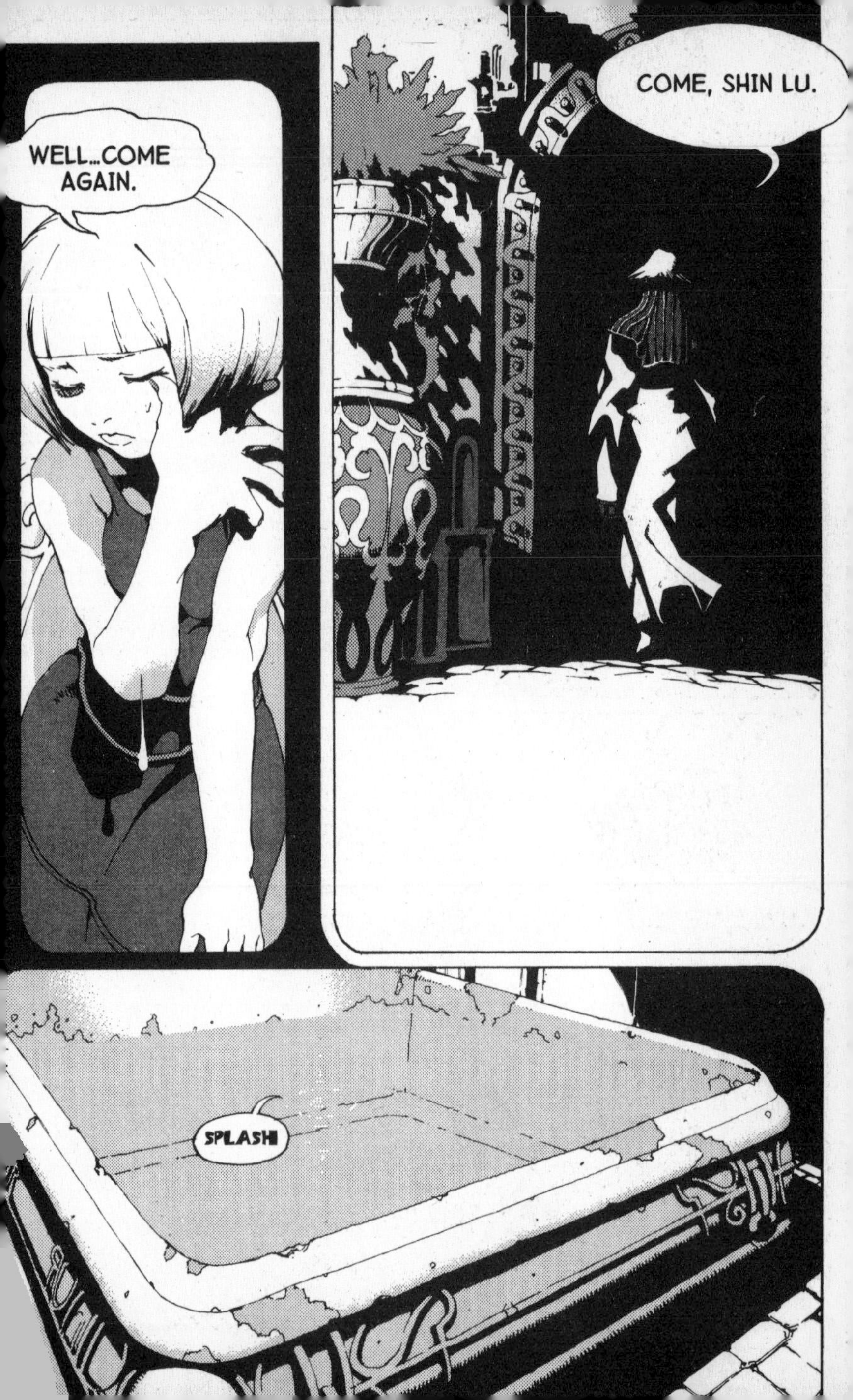
COME, SHIN LU.
WELL...COME AGAIN.
SPLASH

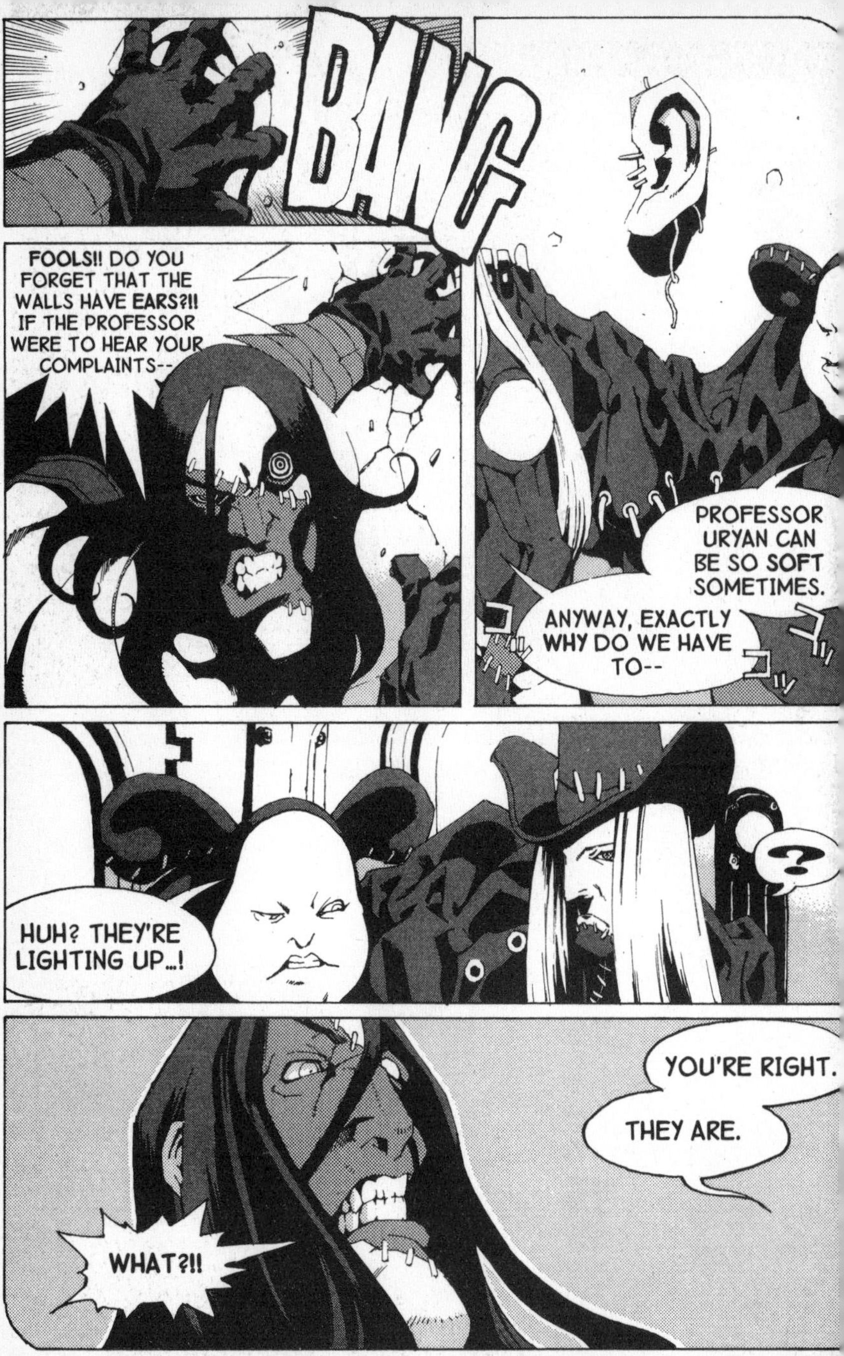
BANG
FOOLS!! DO YOU FORGET THAT THE WALLS HAVE EARS?!! IF THE PROFESSOR WERE TO HEAR YOUR COMPLAINTS--
PROFESSOR URYAN CAN BE SO SOFT SOMETIMES.
ANYWAY, EXACTLY WHY DO WE HAVE TO--
?
HUH? THEY'RE LIGHTING UP...!
YOU'RE RIGHT.
THEY ARE.
WHAT?!!

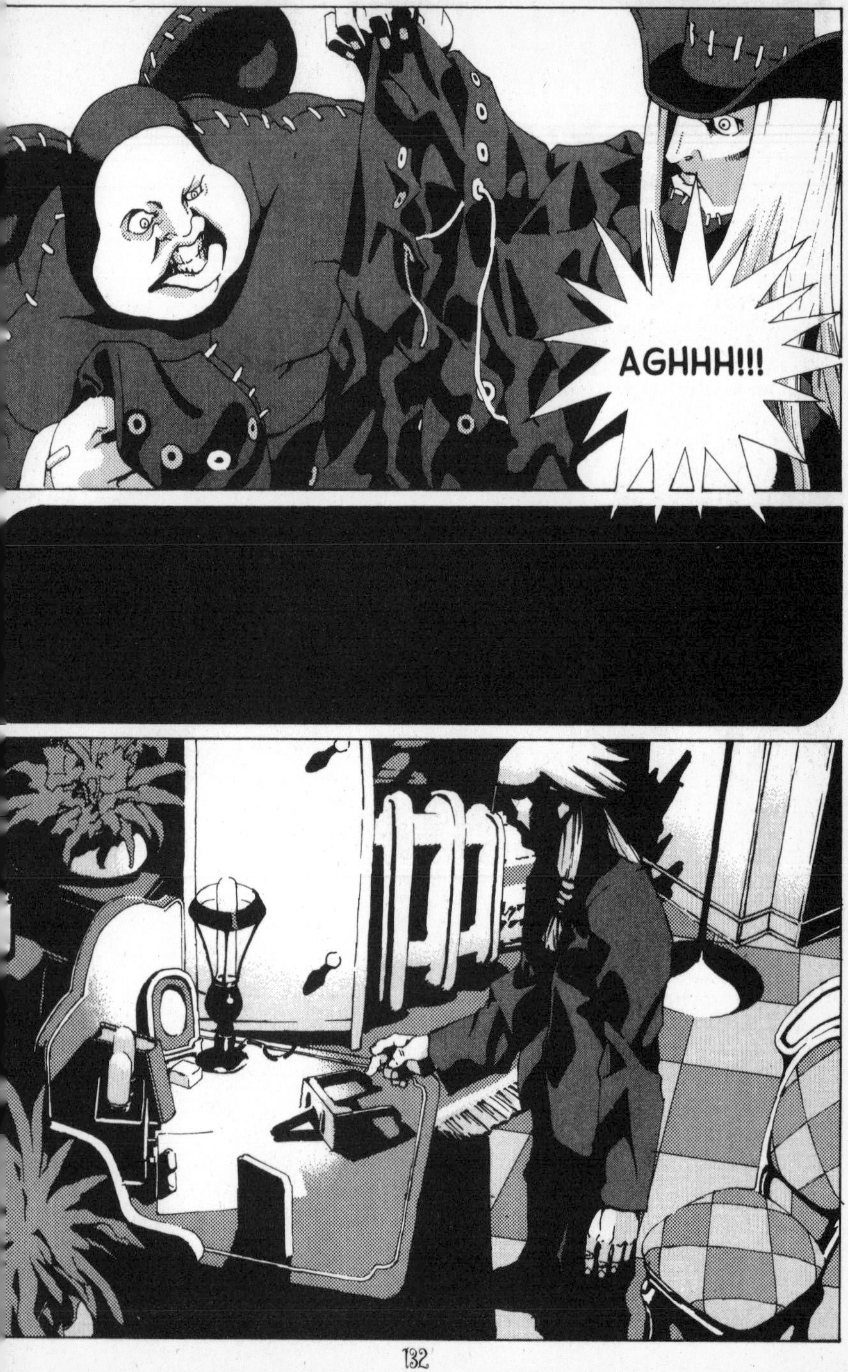
AGHHH!!!

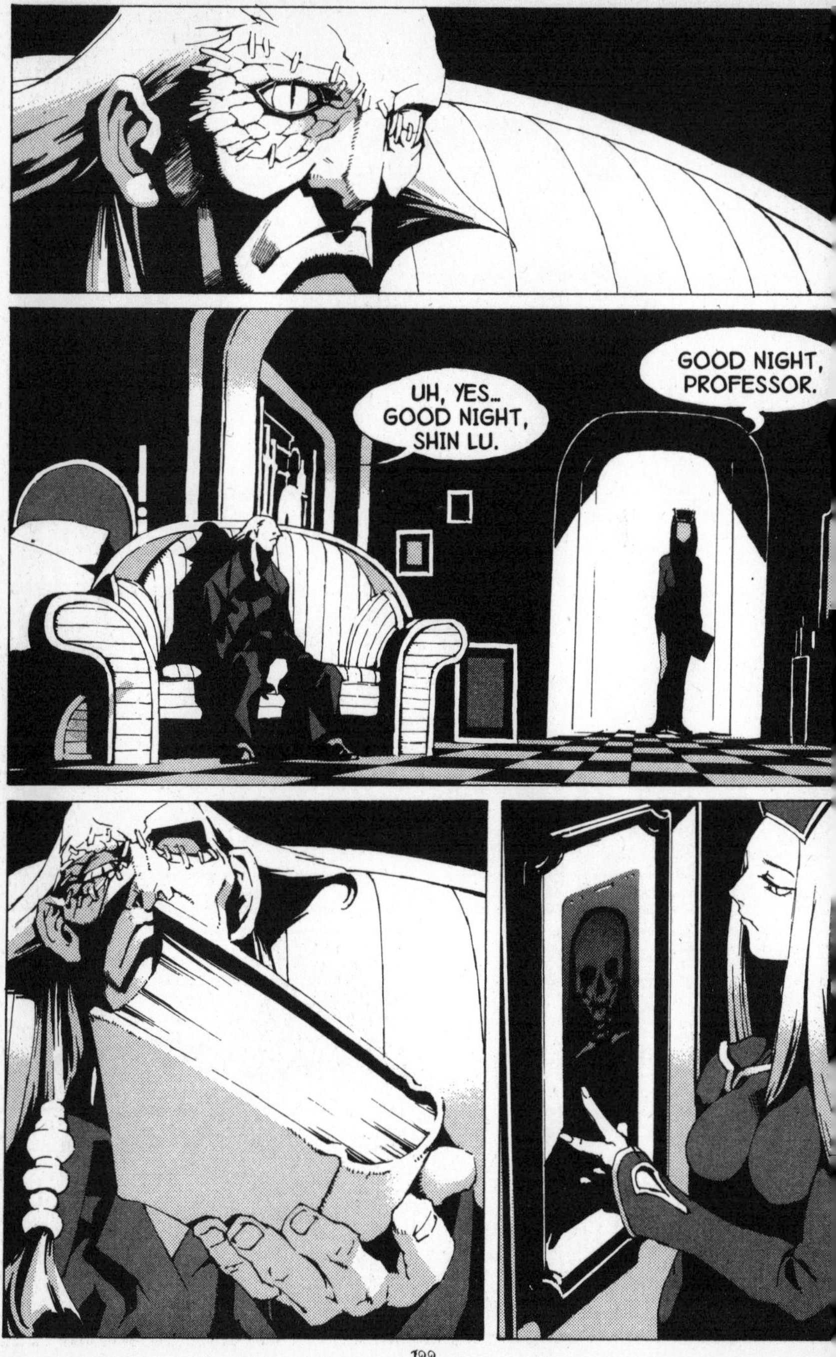
GOOD NIGHT, PROFESSOR.
UH, YES... GOOD NIGHT, SHIN LU.

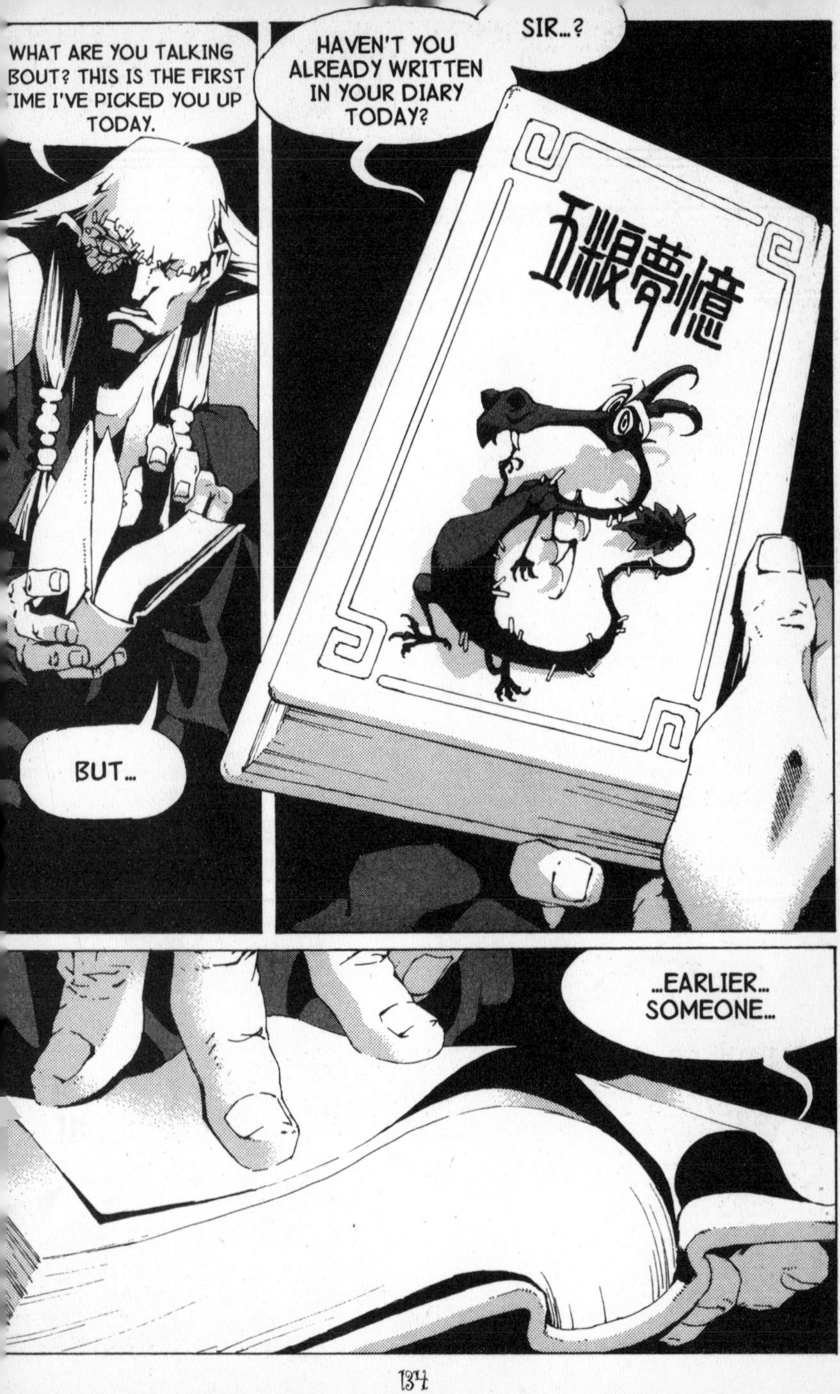
SIR...?
HAVEN'T YOU ALREADY WRITTEN IN YOUR DIARY TODAY?
WHAT ARE YOU TALKING BOUT? THIS IS THE FIRST TIME I'VE PICKED YOU UP TODAY.
BUT...
...EARLIER... SOMEONE...

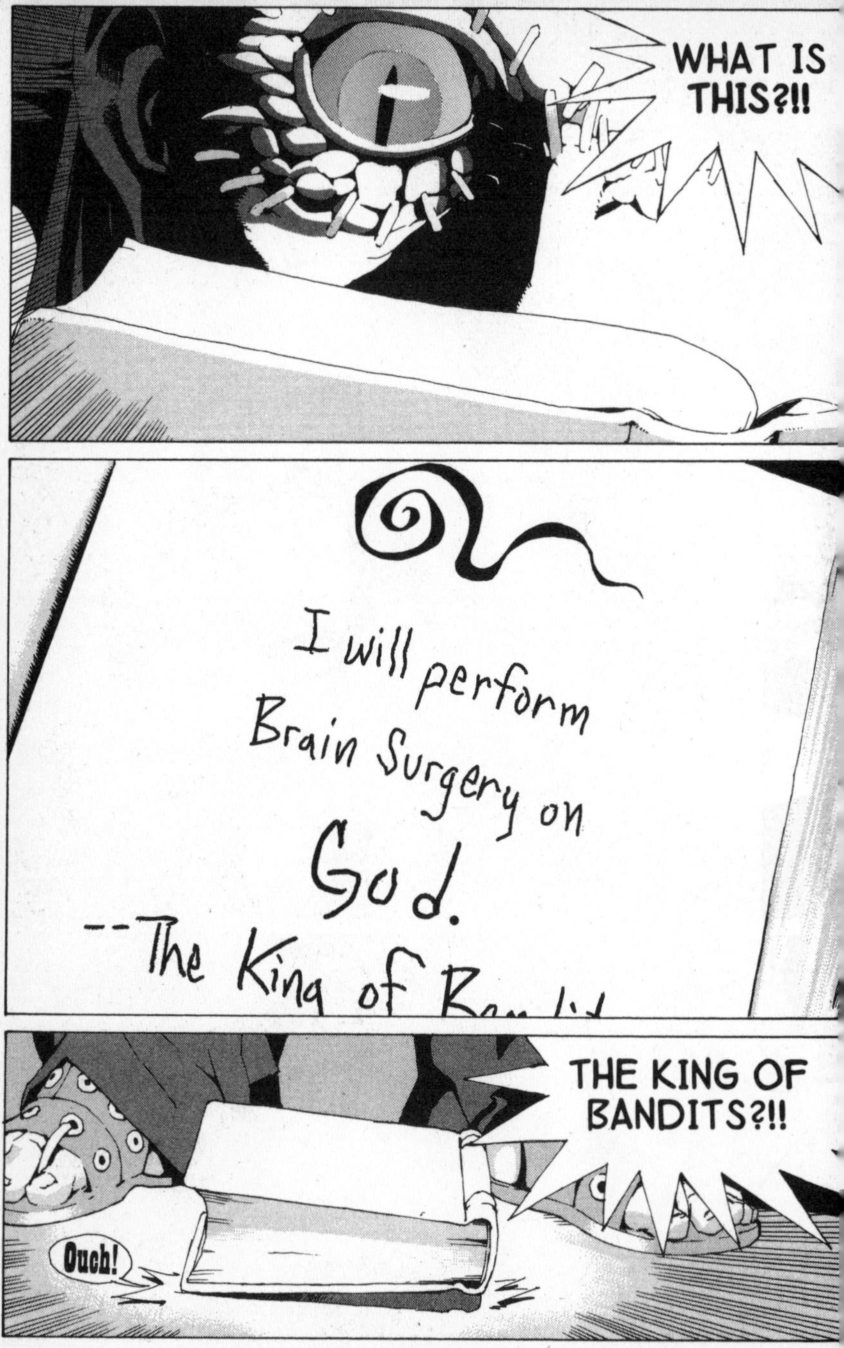
WHAT IS THIS?!!
I will perform Brain Surgery on God.
--The King of
THE KING OF BANDITS?!!
Ouch!

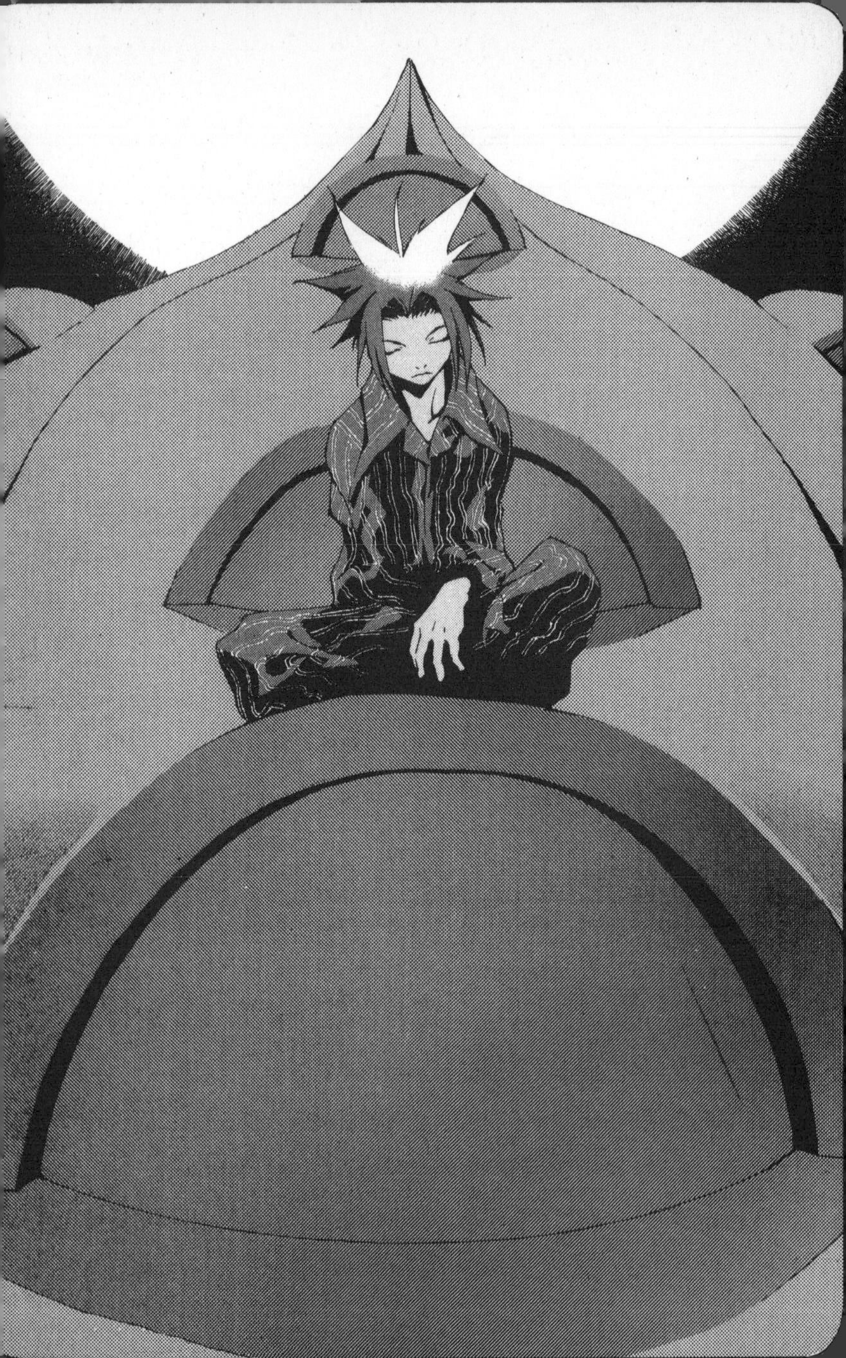

4th Shot - God's Brain

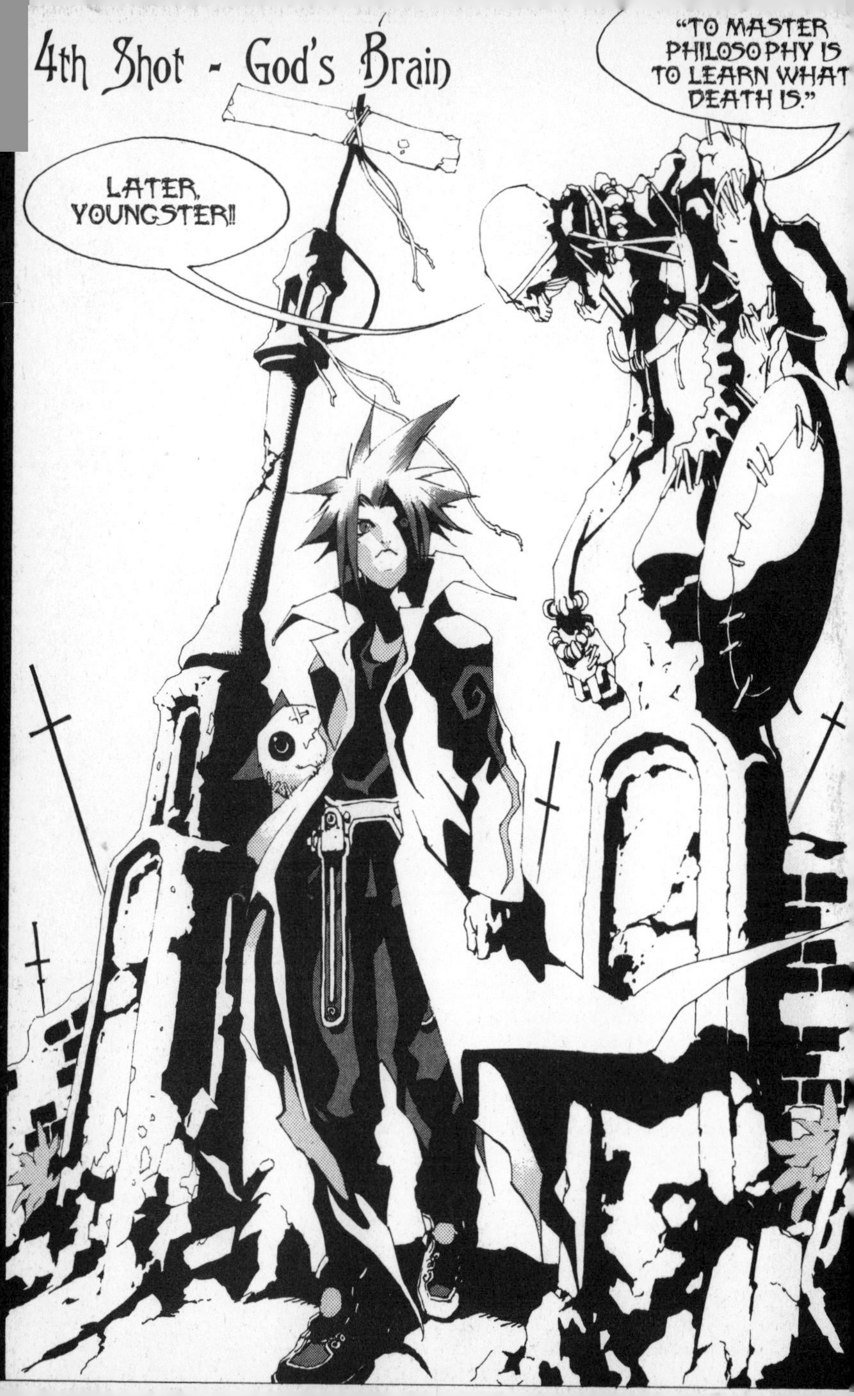
"TO MASTER PHILOSOPHY IS TO LEARN WHAT DEATH IS."
LATER, YOUNGSTER!!

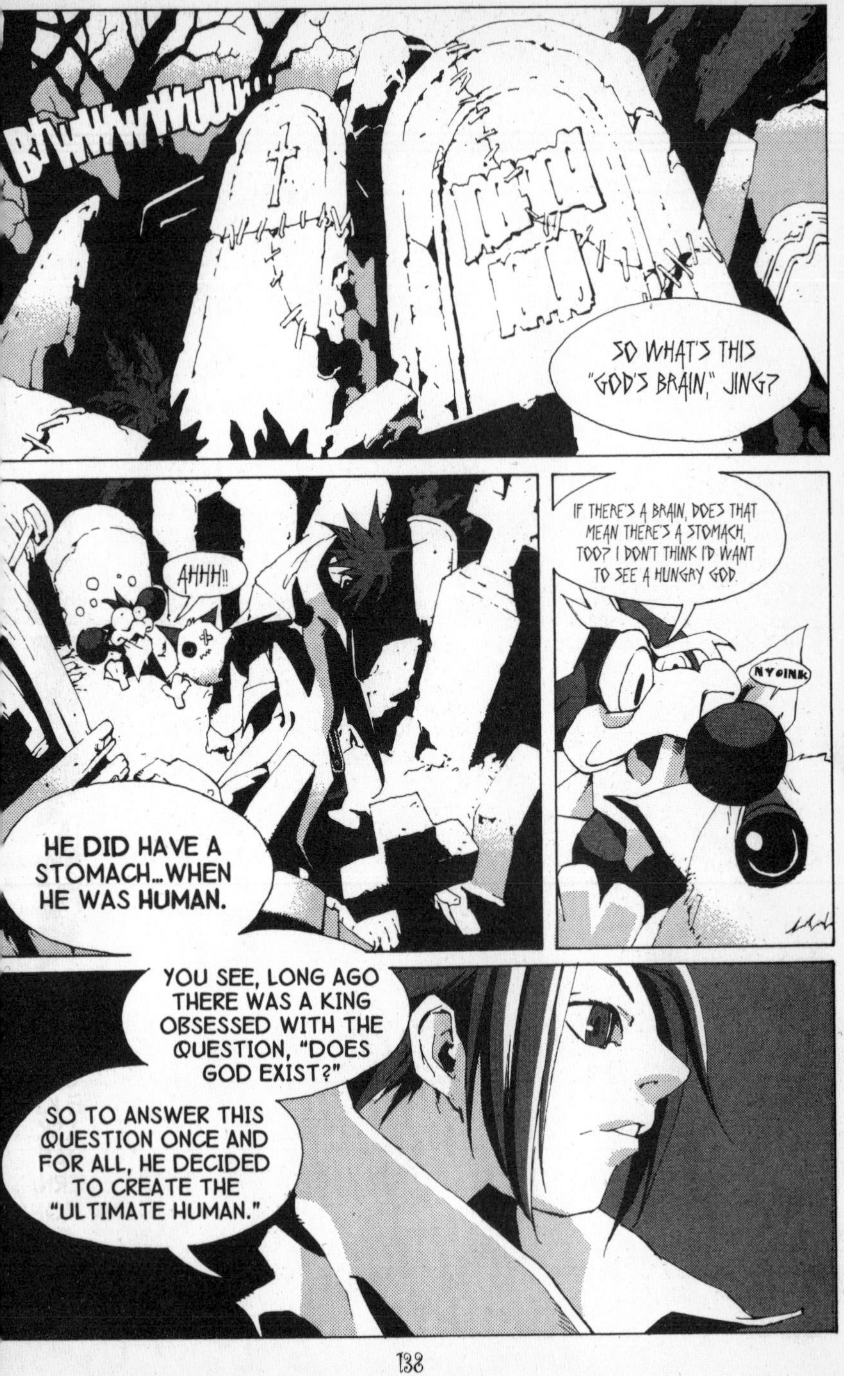

BRWWWWHUUU...
SO WHAT'S THIS "GOD'S BRAIN," JING?
AHHH!!
IF THERE'S A BRAIN, DOES THAT MEAN THERE'S A STOMACH, TOO? I DON'T THINK I'D WANT TO SEE A HUNGRY GOD.
NYOINK
HE DID HAVE A STOMACH...WHEN HE WAS HUMAN.
YOU SEE, LONG AGO THERE WAS A KING OBSESSED WITH THE QUESTION, "DOES GOD EXIST?"
SO TO ANSWER THIS QUESTION ONCE AND FOR ALL, HE DECIDED TO CREATE THE "ULTIMATE HUMAN."

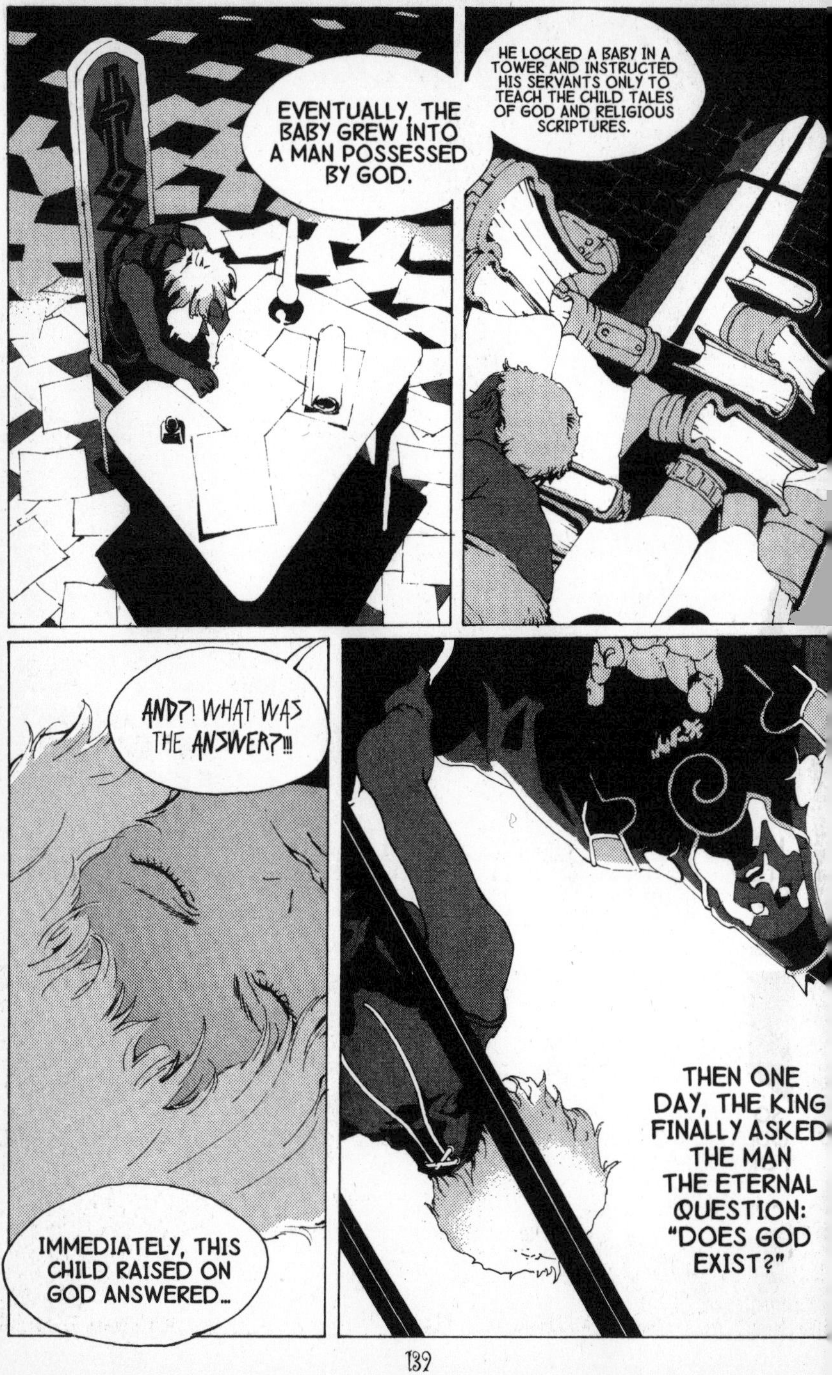
HE LOCKED A BABY IN A TOWER AND INSTRUCTED HIS SERVANTS ONLY TO TEACH THE CHILD TALES OF GOD AND RELIGIOUS SCRIPTURES.
EVENTUALLY, THE BABY GREW INTO A MAN POSSESSED BY GOD.
THEN ONE DAY, THE KING FINALLY ASKED THE MAN THE ETERNAL QUESTION: "DOES GOD EXIST?"
IMMEDIATELY, THIS CHILD RAISED ON GOD ANSWERED...
AND?! WHAT WAS THE ANSWER?!!!

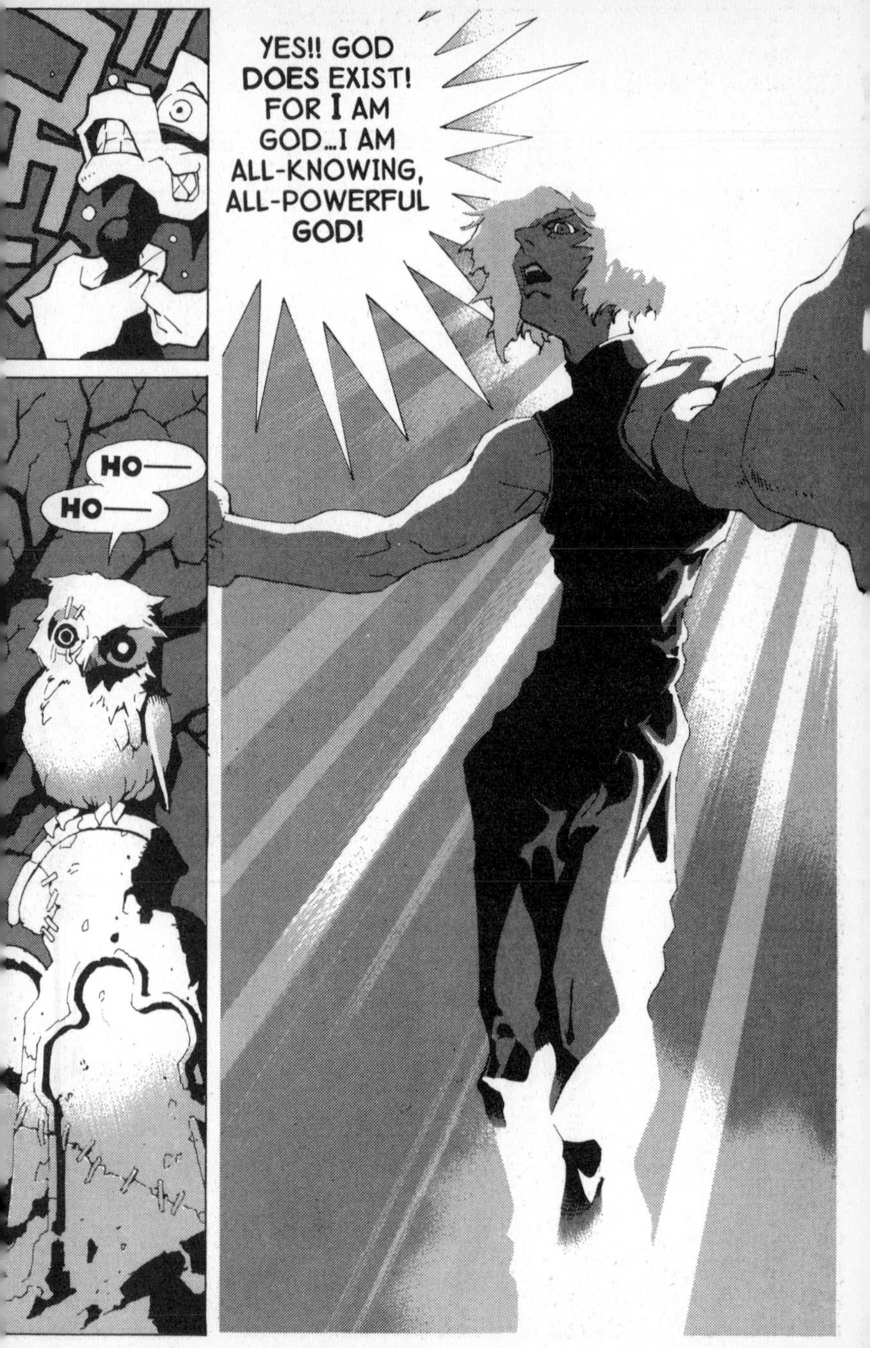
YES!! GOD DOES EXIST! FOR I AM GOD...I AM ALL-KNOWING, ALL-POWERFUL GOD!
HO——
HO——

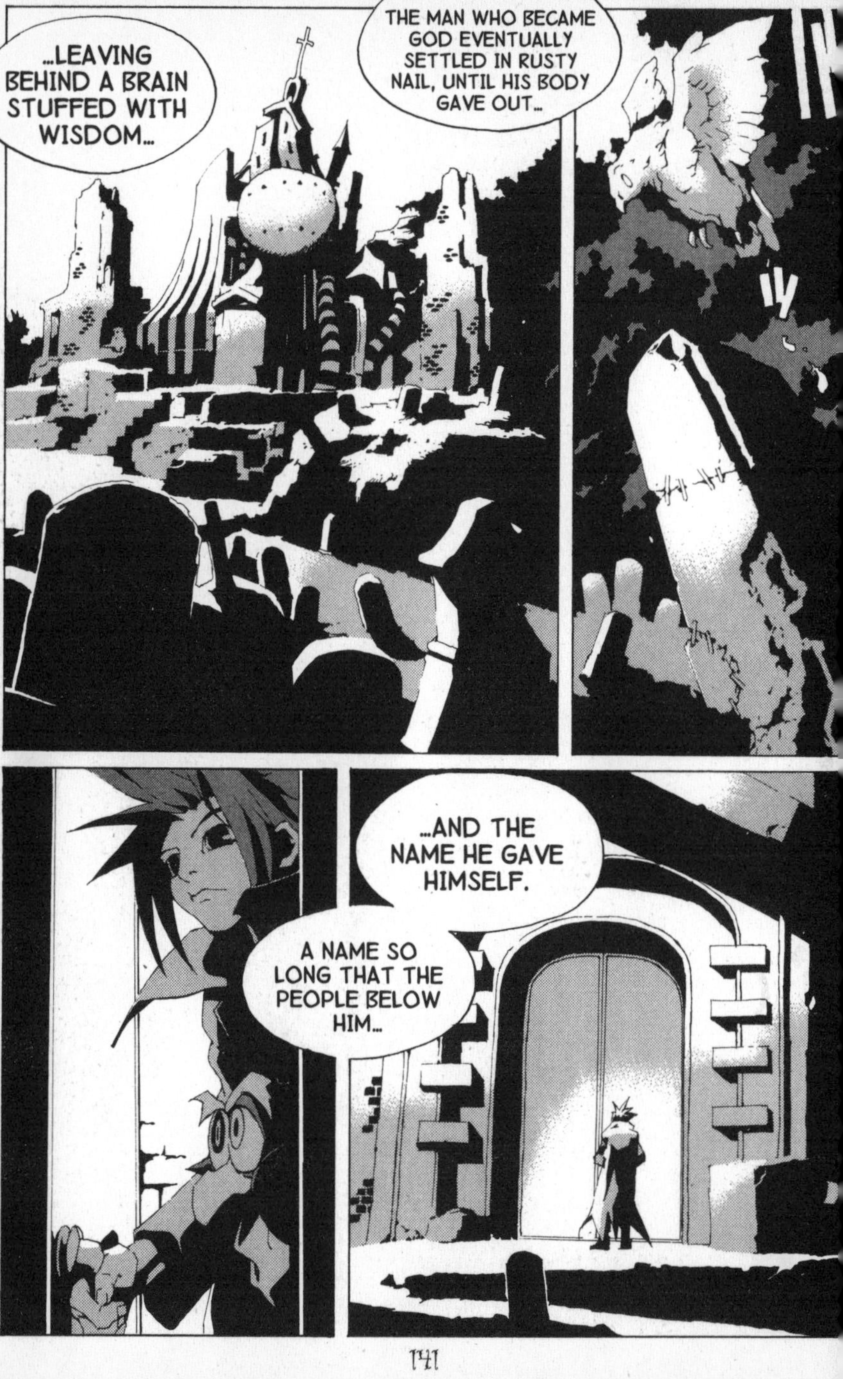
THE MAN WHO BECAME GOD EVENTUALLY SETTLED IN RUSTY NAIL, UNTIL HIS BODY GAVE OUT...
...LEAVING BEHIND A BRAIN STUFFED WITH WISDOM...
...AND THE NAME HE GAVE HIMSELF.
A NAME SO LONG THAT THE PEOPLE BELOW HIM...

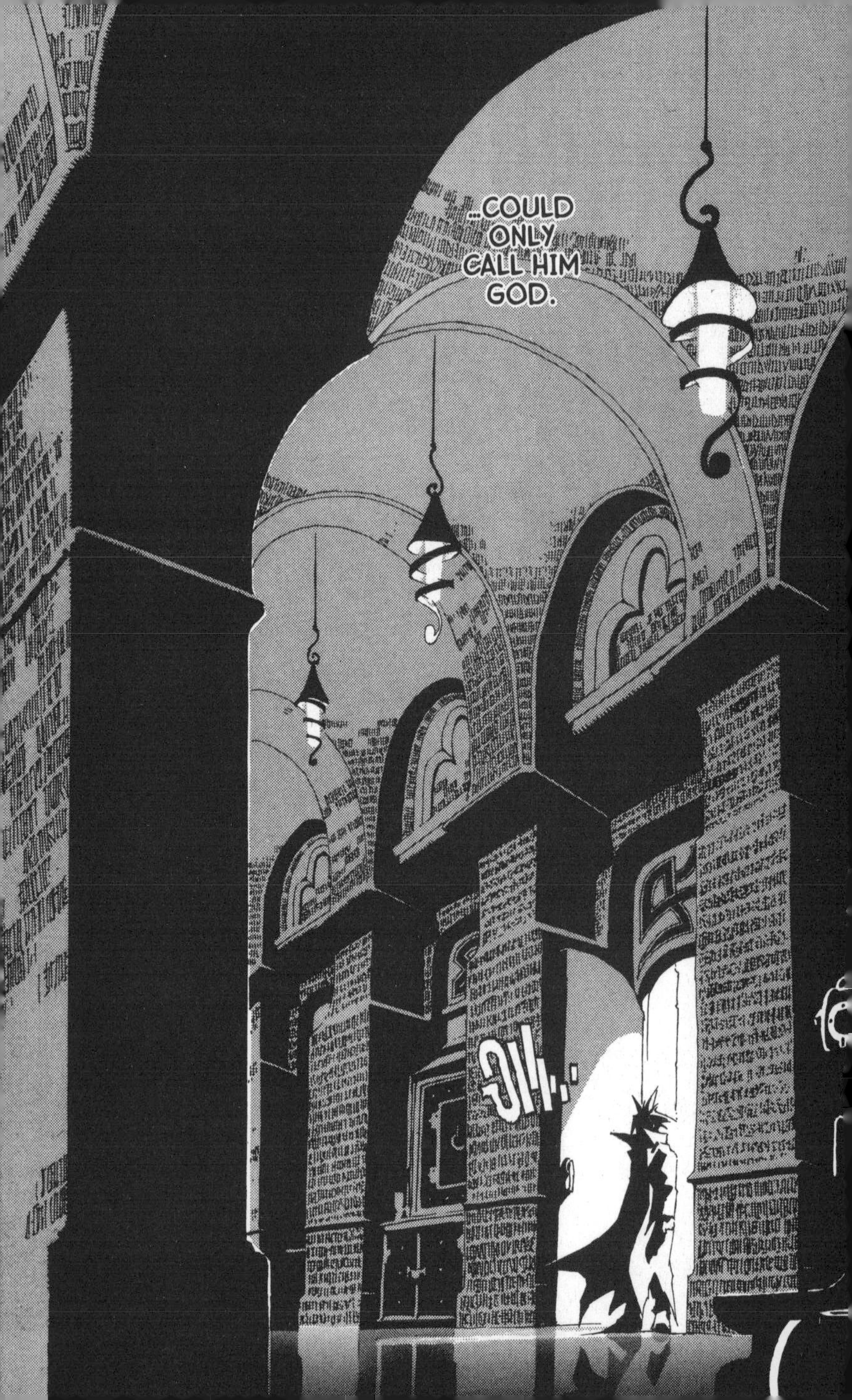
...COULD ONLY CALL HIM GOD.

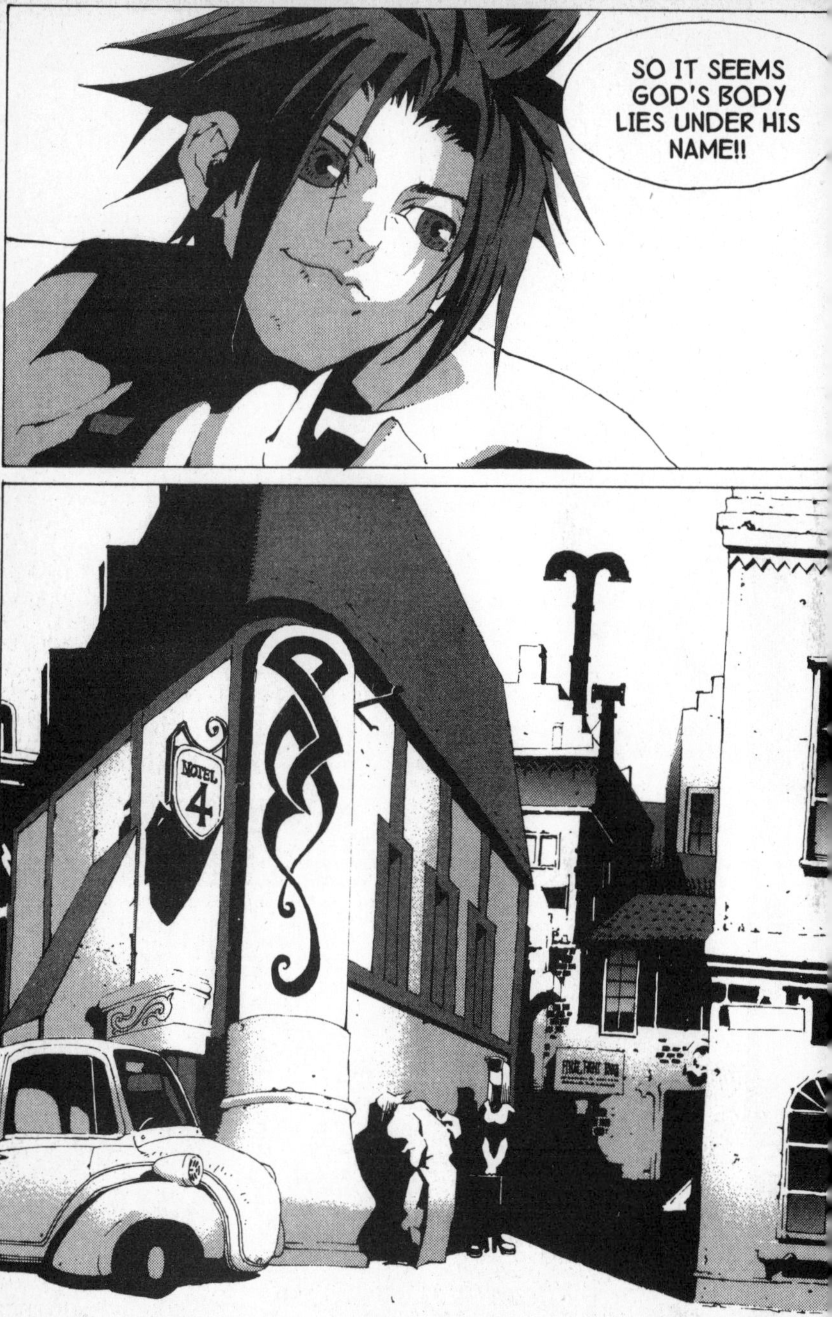
SO IT SEEMS GOD'S BODY LIES UNDER HIS NAME!!
MOTEL 4

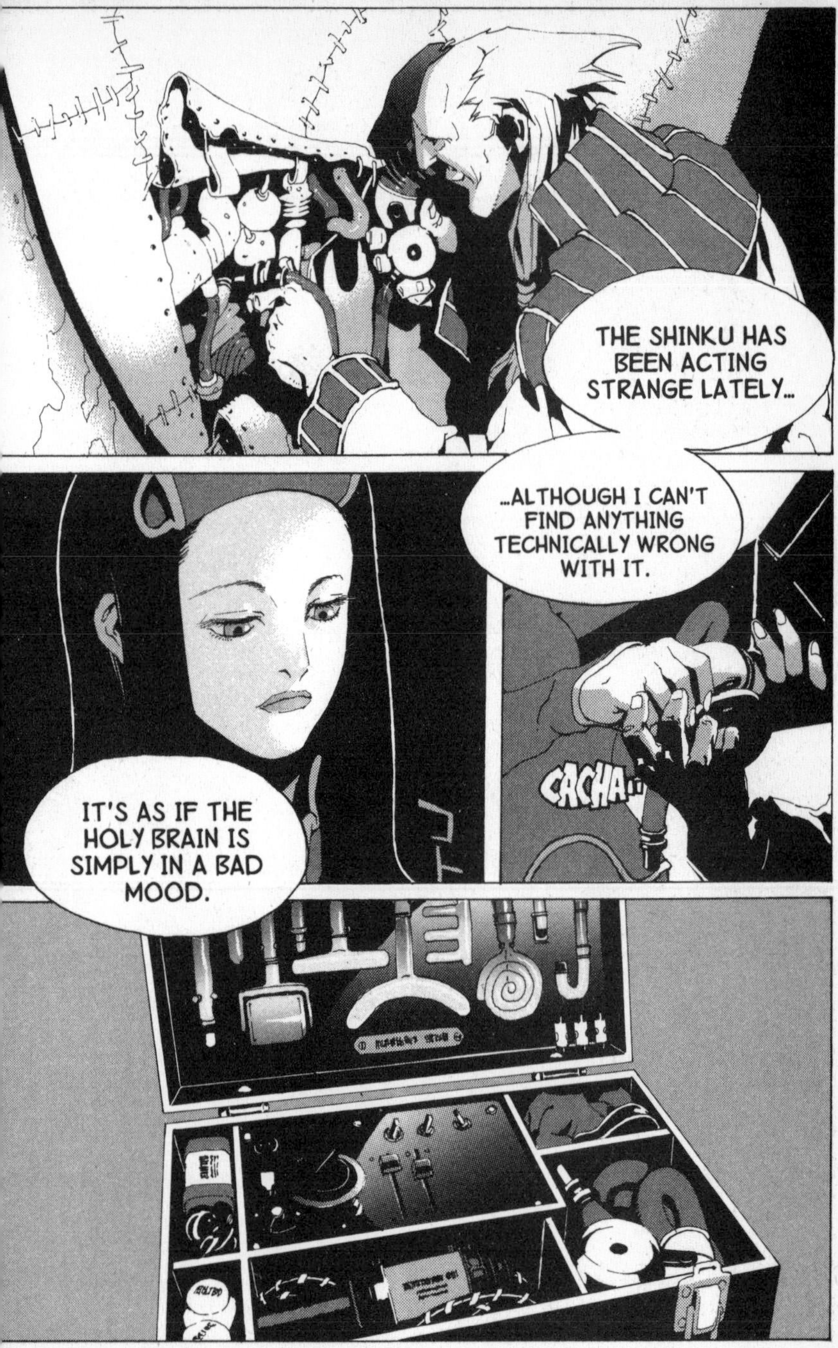
THE SHINKU HAS BEEN ACTING STRANGE LATELY...
...ALTHOUGH I CAN'T FIND ANYTHING TECHNICALLY WRONG WITH IT.
CACHA...
IT'S AS IF THE HOLY BRAIN IS SIMPLY IN A BAD MOOD.

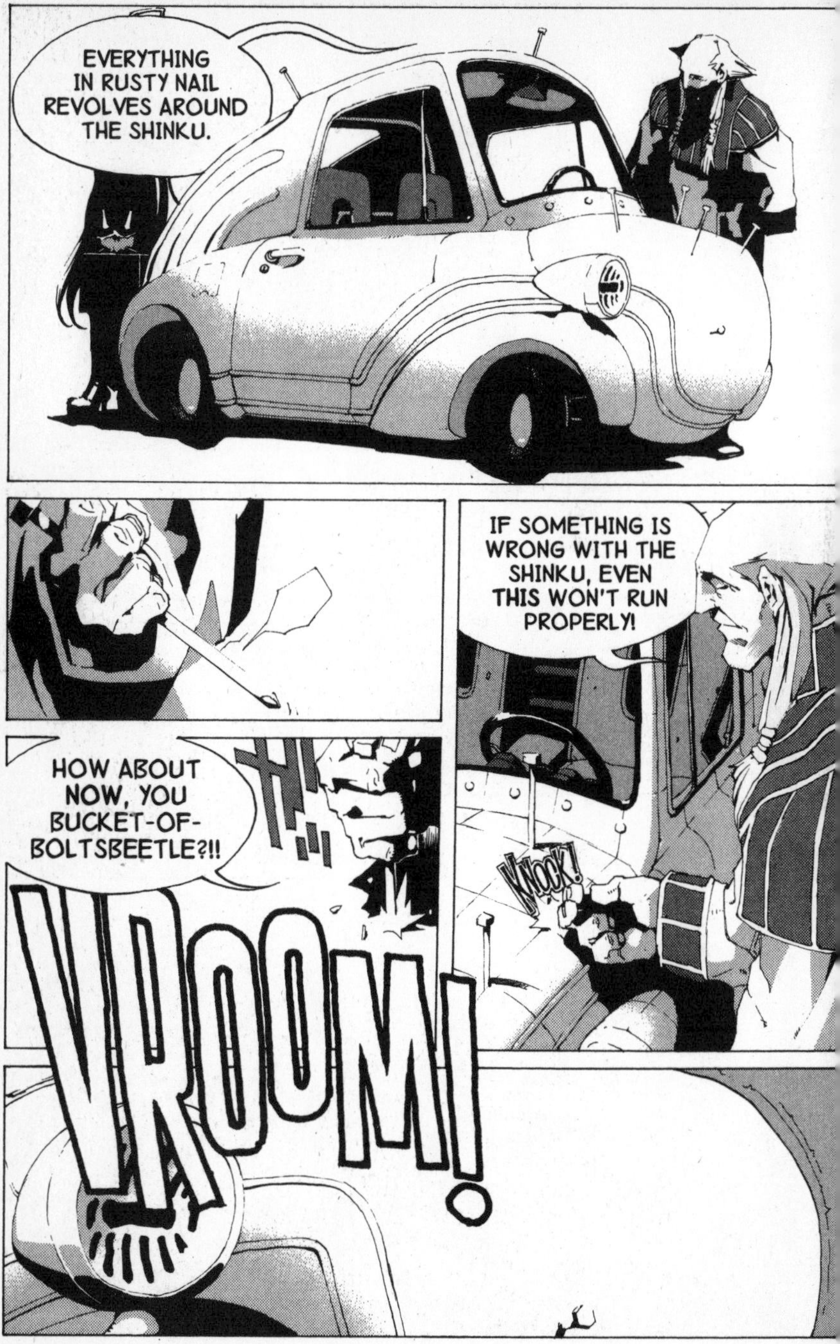
EVERYTHING IN RUSTY NAIL REVOLVES AROUND THE SHINKU.
IF SOMETHING IS WRONG WITH THE SHINKU, EVEN THIS WON'T RUN PROPERLY!
HOW ABOUT NOW, YOU BUCKET-OF-BOLTSBEETLE?!!
KNOCK!
VROOM!

I SEE...SO HE WENT TO THE GRAVEYARD.

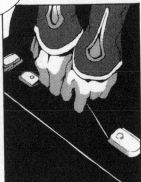

CAN..

CALL THE SPIRITO VOURI!!!

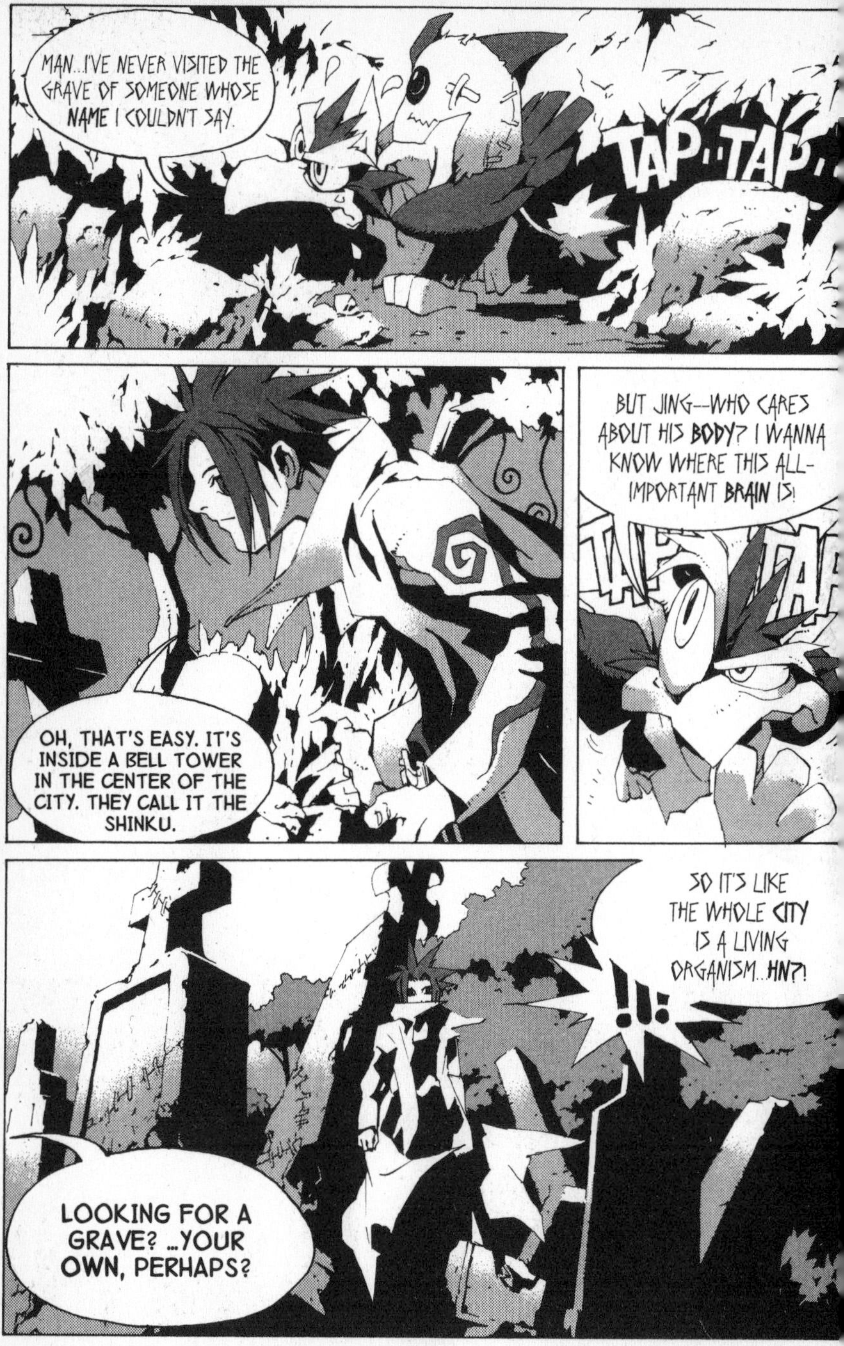
MAN...I'VE NEVER VISITED THE GRAVE OF SOMEONE WHOSE NAME I COULDN'T SAY.
TAP TAP
BUT JING--WHO CARES ABOUT HIS BODY? I WANNA KNOW WHERE THIS ALL-IMPORTANT BRAIN IS!
OH, THAT'S EASY. IT'S INSIDE A BELL TOWER IN THE CENTER OF THE CITY. THEY CALL IT THE SHINKU.
SO IT'S LIKE THE WHOLE CITY IS A LIVING ORGANISM...HN?!
!!
LOOKING FOR A GRAVE? ...YOUR OWN, PERHAPS?

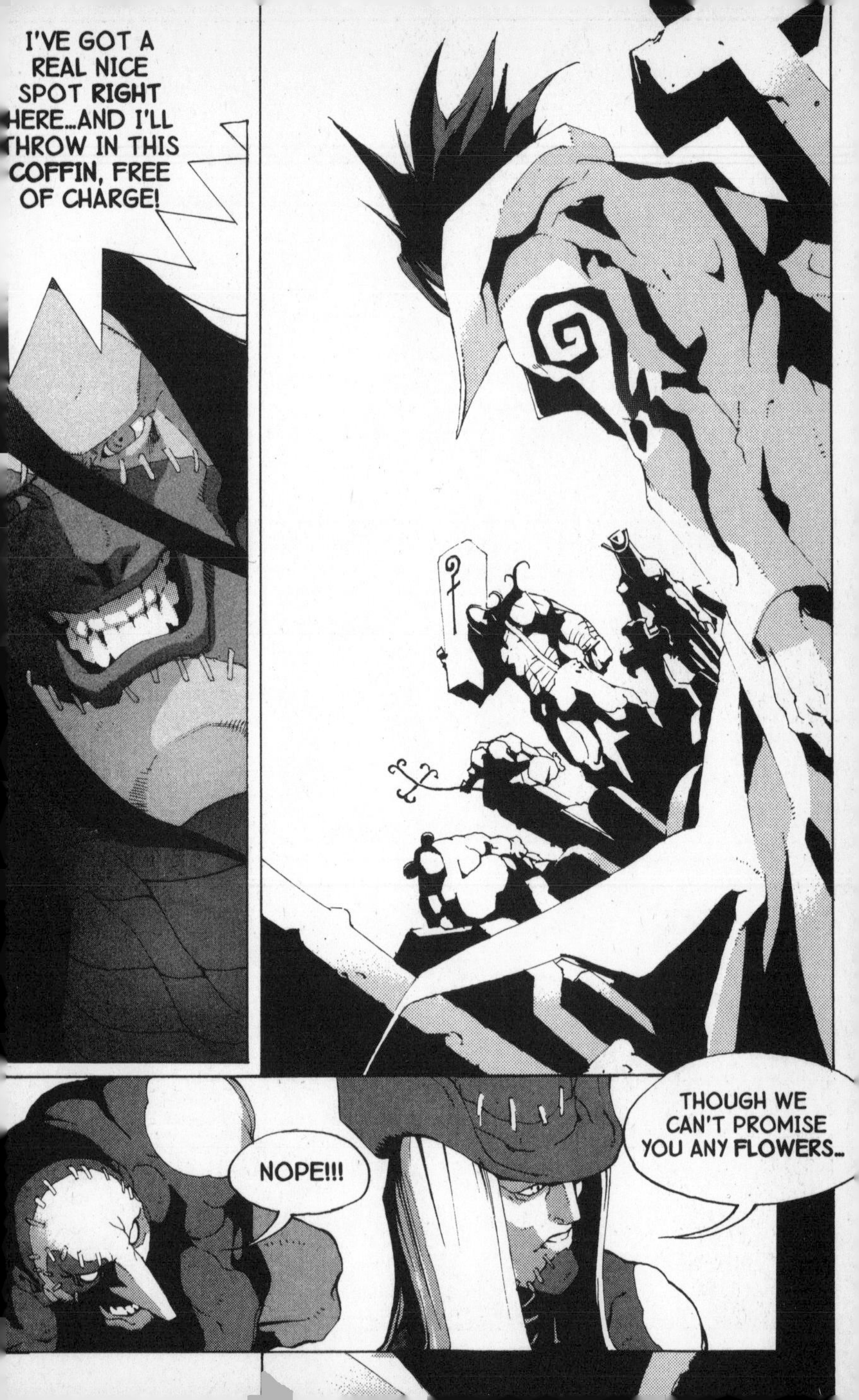
I'VE GOT A REAL NICE SPOT RIGHT HERE...AND I'LL THROW IN THIS COFFIN, FREE OF CHARGE!
THOUGH WE CAN'T PROMISE YOU ANY FLOWERS...
NOPE!!!

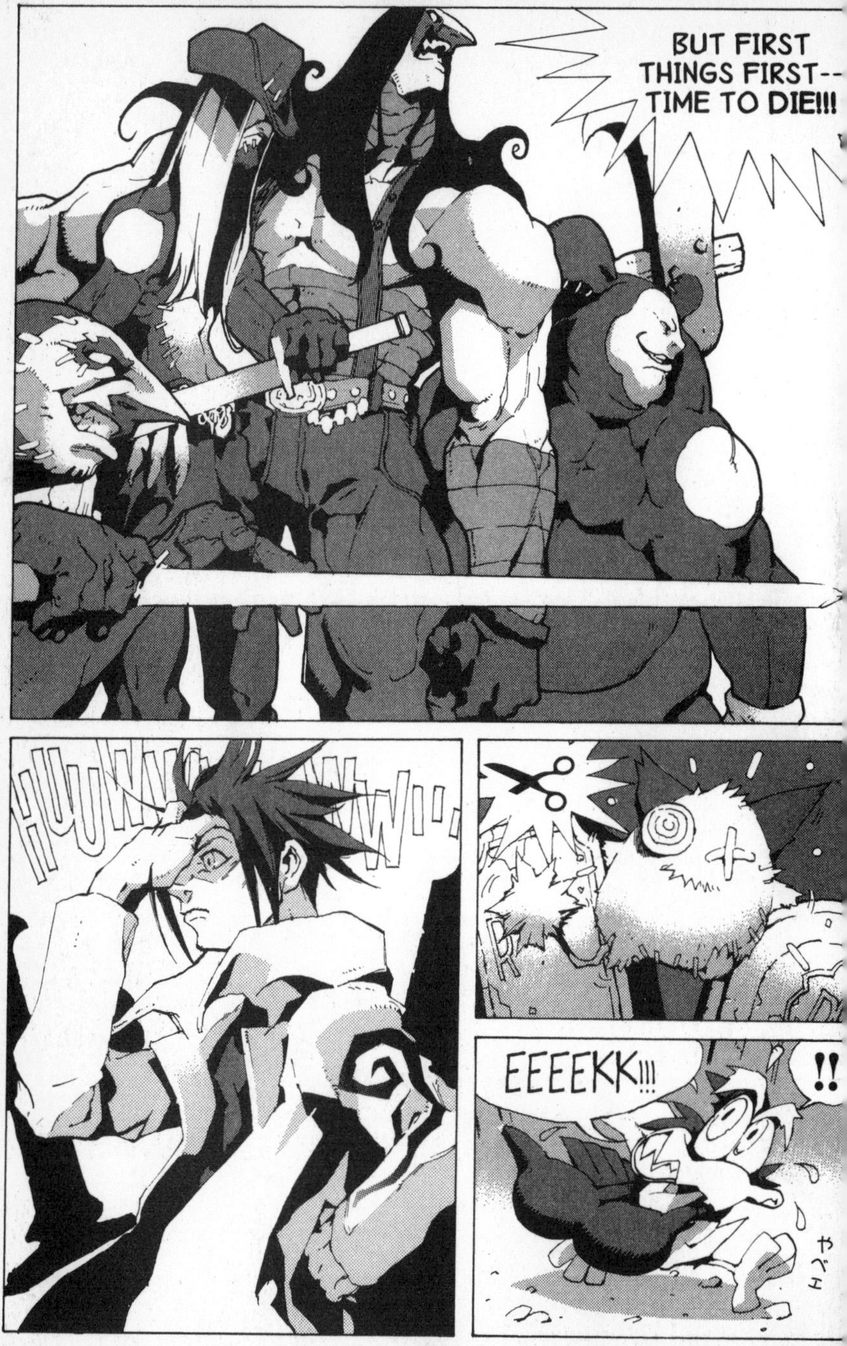
BUT FIRST
THINGS FIRST--
TIME TO DIE!!!
EEEEKK!!!
!!

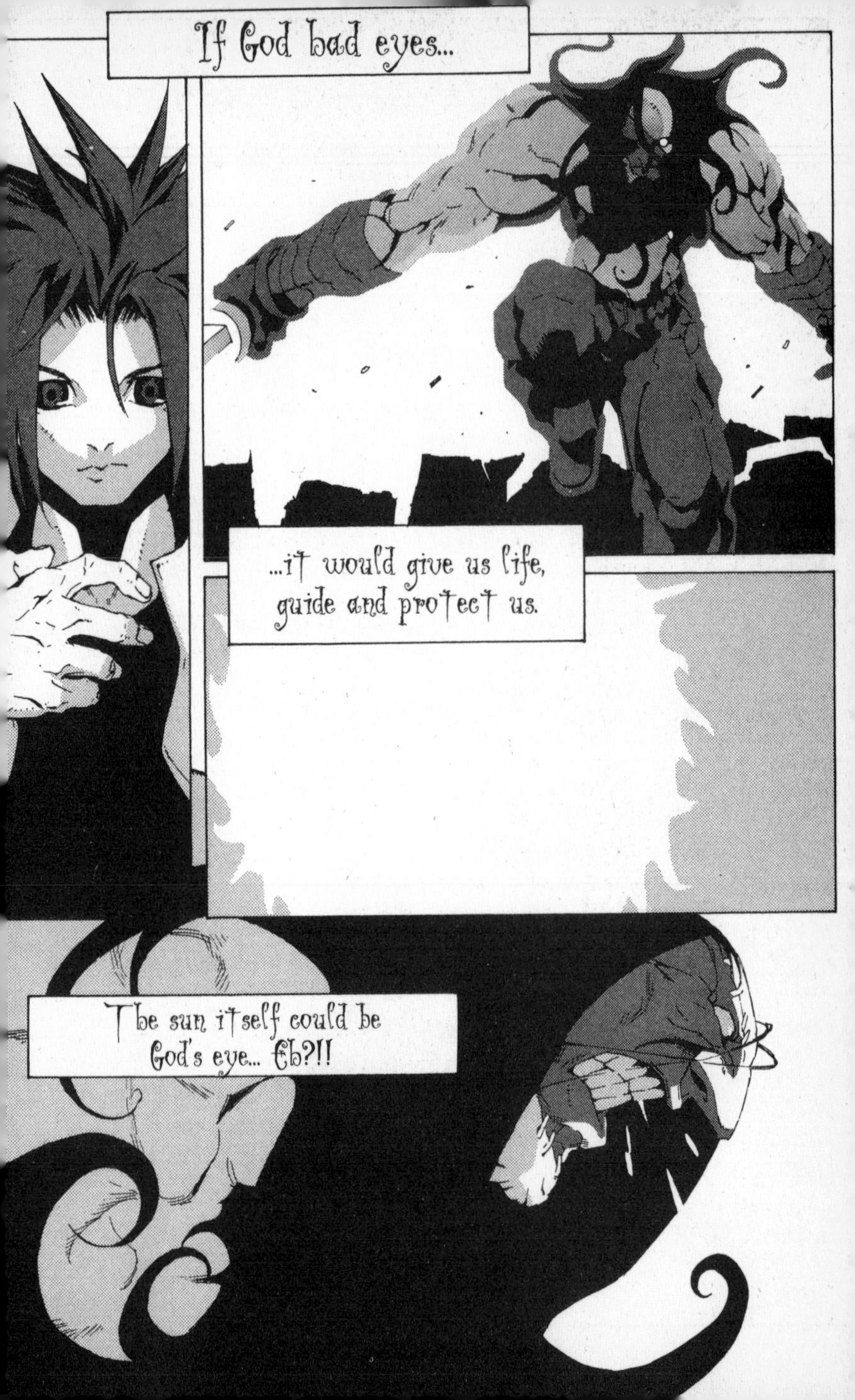
If God had eyes...
...it would give us life, guide and protect us.
The sun itself could be God's eye... Eh?!!

PROFESSOR URYAN SAID TO CAPTURE HIM **ALIVE**!!

BUT IT'S UP TO ME WHETHER HE LIVES OR DIES!

AND IF YOU REALLY WISH TO DIE, JING...

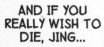

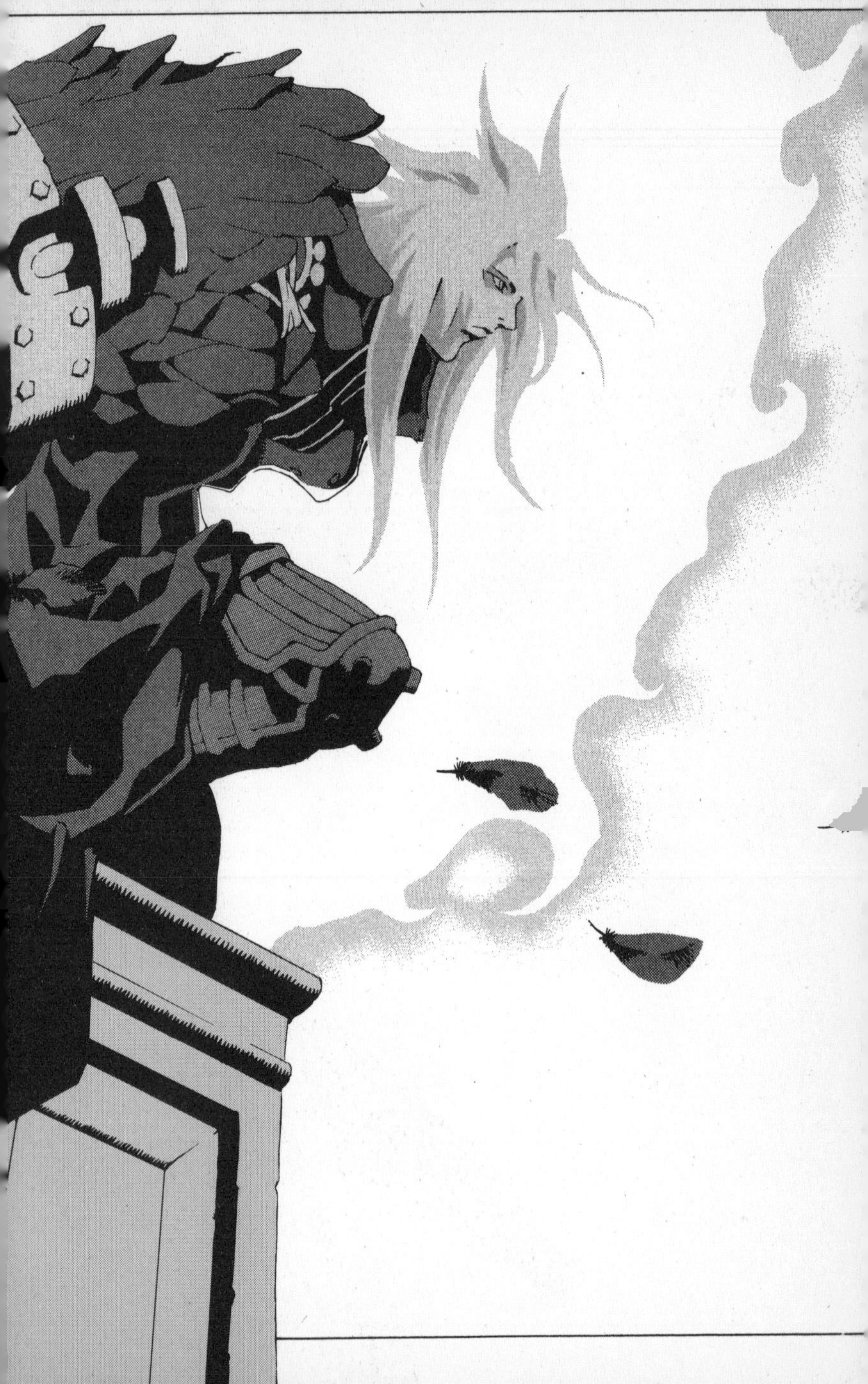

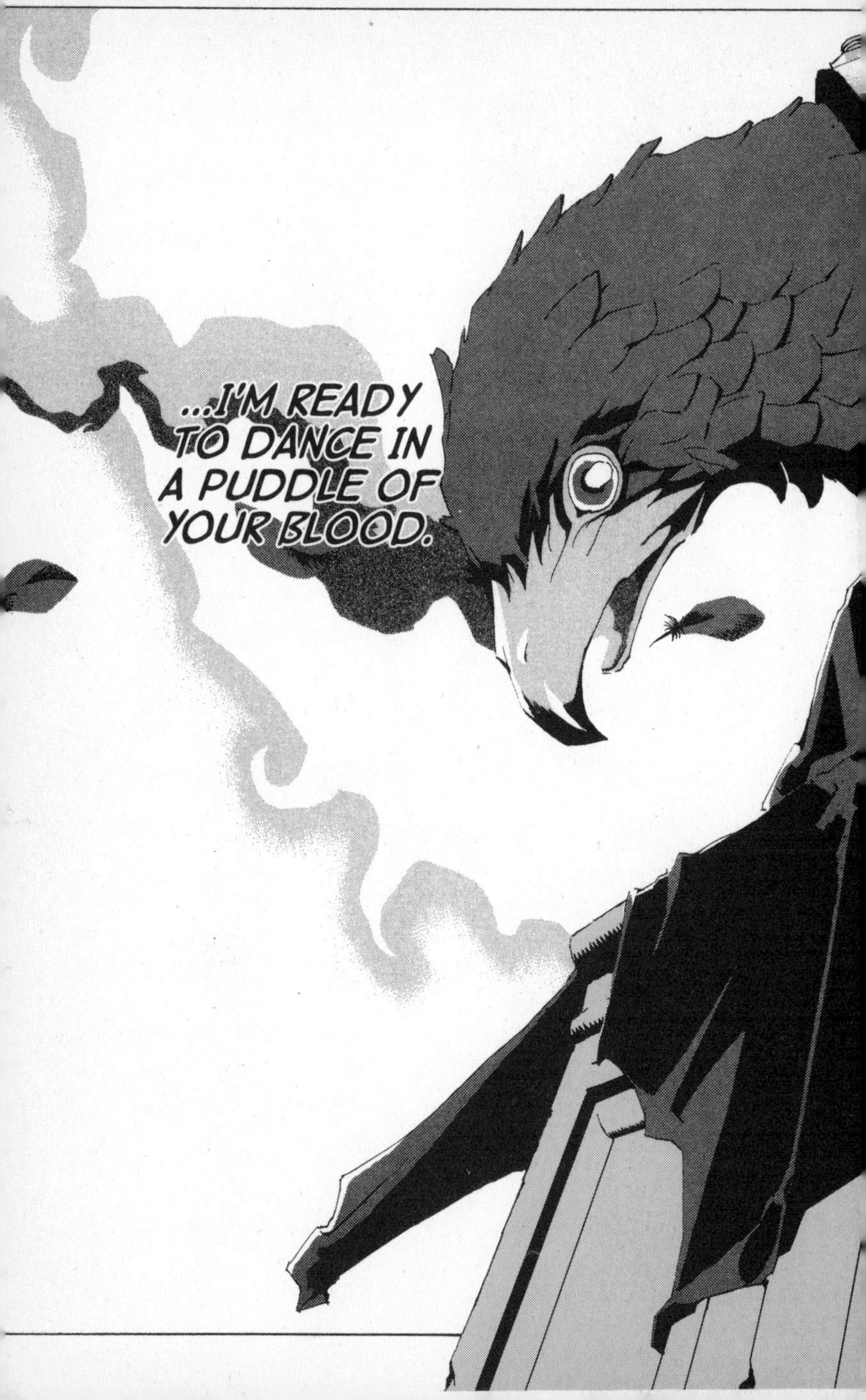
...I'M READY TO DANCE IN A PUDDLE OF YOUR BLOOD.

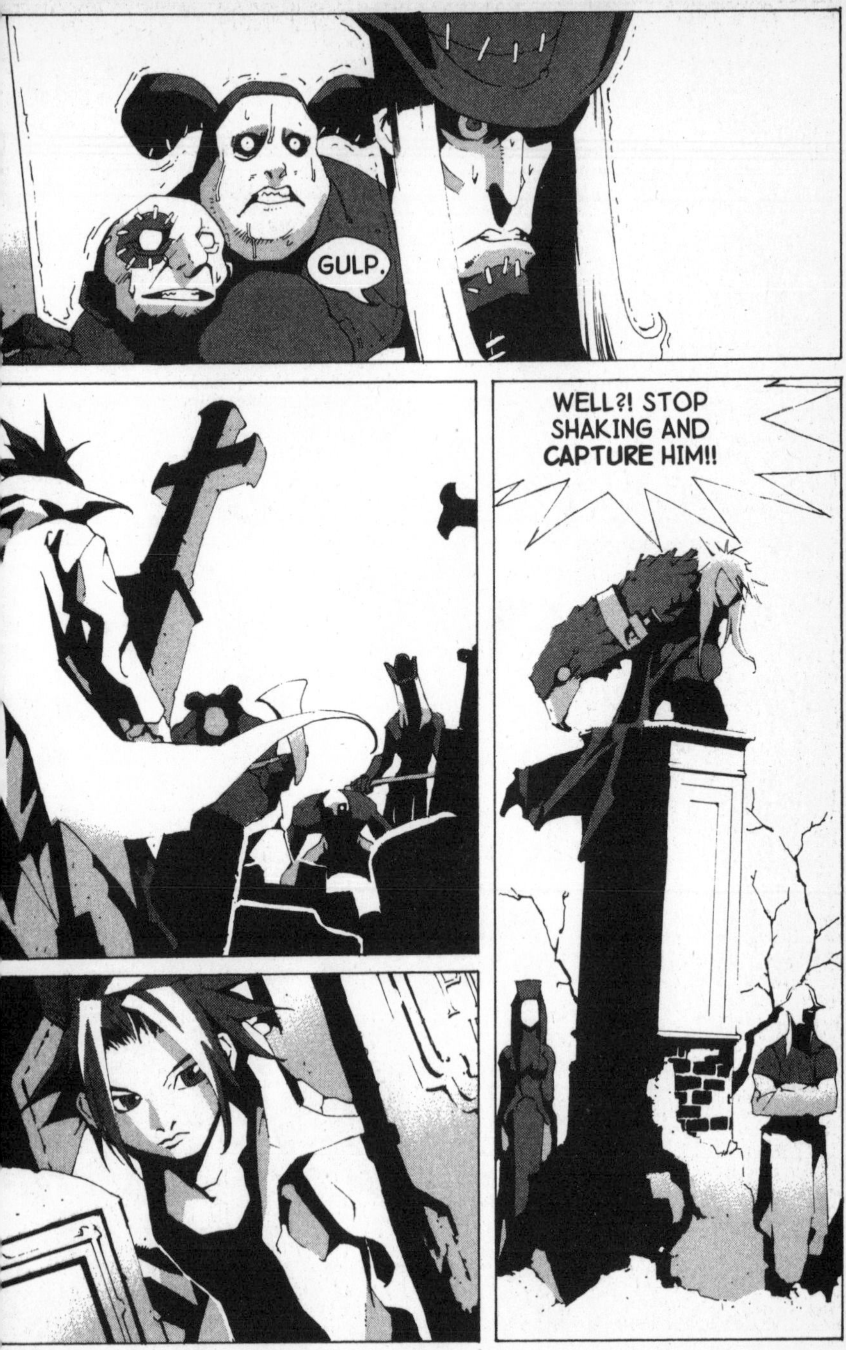
GULP.
WELL?! STOP SHAKING AND CAPTURE HIM!!

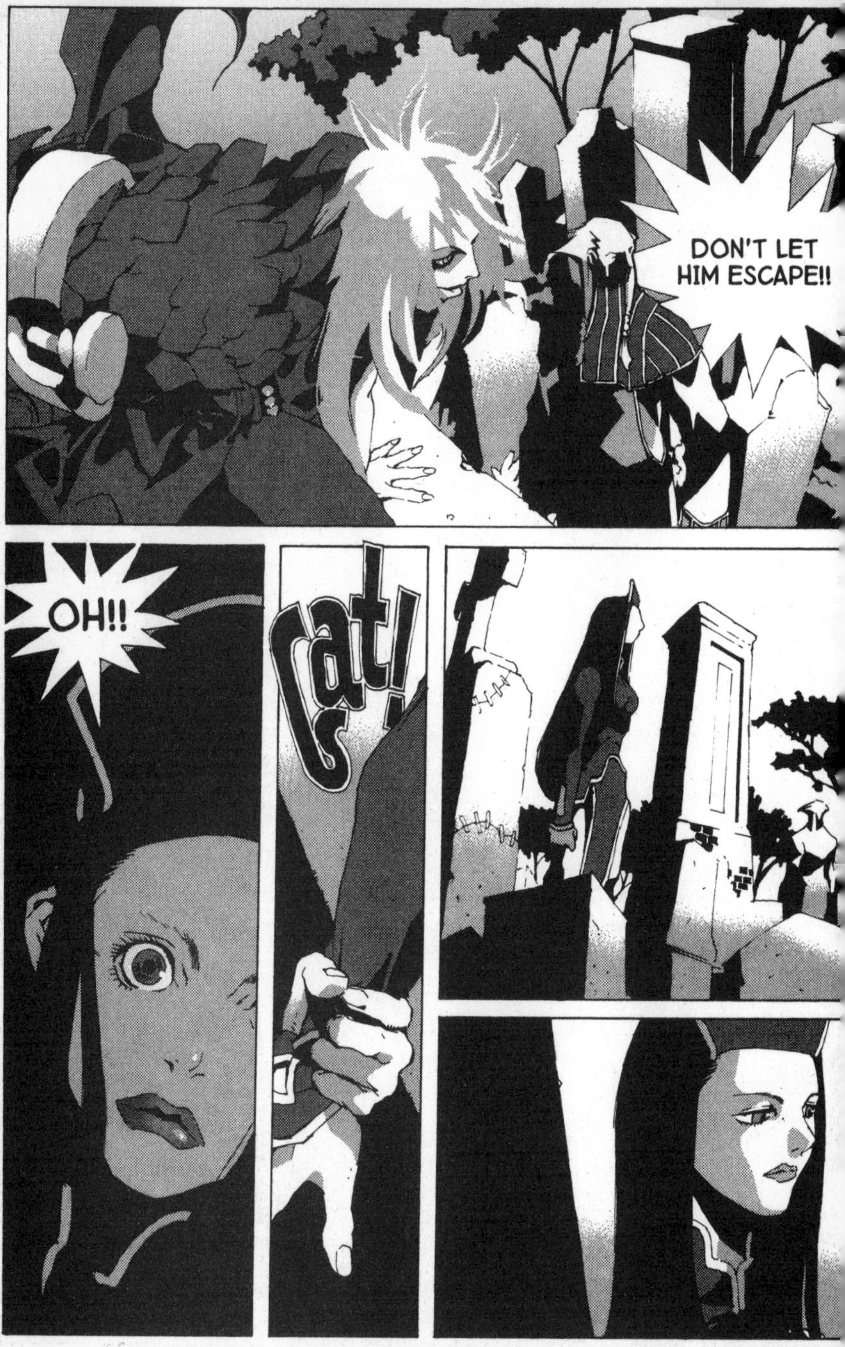
DON'T LET HIM ESCAPE!!
OH!!
cat!

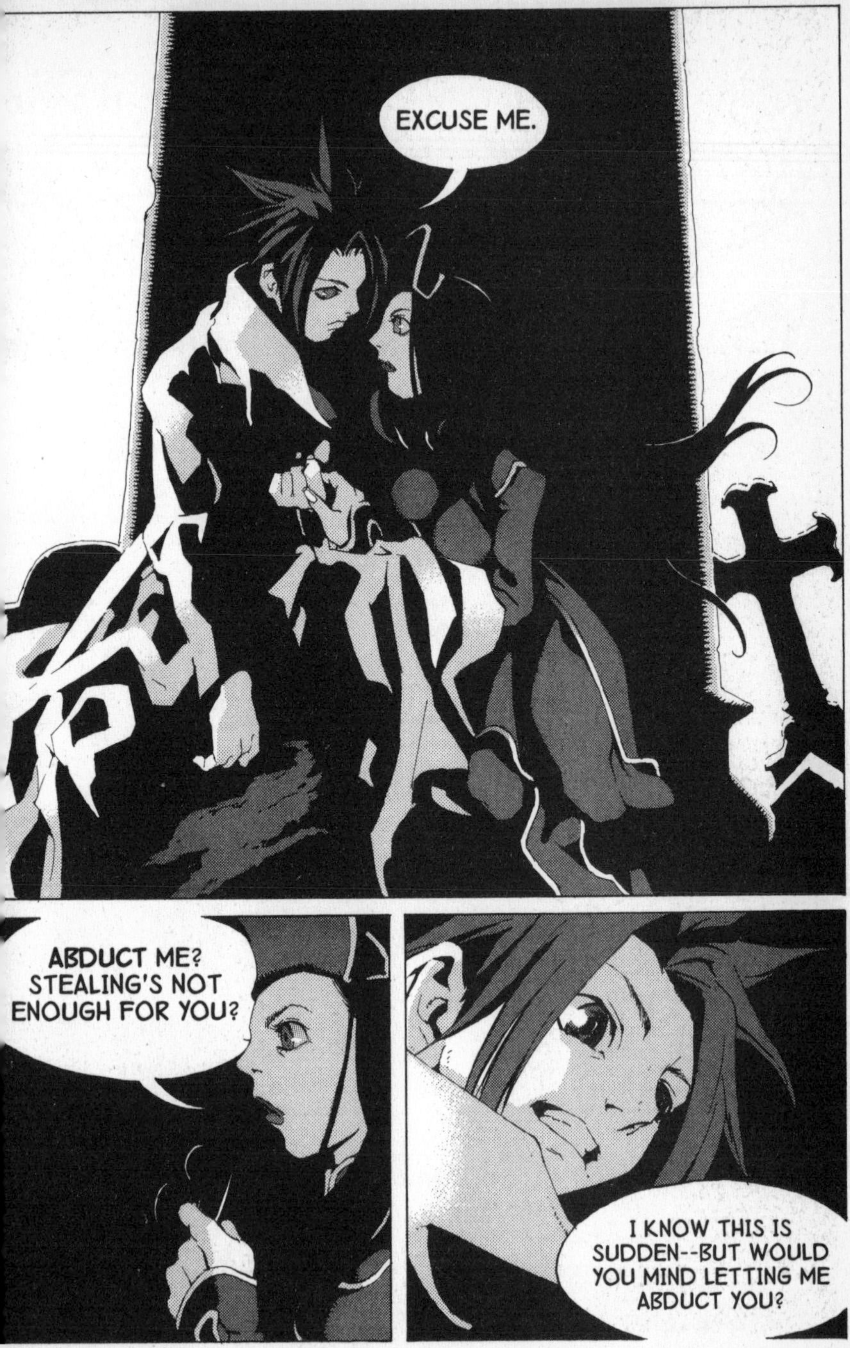
EXCUSE ME.
ABDUCT ME? STEALING'S NOT ENOUGH FOR YOU?
I KNOW THIS IS SUDDEN--BUT WOULD YOU MIND LETTING ME ABDUCT YOU?

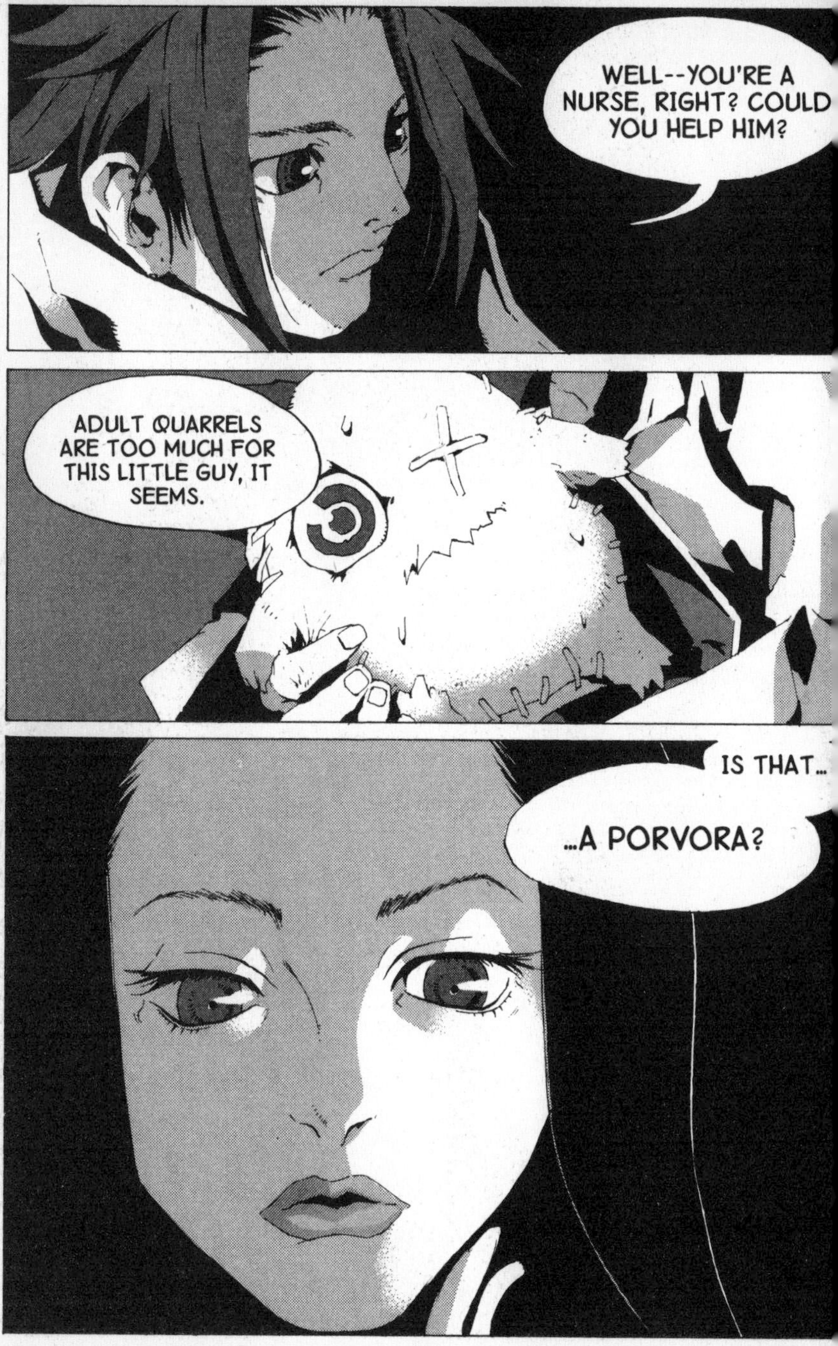
WELL--YOU'RE A NURSE, RIGHT? COULD YOU HELP HIM?
ADULT QUARRELS ARE TOO MUCH FOR THIS LITTLE GUY, IT SEEMS.
IS THAT...
...A PORVORA?

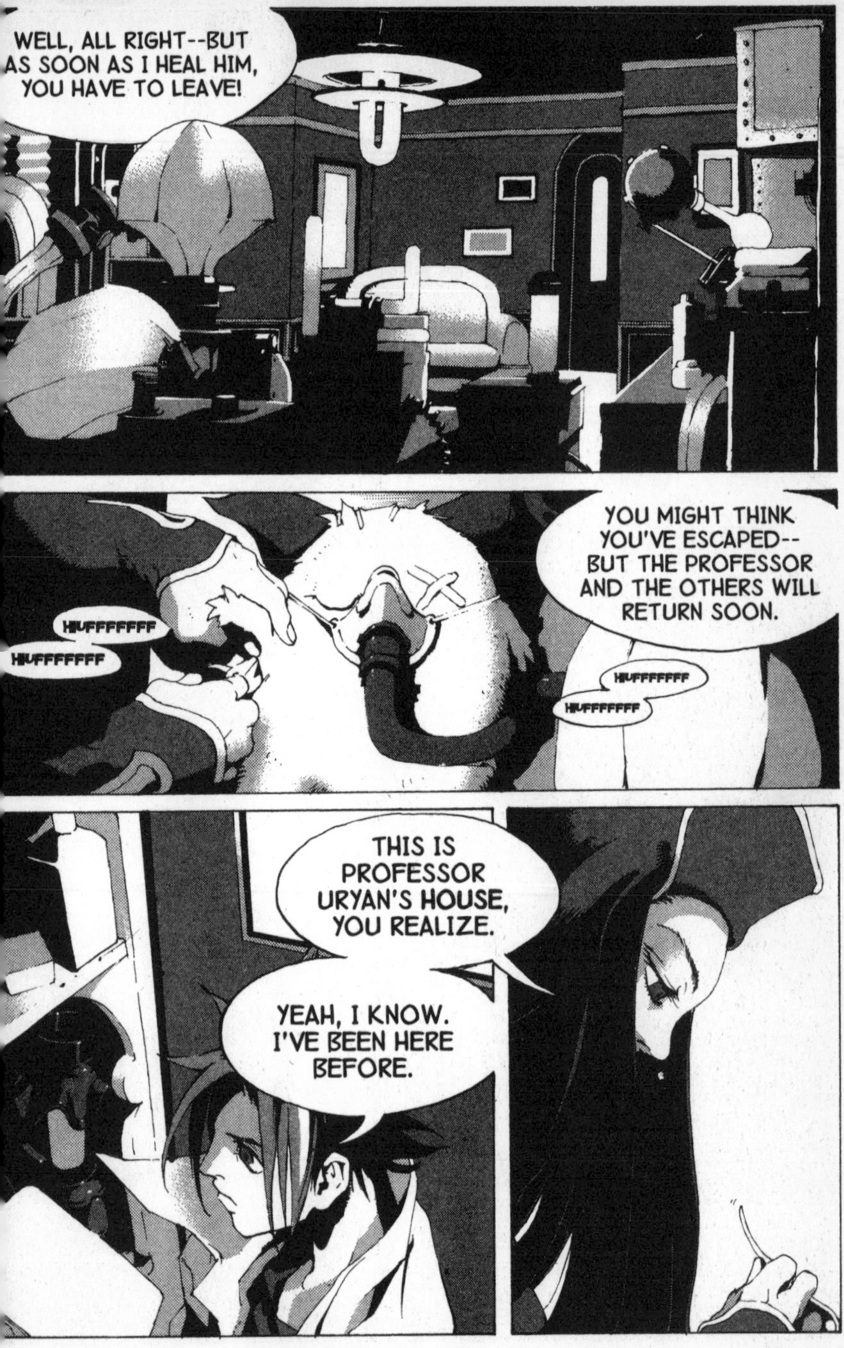
WELL, ALL RIGHT--BUT AS SOON AS I HEAL HIM, YOU HAVE TO LEAVE!
YOU MIGHT THINK YOU'VE ESCAPED-- BUT THE PROFESSOR AND THE OTHERS WILL RETURN SOON.
HUFFFFFFFF
HUFFFFFFFF
HUFFFFFFFF
HUFFFFFFFF
THIS IS PROFESSOR URYAN'S HOUSE, YOU REALIZE.
YEAH, I KNOW. I'VE BEEN HERE BEFORE.

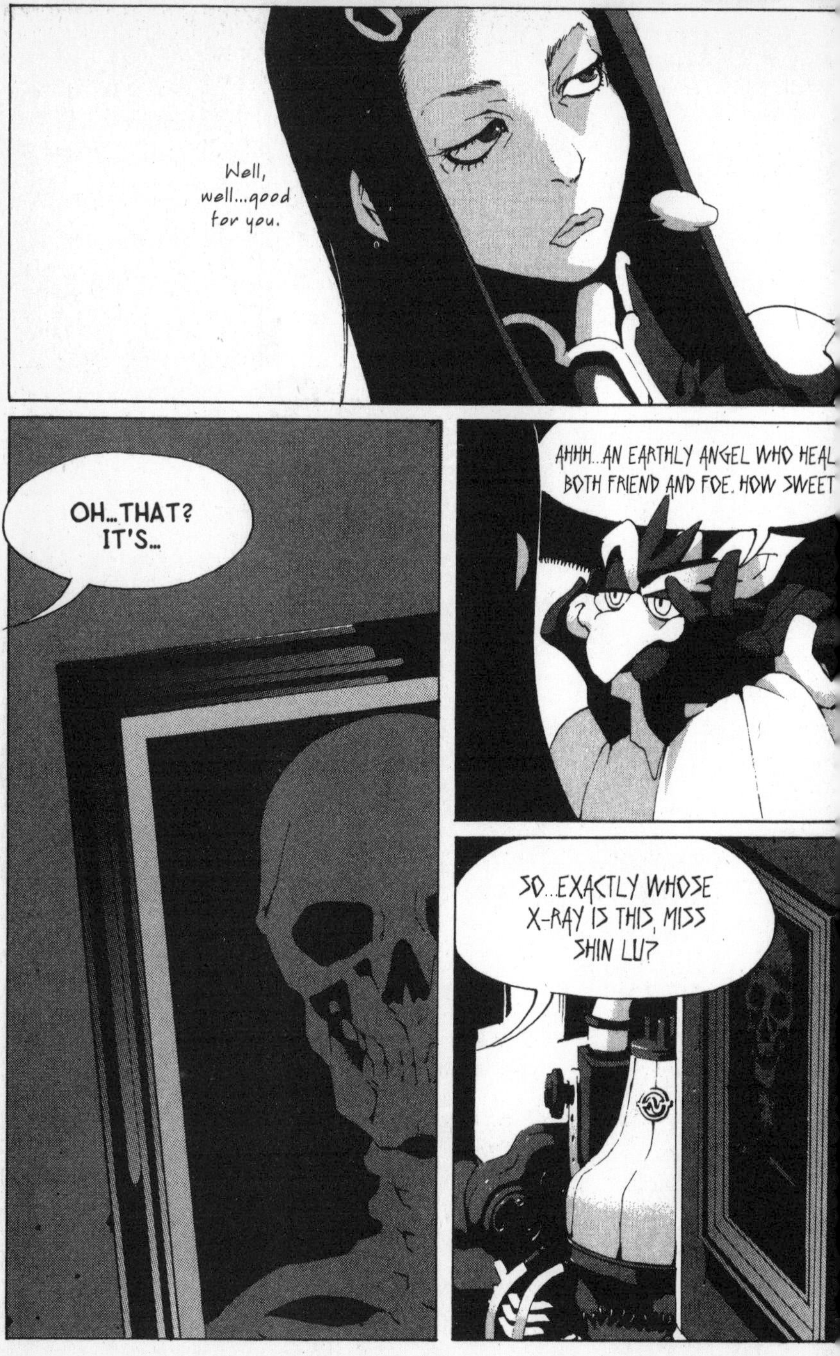
Well, well...good for you.
OH...THAT? IT'S...
AHHH...AN EARTHLY ANGEL WHO HEAL BOTH FRIEND AND FOE. HOW SWEET
SO...EXACTLY WHOSE X-RAY IS THIS, MISS SHIN LU?

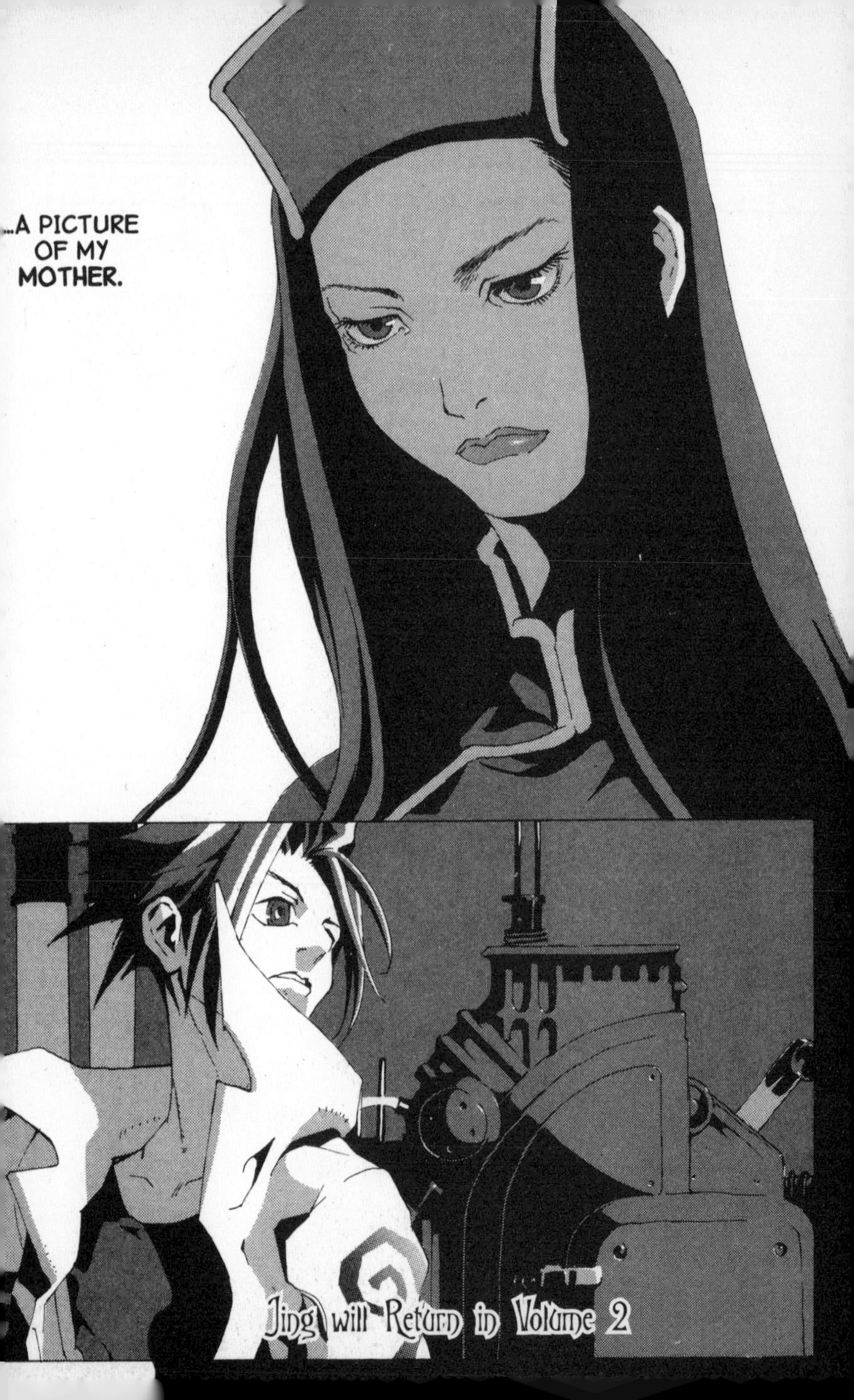
...A PICTURE OF MY MOTHER.
Jing will Return in Volume 2

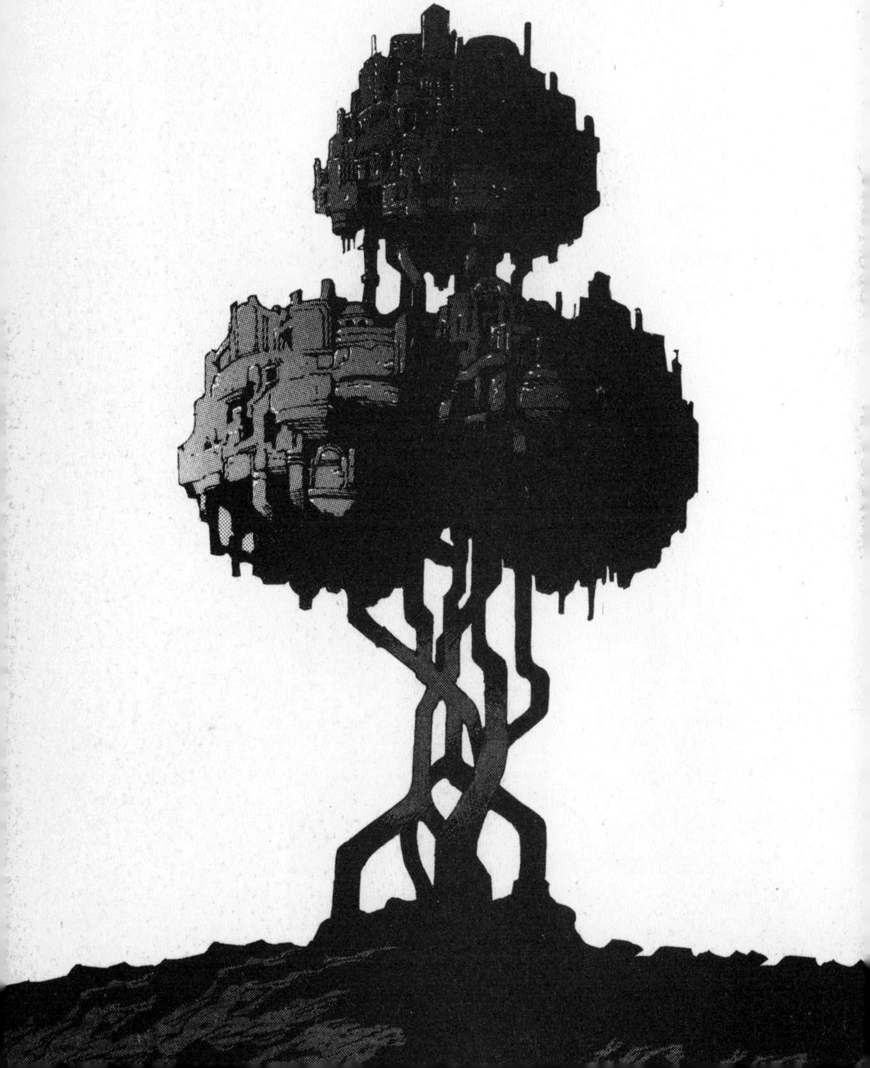

KING OF BANDITS JiNG

TWILIGHT TALES

Volume 2 Preview

BUT BLOODY CAESAR...THEY SAY HE WAS ACTUALLY MADE BY BLENDING CORPSES OF EVERY BLOOD TYPE TOGETHER!

MAYBE THAT EXPLAINS WHY HIS PERSONALITY IS SO ELUSIVE...OR WOULD THAT JUST MAKE HIM PREDOMINANTLY BLOOD TYPE A?

JOKE ABOUT IT IF YOU LIKE. BUT IF YOU DON'T TAKE HIM SERIOUSLY...THERE'LL BE A BLOODBATH.

Rusty Nail is a city with an unusual motto: Give me your tired, your poor, your extra body parts! It's a town that specializes in providing spare limbs to those in need. Rusty Nail's biggest patron is the monstrous Bloody Caesar, a creature composed of more than 30 different people...with room left over for a bit of Jing!

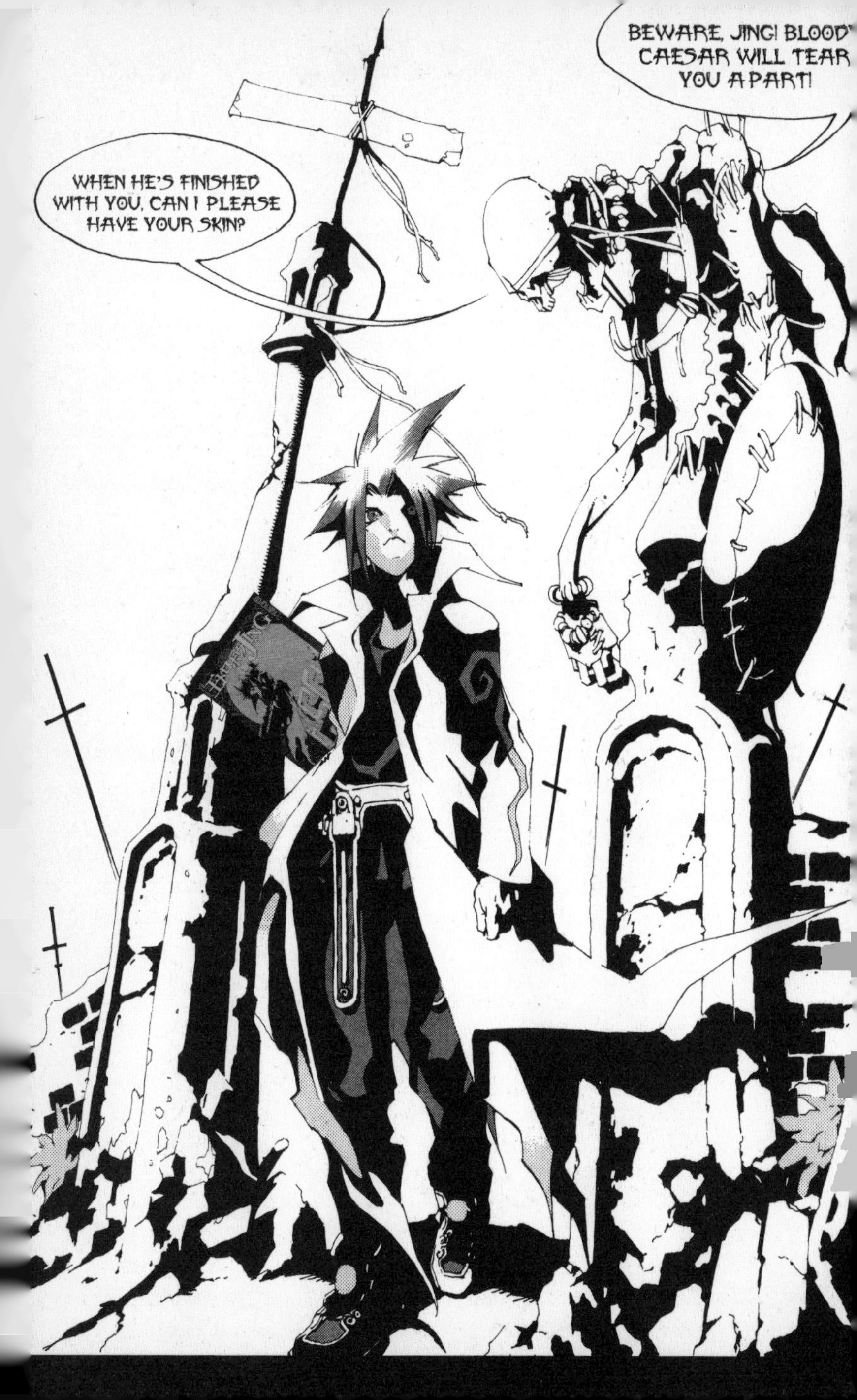
BEWARE, JING! BLOOD
CAESAR WILL TEAR
YOU APART!
WHEN HE'S FINISHED
WITH YOU, CAN I PLEASE
HAVE YOUR SKIN?

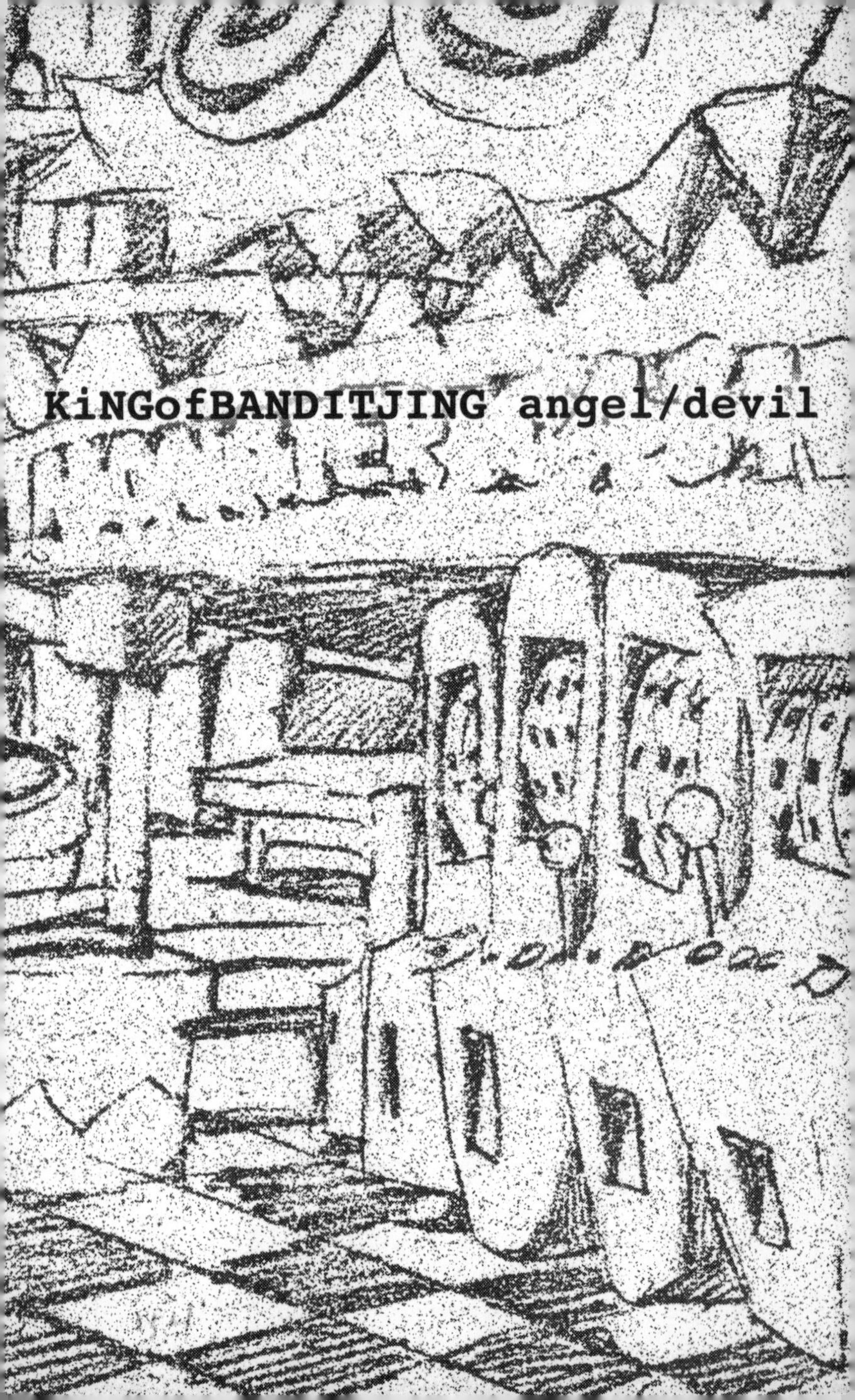
KiNGofBANDITJING angel/devil

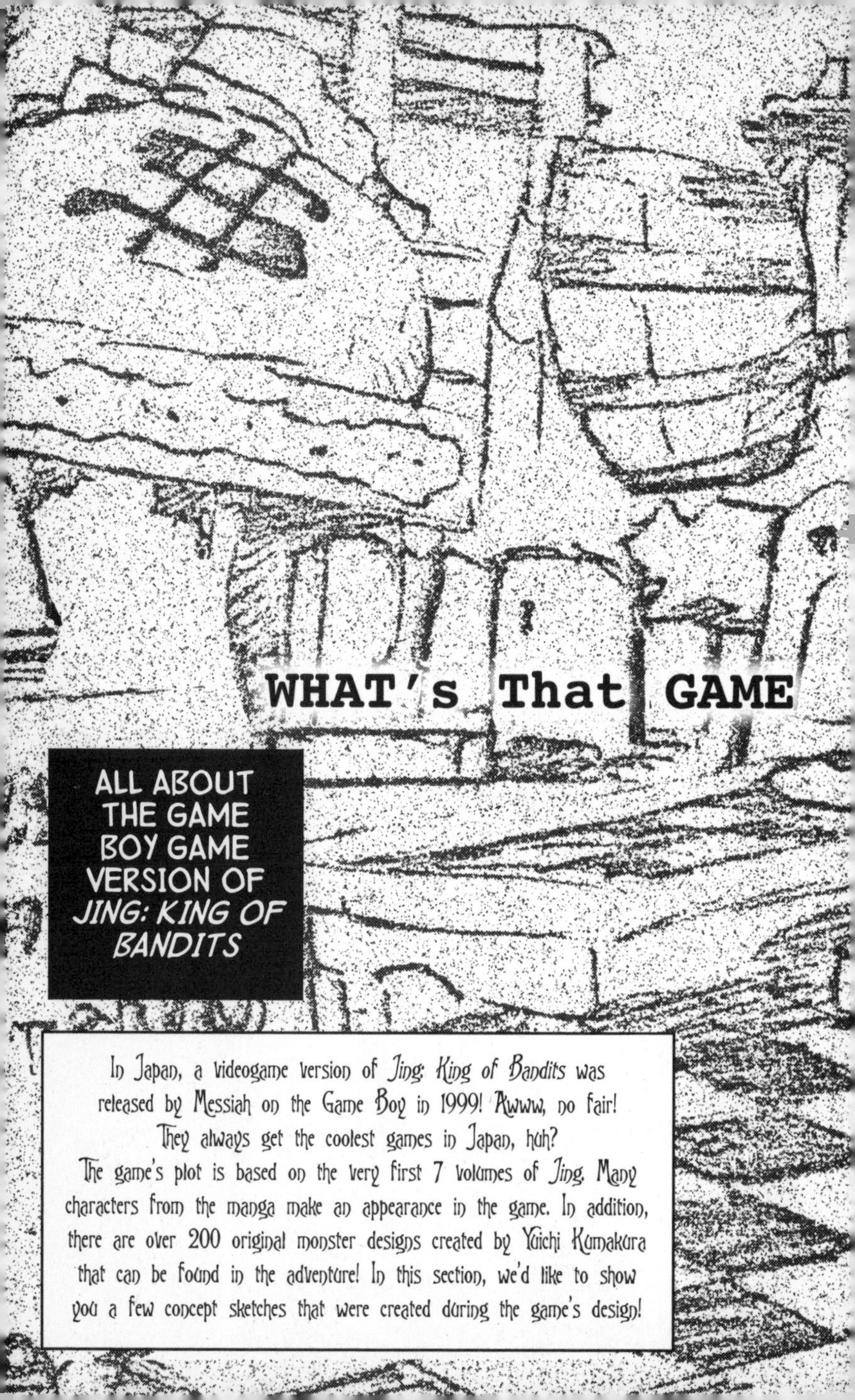

WHAT's That GAME

ALL ABOUT THE GAME BOY GAME VERSION OF *JING: KING OF BANDITS*

In Japan, a videogame version of *Jing: King of Bandits* was released by Messiah on the Game Boy in 1999! Awww, no fair! They always get the coolest games in Japan, huh?
The game's plot is based on the very first 7 volumes of *Jing*. Many characters from the manga make an appearance in the game. In addition, there are over 200 original monster designs created by Yuichi Kumakura that can be found in the adventure! In this section, we'd like to show you a few concept sketches that were created during the game's design!

OPENING

JING ← from RiGHT

The Jing that appears in the game looks very similar to the boy we know and love in the manga. During the game's intro, Jing appears from the right and Kir appears from the left. Then they perform an awesome Kir Royale!

ART FROM THE GAME'S INTRO

romLEFT → KIR

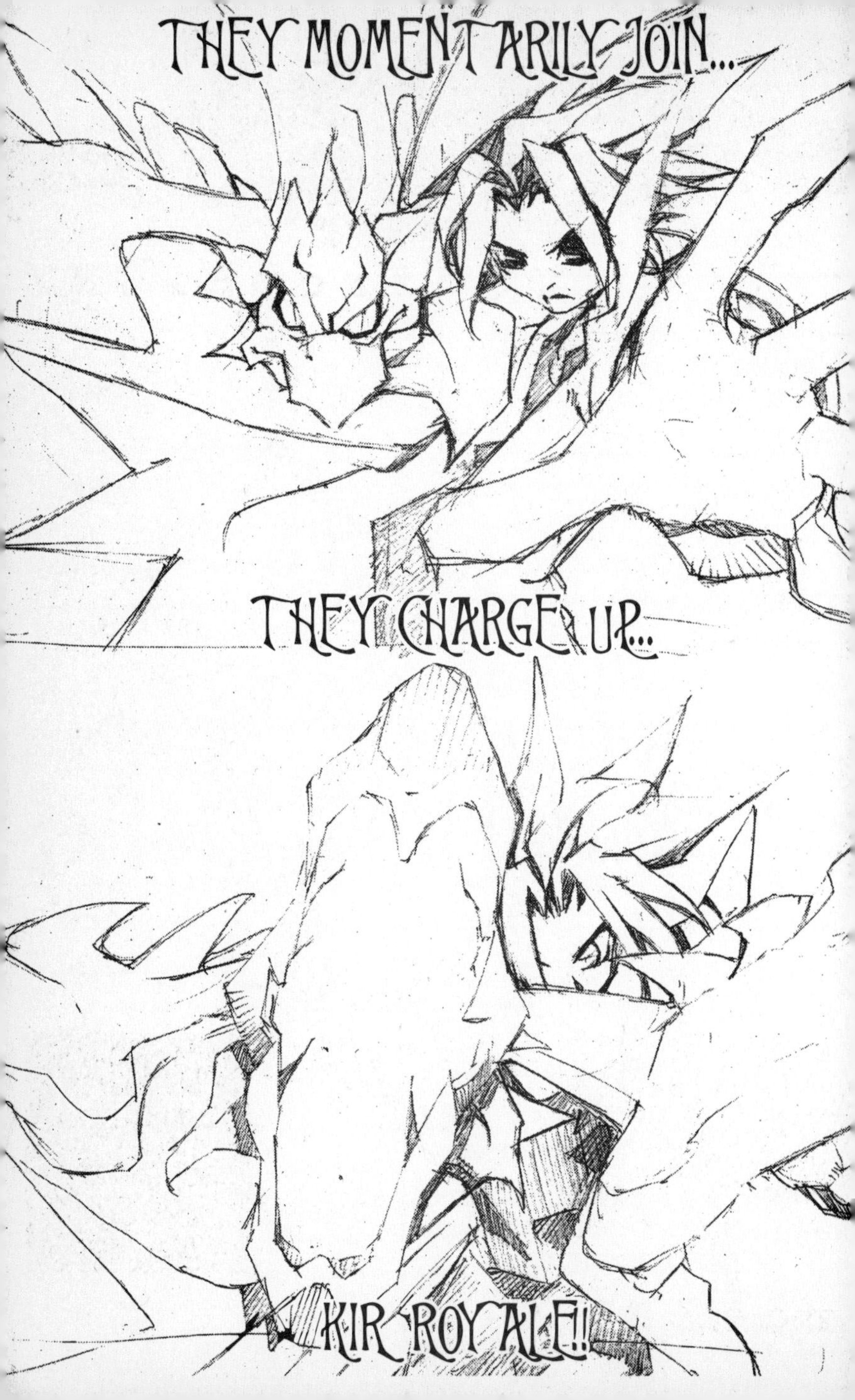
THEY MOMENTARILY JOIN...
THEY CHARGE UP...
KIR ROYALE!!

JiNG & KIR

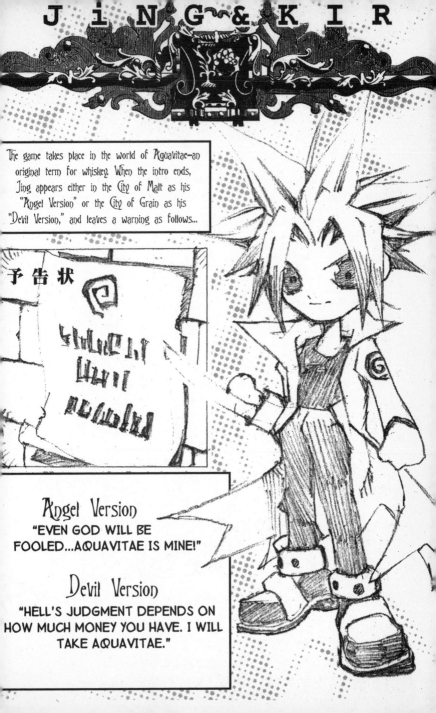

The game takes place in the world of Aquavitae—an original term for whiskey. When the intro ends, Jing appears either in the City of Malt as his "Angel Version" or the City of Grain as his "Devil Version," and leaves a warning as follows...

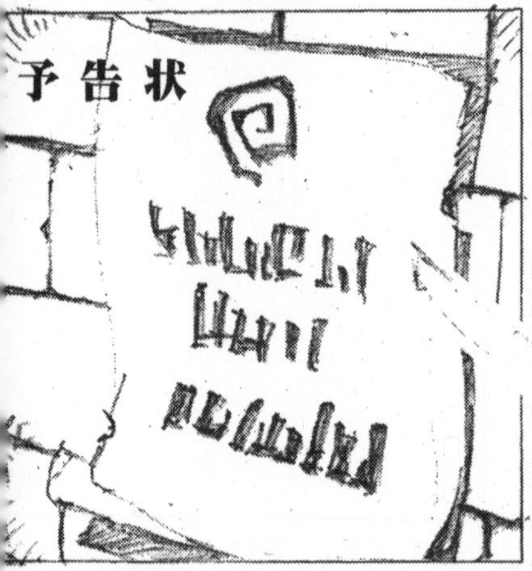
予告状

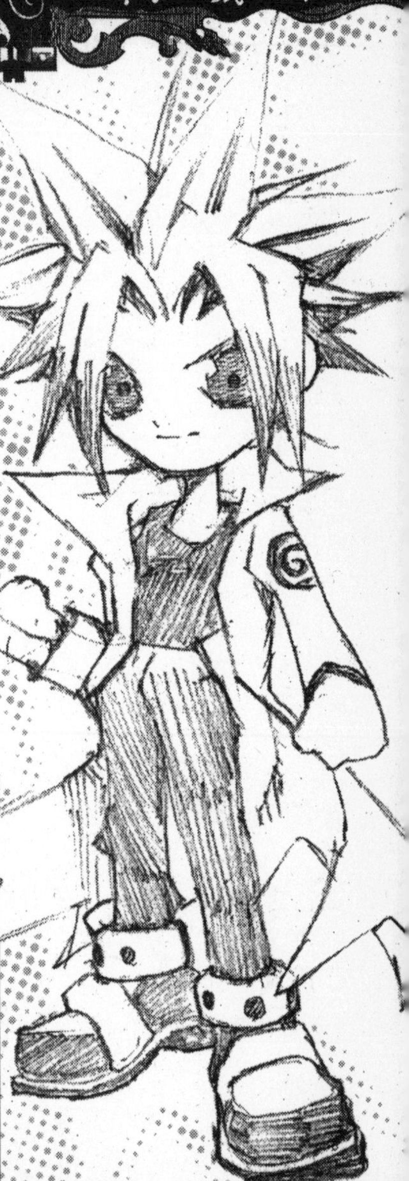

Angel Version

"EVEN GOD WILL BE FOOLED...AQUAVITAE IS MINE!"

Devil Version

"HELL'S JUDGMENT DEPENDS ON HOW MUCH MONEY YOU HAVE. I WILL TAKE AQUAVITAE."

All the faces depicted in the game's "talking-windows" scenes were specially drawn. You can really see the Kumakura style, in even the goofy faces.

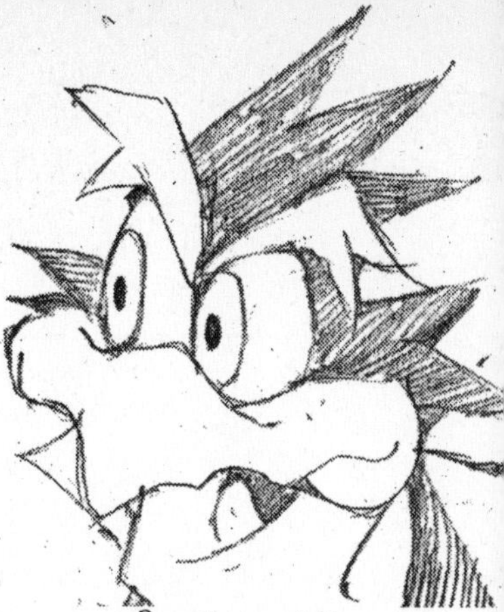

Basic Version of Kir.
Kir always looks relaxed...or drunk.

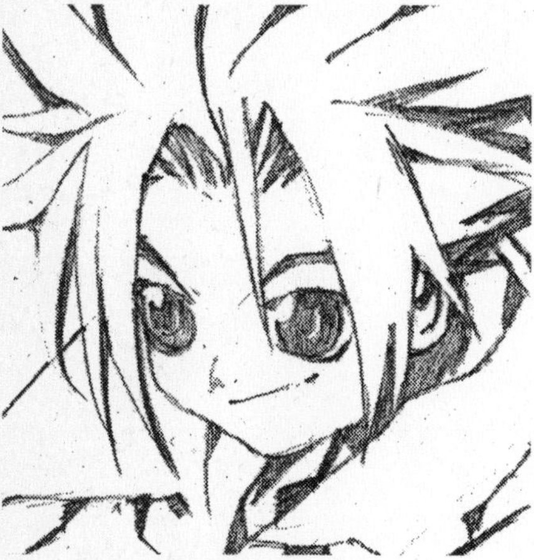

Basic Version of Jing.
He always has that confident look!

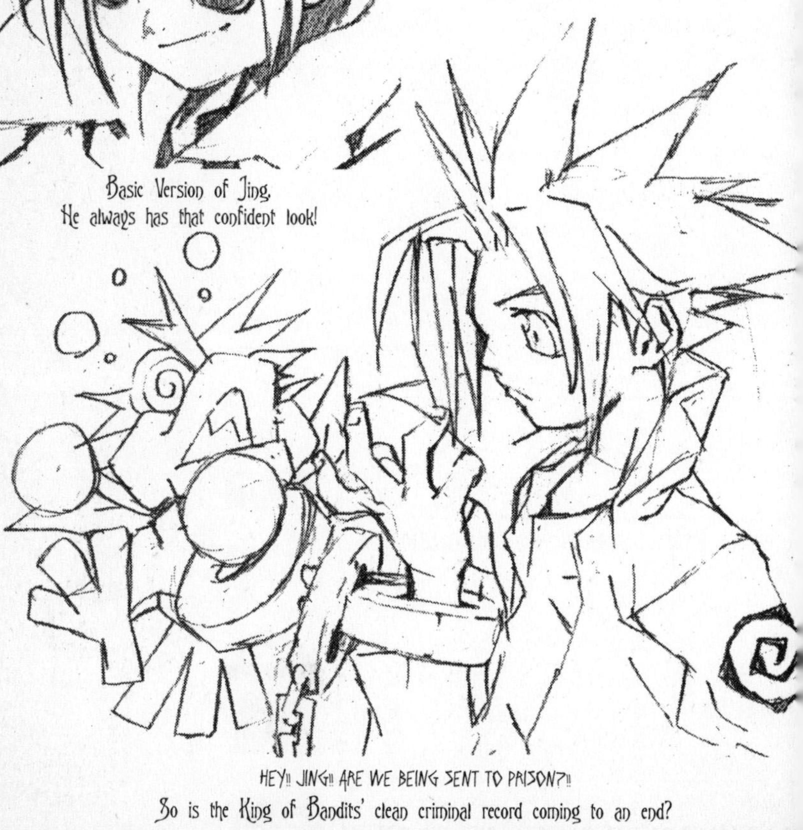

HEY!! JING!! ARE WE BEING SENT TO PRISON?!!
So is the King of Bandits' clean criminal record coming to an end?

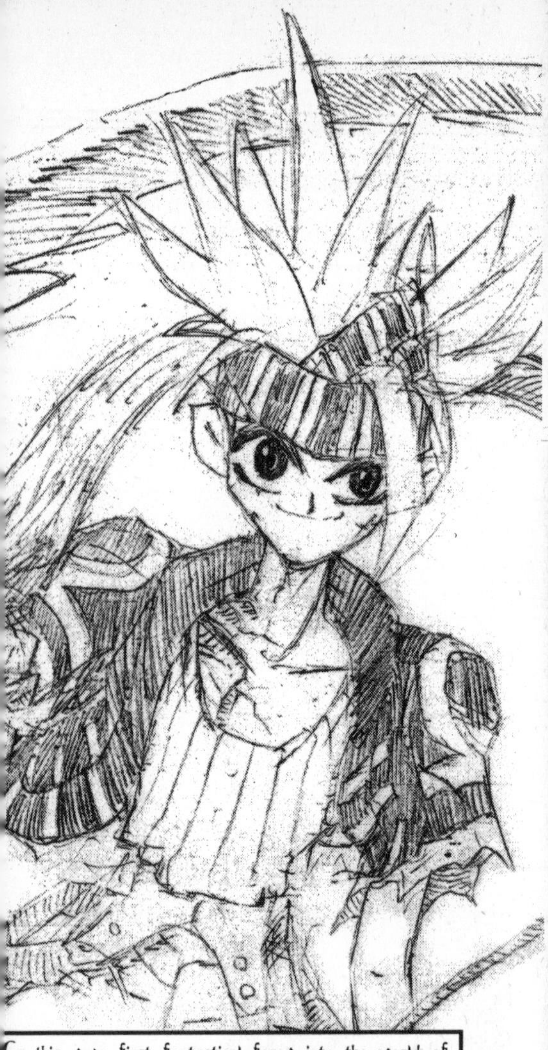

as this your first fantastical foray into the world of ing? Did he completely steal your heart? Well, you've me to the party late, my friend! Oodles of fans have eady fueled their hunger for filching by reading Jing's irst series. That's right! There are 7 volumes of the evious *Jing: The King of Bandits* series just waiting to fall into your eager fingers!

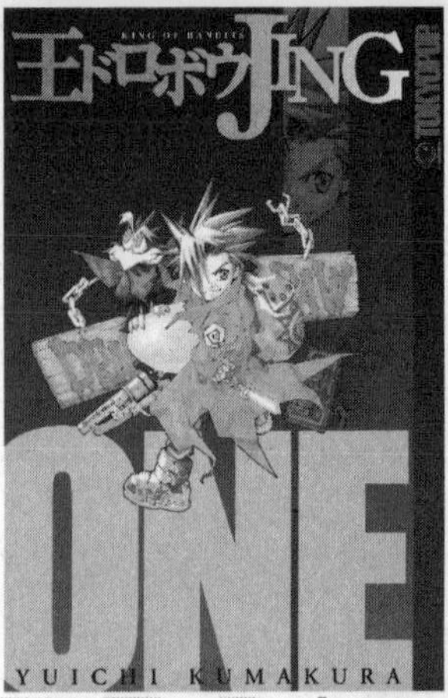

KING OF BANDITS
王ドロボウJING
TOKYOPOP
ONE
YUICHI KUMAKURA

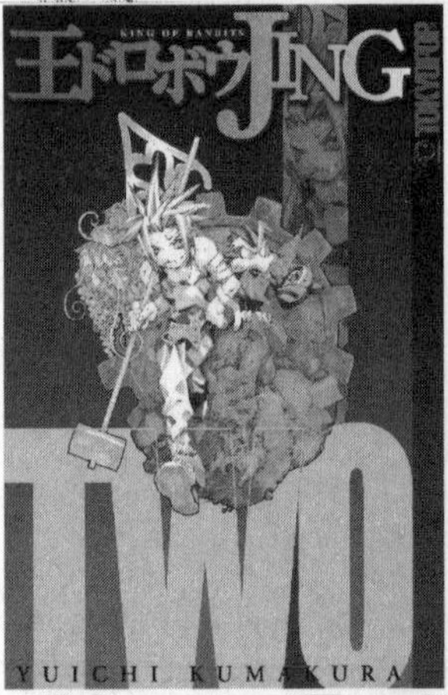

王ドロボウJING
TOKYOPOP
TWO
YUICHI KUMAKURA

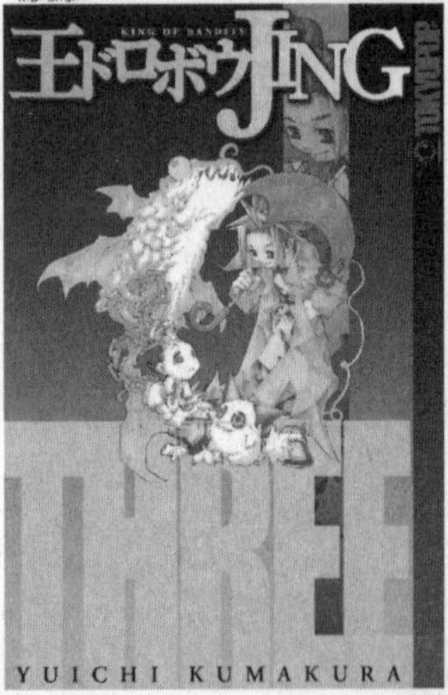

王ドロボウJING
TOKYOPOP
THREE
YUICHI KUMAKURA

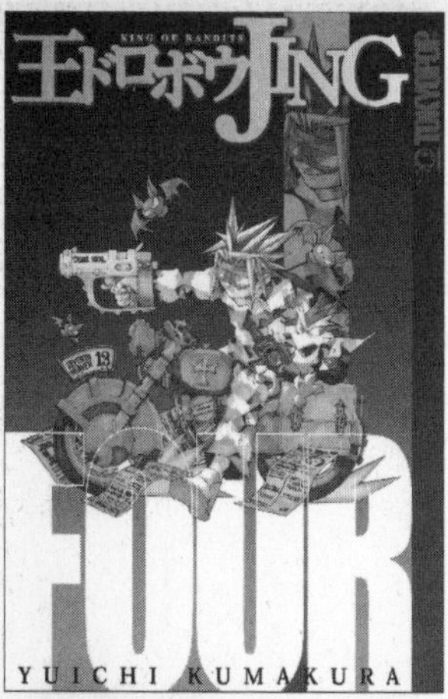

KING OF BANDITS
王ドロボウJING
TOKYOPOP
FOUR
YUICHI KUMAKURA

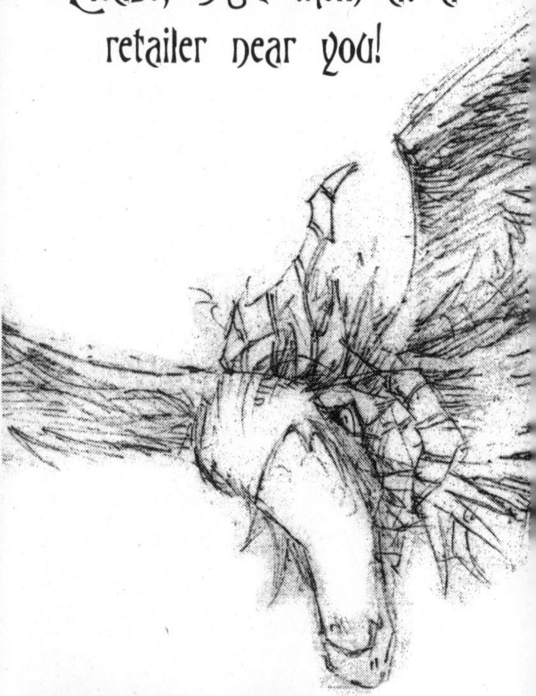

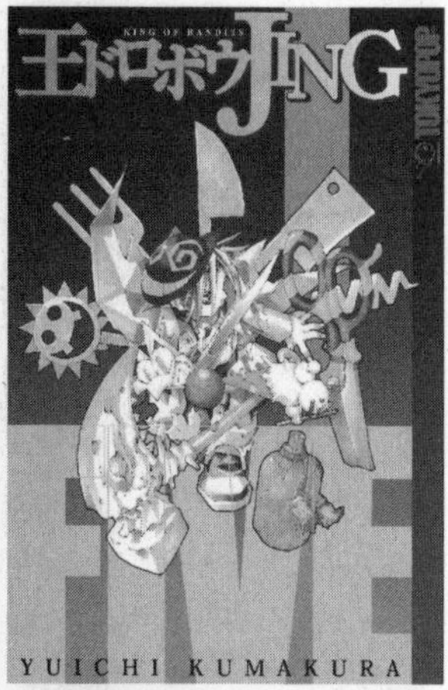

KING OF BANDITS
王ドロボウJING
TOKYOPOP
FIVE
YUICHI KUMAKURA

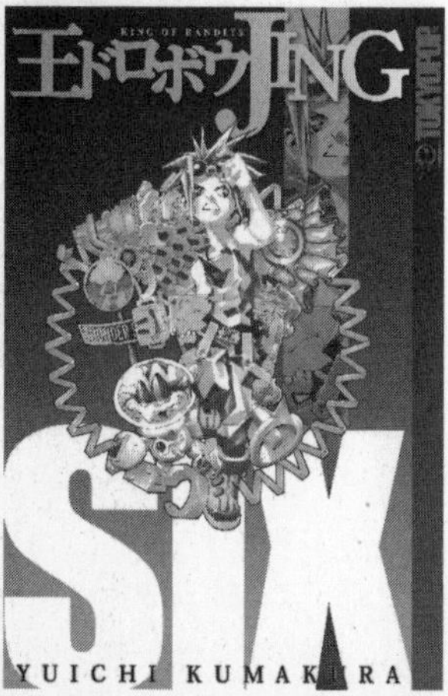

KING OF BANDITS
王ドロボウJING
TOKYOPOP
SIX
YUICHI KUMAKURA

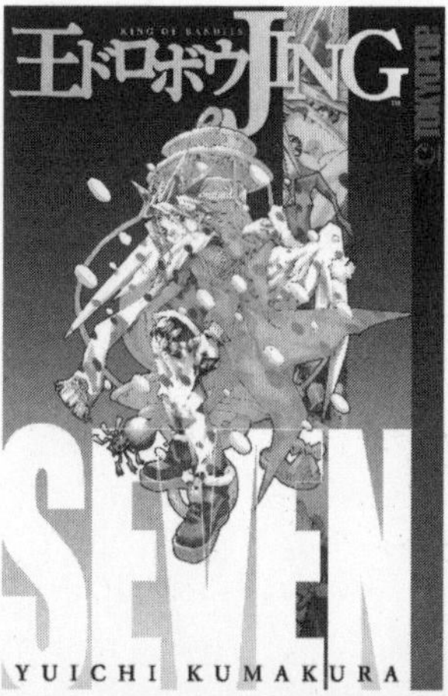

KING OF BANDITS
王ドロボウJING
TOKYOPOP
SEVEN
YUICHI KUMAKURA

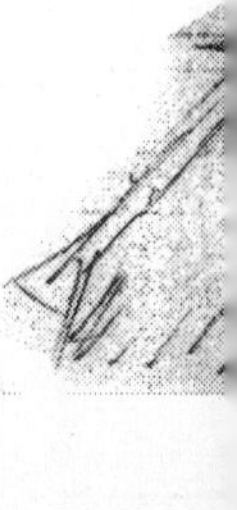

CHRONICLES OF THE CURSED SWORD

BY YEO BEOP-RYONG

A living sword forged in darkness
A hero born outside the light
One can destroy the other
But both can save the world.

TOKYOPOP®

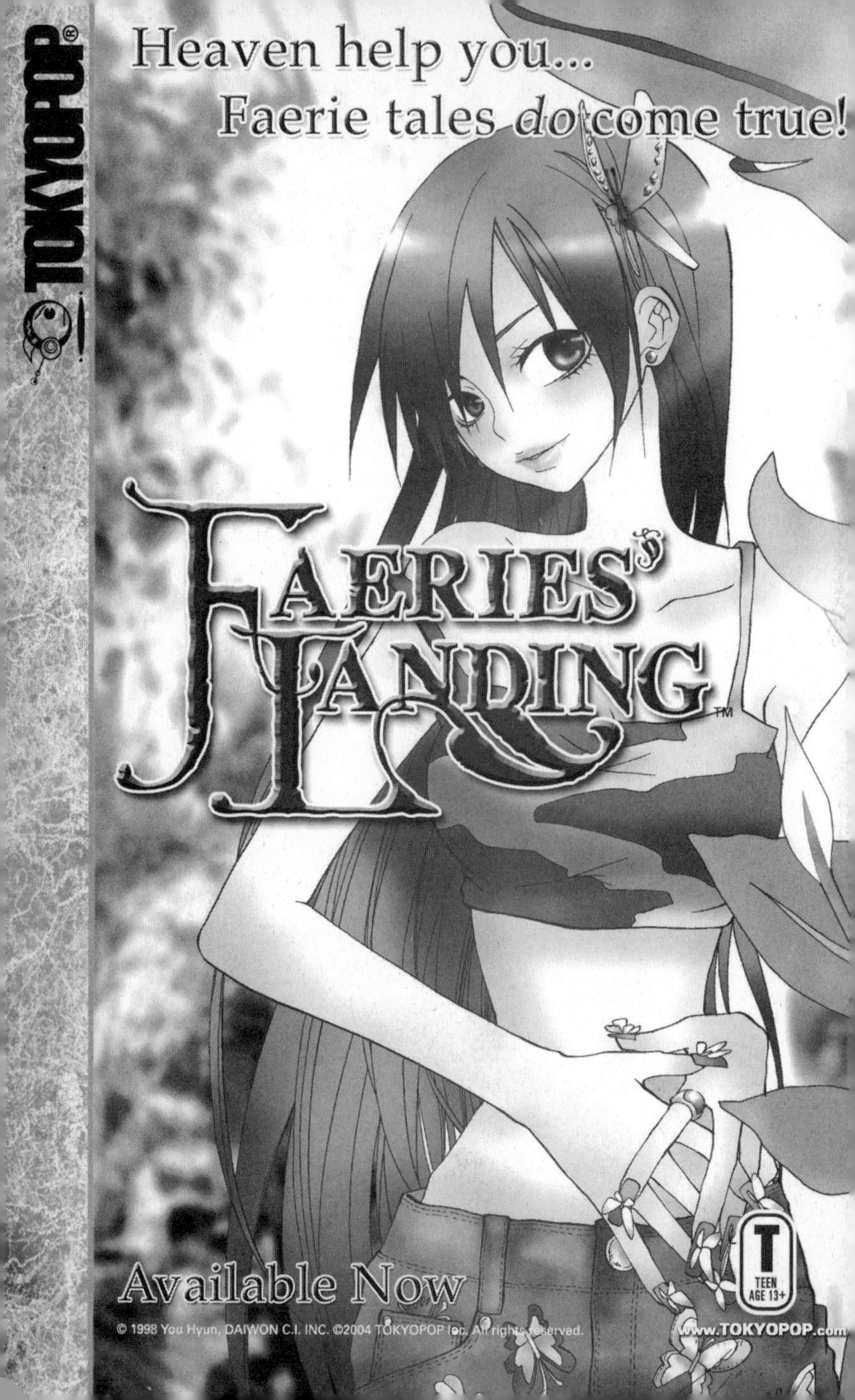

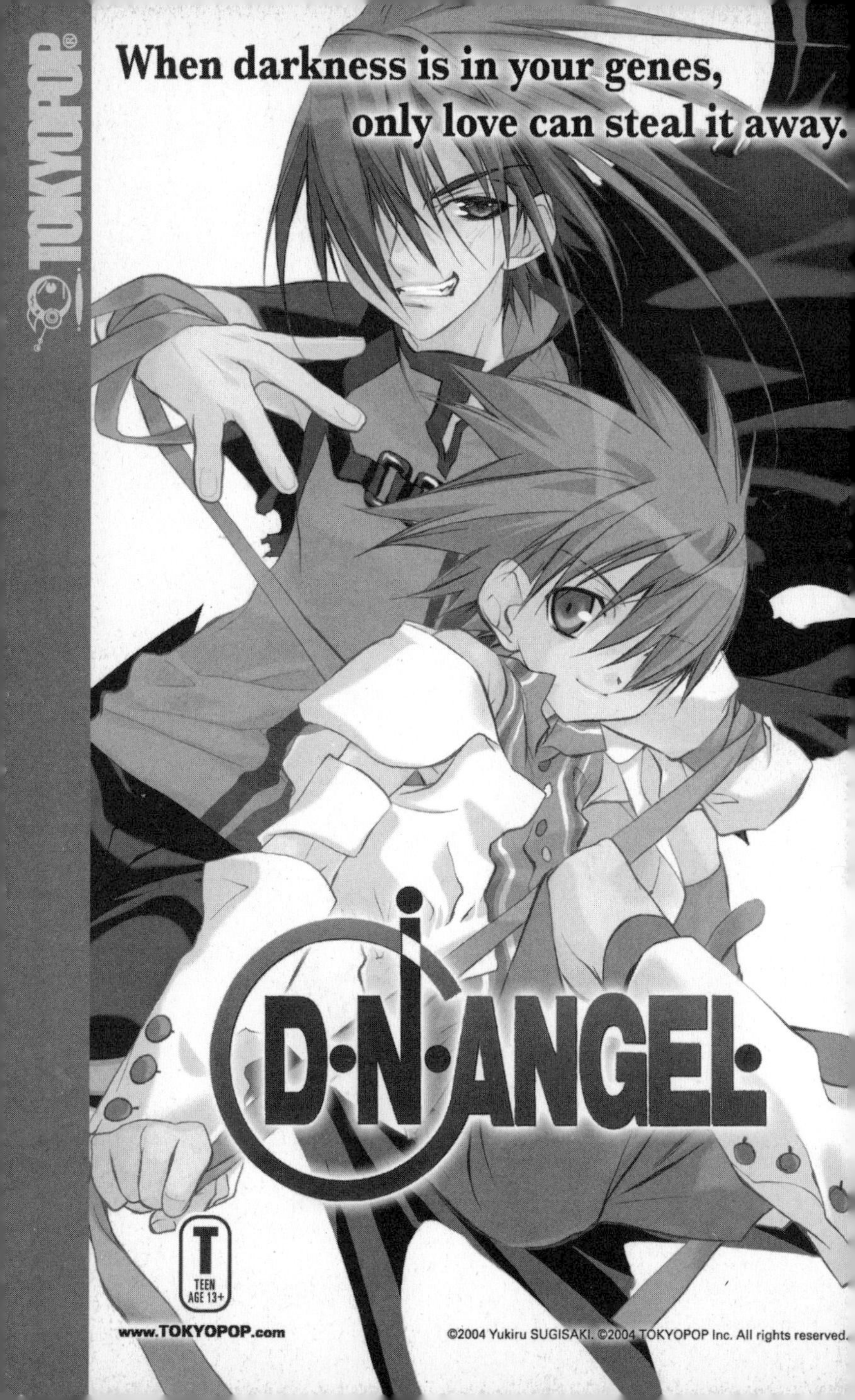
TOKYOPOP®
When darkness is in your genes,
only love can steal it away.
D·N·ANGEL
T
TEEN
AGE 13+
www.TOKYOPOP.com
©2004 Yukiru SUGISAKI. ©2004 TOKYOPOP Inc. All rights reserved.

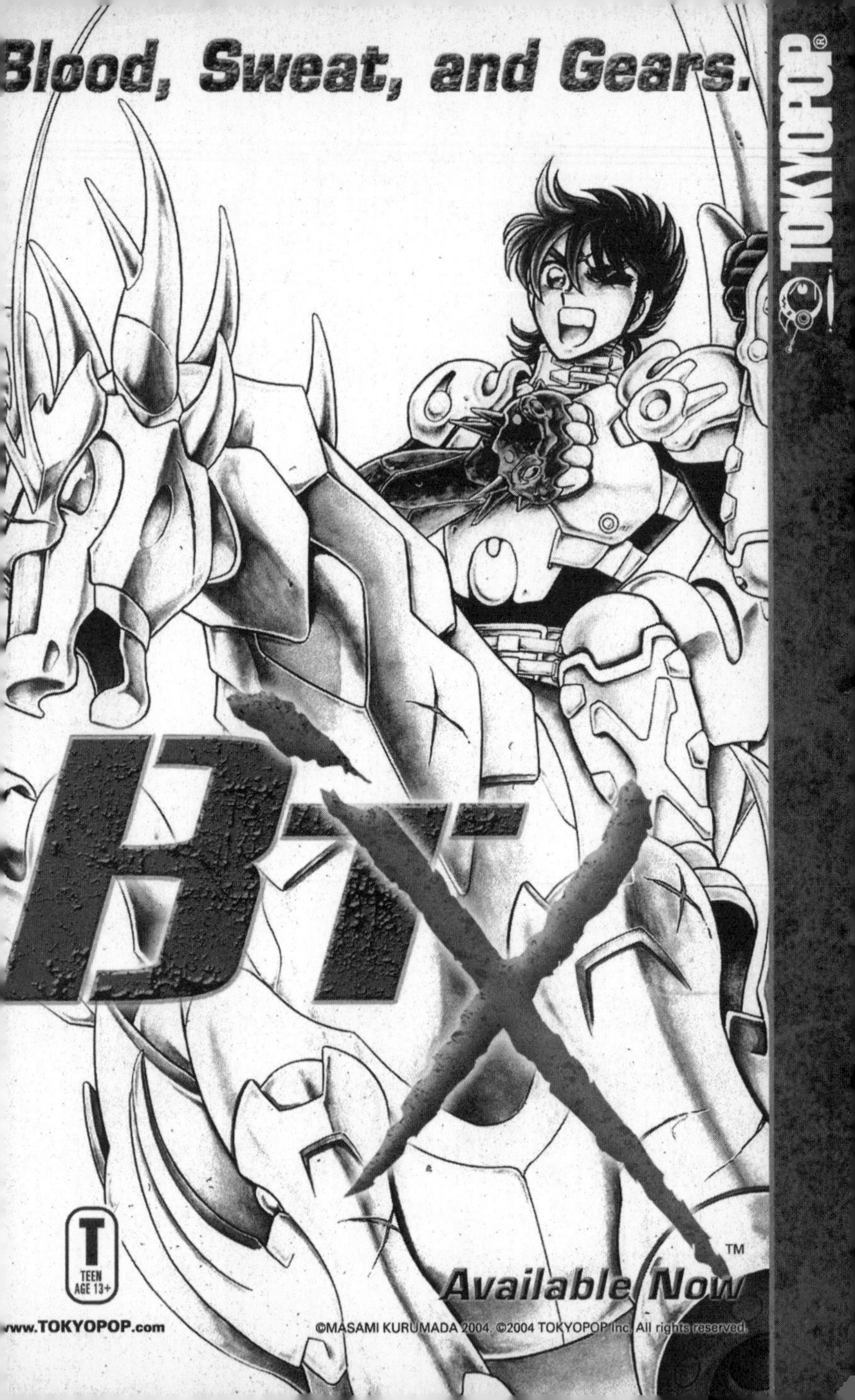
Blood, Sweat, and Gears.
TOKYOPOP®
B'TX™
T
TEEN
AGE 13+
Available Now
www.TOKYOPOP.com
©MASAMI KURUMADA 2004. ©2004 TOKYOPOP Inc. All rights reserved.